HISTORY OF THE
20TH CENTURY

WORLD WAR II

HISTORY OF THE
20TH CENTURY

WORLD WAR II

1939-1945

CHANCELLOR
PRESS

Project editor Peter Furtado

Project art editor Ayala Kingsley

Text editors Robert Peberdy, Mike March, Sue Martin

Cartographic manager Olive Pearson

Cartographic editor Zoë Goodwin

Designers Frankie Wood, Janet McCallum, Wolfgang Mezger, Gill Mouqué, Niki Overy, Linda Reed, Nicholas Rous, Tony de Saulles, Dave Sumner, Rita Wütrych

Picture research manager Alison Renney

Picture research Jan Croot, Diane Hamilton, Rebecca Hirsh, Angela Murphy, Diana Phillips, Linda Proud, Christine Vincent, Charlotte Ward-Perkins

Editorial assistants Elaine Welsh, Monica Byles

AN EQUINOX BOOK

First published by Andromeda Oxford Ltd

This edition published by Chancellor Press, an imprint of Reed Books Limited Michelin House, 81 Fulham Road, London, SW3 6RB and Auckland and Melbourne

© Copyright Andromeda Oxford Ltd 1992

ISBN 0 75370 016 6

Printed in China

ADVISORY EDITORS

Alan Borg
Imperial War Museum, London

Asa Briggs
Worcester College, Oxford

Carlo Cipolla
University of California, Berkeley, USA

Sir Napier Crookenden
Formerly Lieutenant of Her Majesty's Tower of London

Andrew J. Goodpaster
US Army (retired)

Wolfgang Krieger
Ebenhausen, Germany

David Landes
Harvard University, USA

William McNeill
University of Chicago, USA

Peter Pulzer
All Souls College, Oxford

Hartmut Pogge von Strandmann
University College, Oxford

Philip Waller
Merton College, Oxford

Geoffrey Warner
Open University

M.L.H.L. Weaver
Linacre College, Oxford

Charles Webster
All Souls College, Oxford

EDITORS

John Campbell
Freelance writer, London

John Harriss
London School of Economics

Richard Maltby
University of Exeter

C. S. Nicholls
St Antony's College, Oxford

Sidney Pollard
Formerly of University of Bielefeld, Germany

J. M. Winter
Pembroke College, Cambridge

CONTRIBUTORS

Gerold Ambrosius
University of Bremen, Germany

Duncan Anderson
Royal Military Academy, Sandhurst

Ian Beckett
Royal Military Academy, Sandhurst

Geoffrey Best
Formerly of University of Sussex

Robert Bideleux
University of Swansea

Simon Boughey
Corpus Christi College, Cambridge

Gail Braybon
Freelance writer

Sir Julian Bullard
All Souls College, Oxford

Kathleen Burk
Imperial College, London

Angus Calder
Open University

Peter Carey
Trinity College, Oxford

Jane Carmichael
Imperial War Museum, London

Malcolm Cooper
Formerly of Newfoundland University, Canada

P. L. Cottrell
University of Leicester

Robert Dare
University of Adelaide, Australia

Martin Dean
Formerly of University of Cambridge

Anne Deighton
University of Reading

John Erickson
University of Edinburgh

David Fletcher
The Tank Museum, Wareham

CONTENTS

James Foreman-Peck
University of Hull

Brian Foss
Freelance writer

Michael Geyer
University of Chicago, USA

Robert Gildea
Merton College, Oxford

Anthony Glees
Brunel University

Roger Griffin
Oxford Polytechnic

Jennifer Hargreaves
Roehampton Institute, London

Nathaniel Harris
Freelance writer

Nigel Harris
University College, London

Gundi Harriss
Birkbeck College, London

David Horn
University of Liverpool

Julian Jackson
University College of Swansea

Keith Jeffrey
University of Ulster

Matthew Jones
St Antony's College, Oxford

Paul Kennedy
Yale University, USA

Ghislaine Lawrence
National Museum of Science and Industry, London

Peter Lowe
University of Manchester

Keith Lyons
London School of Economics

Dermott MacCann
Brunel University

Peter Martland
Corpus Christi College, Cambridge

Roger Morgan
London School of Economics

Lucy Newton
Leicester University

A. J. Nicholls
St Antony's College, Oxford

David Penn
Imperial War Museum, London

Brian Holden Reid
King's College, London

Catherine Reilly
Freelance writer

Denis Ridgeway
Formerly of Royal Navy Scientific Service

Gowher Rizvi
University of Warwick

Keith Sainsbury
University of Reading

Harry Shukman
St Antony's College, Oxford

Penny Sparke
Royal College of Art, London

Jill Stephenson
University of Edinburgh

Stanley Trapido
Lincoln College, Oxford

T.H.E. Travers
University of Calgary, Canada

S.B. Whitmore
Formerly British Army of the Rhine, Germany

Paul Wilkinson
University of Aberdeen

Elizabeth Wilson
North London Polytechnic

Roger Zetter
Oxford Polytechnic

CARTOGRAPHIC ADVISORS

Colin Bruce
Imperial Collge, London

John Pimlott
Royal Military Academy, Sandhurst

INTRODUCTION

What we call World War II began as two separate wars, which had quite different origins and were fought in different continents. The war in Asia arose from the slow disintegration of the ancient empire of China and the ambition of a dynamic new power, Japan, to move into the resulting vacuum. The war in Europe was essentially a resumption of the Great War of 1914–18, caused by a revival of the military power and territorial ambition of Germany. The story of World War II is the way that these two regional conflicts merged into a single global conflict, resulting in a new world order dominated by two victorious – but very soon rival – superpowers.

The rise of Japan

The emergence of Japan as a world power had been bewilderingly rapid. Within a single lifetime many Japanese had witnessed the self-contained agrarian Japan of their childhood transformed into the world's seventh largest industrial producer. Western penetration in the 1860s had provided the catalyst: in 1868 young Samurai noblemen, smarting from the humiliation, centralized power in the hands of the Emperor Meiji and subsequently engineered a political, economic and military revolution. By the 1870s Japan had a modern army and navy which defeated China in 1895, the Russian Empire in 1905 and in 1914 overran Germany's eastern and Pacific colonies. By 1933 Japan's new empire covered Formosa, Korea, Manchuria and the Marshall, Caroline and Mariana islands in the Pacific.

But by the late 1920s the strain of rapid modernization was beginning to tell. Japan's population explosion – from 30 million in 1870 to 55 million by 1920 and 80 million by 1937 – led to the fragmentation of the land into smaller and smaller holdings, the migration of the population to huge new industrial cities and phenomenal economic growth, concentrated in heavy industry (shipbuilding in particular) and textiles. Export of the latter provided some 70 percent of Japan's foreign earnings, which went to feed its population and pay for industrial raw materials. But in 1930 its overseas textile markets vanished as western nations tried to protect their own hard-hit industries from the depression behind high tariff walls. The effect on Japan was devastating.

Hitherto industrial growth had gone hand-in-hand with the development of political democracy. Seventy years earlier Japan had been as feudal as medieval England. In 1889, however, the Samurai responsible for the Meiji restoration introduced a constitution based on that of imperial Germany. Power remained in the hands of the emperor and his cabinet, but a diet was established, elected on a limited franchise. Universal (male) suffrage came in 1924. Mass political parties began to evolve and in normal circumstances the elected diet should have exerted steadily increasing influence over the executive.

But the crisis of the 1930s put a halt to democratization. Disillusion with western ideals, and the social tensions of rapid modernization, gave birth to ultra-conservative patriotic societies. In a more advanced political system these might have evolved into a national socialist party. Instead they formed alliances with the army and navy, which were developing their own rival ambitions – the army for expansion on the mainland at the expense of China and Russia, the navy to make Japan self-sufficient in a raw materials by the conquest of British Malaya and the Dutch East Indies. In 1935 Japan repudiated the Washington Naval Treaty, negotiated in 1922 by a civilian government, and began building a modern fleet which should challenge British and American domination of the Pacific. In 1936 an army revolt was put down, but henceforth the government was effectively under the thumb of the armed forces and an attempt to solve Japan's problems by war became increasingly inevitable.

The recovery of Germany

The growing power of imperial Germany had made its first bid to dominate the European continent in 1914–18. Following the surrender of Wilhelm II's armies in November 1918, the victorious western Allies – France, the UK and the USA – had tried to prevent any renewal of the attempt by means of the punitive Treaty of Versailles. The German army was to be limited to 100,000 men, with no general staff, no heavy artillery and no aircraft; the navy to ships under 10,000 tons, with no submarines. The territory of Alsace-Lorraine was returned to France, the Rhineland demilitarized, and the union of Germany with Austria (Anschluss) was forbidden. The leaders of the new German republic signed the Treaty, under protest, on 28 June 1919.

But, apart from the loss of Alsace-Lorraine and the temporary occupation of the Rhineland, Germany was not dismembered and many Germans did not believe that they had been militarily defeated. Over the next ten years a powerful myth of national betrayal was fed by economic depression. In 1932, following spectacular inflation and high unemployment, the National Socialist ("Nazi") party, led by Adolf Hitler, won 37 percent of the popular vote, becoming by far the largest party in the German parliament, the Reichstag. In 1933 Hitler was appointed chancellor. Once in power, he quickly swept aside the discredited democracy of the Weimar Republic and set about overturning the provisions of Versailles, taking advantage of the reluctance or inability of the other powers to prevent him. France and the UK were exhausted by the last war and unwilling to contemplate another, preferring to believe that Hitler's legitimate desire to restore German pride could be met by reasonable concessions; the old Austro-Hungarian Empire had fragmented in 1918, leaving only a string of vulnerable successor states on Germany's eastern borders; Soviet Russia had turned in on itself following defeat and revolution in 1917; and the United States, after its decisive contribution to the defeat of Germany in 1917–18, had withdrawn back into its traditional isolationism. There was thus a power vacuum in the heart of Europe which Hitler was able to exploit to create the "living space" (Lebensraum) he claimed Germany needed. He rearmed, remilitarized the Rhineland in 1936, engineered Anschluss with Austria in 1938, and bluffed and bullied the western democracies into letting him take over much of Czechoslovakia in 1938–39; then – still calculating that France and Britain would stand aside – he invaded Poland. By the time the democracies were finally driven to declare war in September 1939 they were helpless to prevent Germany overrunning practically the whole of continental Europe.

From regional conflicts to world war

Fighting in Asia had actually begun in July 1937 when – to the fury of the Japanese admirals – Japanese troops invaded northern China, where they soon became bogged down. But the wider war in Asia really stemmed from Japanese naval expansionism, which quickly ran into conflict not only with the old European empires in Asia – the British in India, Burma and Malaya, the French in Indochina and the Dutch in Indonesia – which offered little resistance, but more importantly with the other rising power in the Pacific – the USA. Japan's military leaders sought to preempt the American response by striking first at the US navy at Pearl Harbor in December 1941. But this was a desperate gamble whose initial success only served to ensure the inevitability of Japan's ultimate destruction when the whole industrial and military power of the United States was eventually mobilized against it.

The aggressive ambitions of both Japan and Germany were motivated by a similar mixture of resurgent national pride, contempt for inferior races and glorification of militarism, exacerbated by the effects of economic recession. The crucial element which linked the two regional conflicts into a world war, however, was not ideology but the military involvement of the United States – and to a lesser extent the UK – in both Asia and Europe. This is not to underrate the immense part played in the defeat of Hitler by the Soviet Union. In 1940 the UK, fighting for its life in lone resistance to Germany in Europe, had successfully resisted German invasion but could do nothing by itself to encompass Hitler's defeat. In June 1941 Hitler took the first step to ensuring his own defeat by invading the Soviet Union. In August 1939 he had been careful to neutralize the latent power of the Soviet Union by means of the Soviet-German Nonaggression Pact before he launched his

▲ The rise of German fascism: Nazi supporters at a Nuremberg rally, 1936.

attack on Poland; but now he wantonly provoked it. Like the French emperor Napoleon's *Grande armée* in 1812, his armies penetrated deep into Russia and then foundered; more men and materiel were expended in Russia than on any other front in World War II before the Red Army rolled westward in 1944–45 to occupy half of what had been Hitler's Reich. The USSR unquestionably made the major contribution to the Allied victory over Germany. But from 1943 – as in 1917–18 – the equal and opposite power of the United States made the decisive contribution in western Europe. This too Hitler largely brought upon himself by quite unnecessarily declaring war on the United States following the Japanese attack on Pearl Harbor – an act of suicidally insane bravado which made it enormously easier for President Roosevelt not merely to bring the US into the Euro-pean war, overcoming the still strong isolationist instinct of much American opinion, but also to agree with his British and Soviet allies to make the defeat of Germany, rather than Japan, America's first priority. It was the simultaneous global involvement of the United States in both theaters that made 1941–45 a single war and truly a world war.

There was no necessity for Hitler to declare war on the United States. His action was no more than a gesture of support for an ally who he hoped would help defeat the British for him in their empire while keeping the Americans occupied in the Pacific. Beyond a superficial identity of interest between two militaristic regimes with complementary territorial ambitions in their own spheres, there was no genuine alliance between Germany and Japan. There was little in practice they could do to help each other and they made no attempt to coordinate their strategy. The British, Soviets and Americans, on the other hand, did establish a Grand Alliance with regular summit meetings between the leaders. Between the American and British forces in Europe there was a complete coordination of strategic planning under a single joint command. For reasons of both geography and politics this was not possible between the Red Army and the western democracies. But the UK and America sent vast quantities of material supplies to the USSR; and with the Soviet Union posing as a democratic nation they fought supposedly for shared values against a common enemy, loosely defined as Fascism. Behind the high-flown rhetoric, naturally, they fought at the same time for their own national security and economic interest. In places the interests even of the English-speaking democracies conflicted, notably in Asia where American anticolonialist rhetoric and economic imperialism clashed with Britain's vain concern to preserve the British Empire.

To this extent the war remained two wars, with the Americans and British pursuing somewhat different objectives in each theater. Though the Soviets formally and belatedly joined in the war against Japan just before Hiroshima, there was no serious territorial overlap between the two conflicts. The Soviets and Americans (with the British), converging on Berlin simultaneously from east and west, jointly won the war in Europe and divided the continent between their respective spheres of influence. But the Americans won the war in Asia essentially by themselves and were left – until China and Japan recovered – the predominant power in Asia as well. The conclusive event of the entire war was the American development and use of the atomic bomb. This achievement – matched within a few years by the Soviet Union – changed the nature of the postwar world. Where before the wars in both Asia and Europe there had been power-vacuums waiting to be filled, after 1945 the two nuclear superpowers were omnipresent, locked in worldwide ideological competition and maintaining the peace only through a balance of terror.

The Course of World War II

CANADA

UNITED STATES

Pearl Harbor
★ 7 Dec 1941

★ Major battle, with date

Area of conflict

▨ Land

▨ Sea

ASIA/PACIFIC

1937

On 7 July 1937, Japanese troops invade China. From August to November they also fight for and take Shanghai.

1938

From March to October the Japanese advance south and take Hankou. In the autumn (October-November) they systematically seize Chinese ports.

1939

The seizure of Chinese ports continues. In September a Japanese offensive against Changsha fails, bringing Japanese expansion to an end. In November the Japanese cut the railroad from Hanoi.

1940

In June the USA begins a massive expansion of the navy. In September Vichy France allows Japanese troops to land in Indochina. The USA responds with a trade embargo.

1941

In July Japan declares a Franco-Japanese protectorate over Indochina and occupies the country: the USA, UK and Netherlands stop exports of oil to Japan. On 7 December Japan attacks the US Pacific Fleet in Pearl Harbor. It also starts a conquest of SE Asia.

1942

Japanese expansion in SE Asia continues. Singapore falls in February, Mandalay in April. On the Philippines organized resistance ceases in May. But Japan begins to suffer reverses. US success in the Battle of the Coral Sea in May saves Australia. In June, in the Battle of Midway, the USA destroys four of Japan's carriers. In August US marines capture and hold the Japanese airfield on Guadalcanal in the Solomons.

1943

The Japanese evacuate Guadalcanal in

NORWAY **FINLAND**

SOVIET UNION

UNITED KINGDOM

Bulge
16 Dec 1944 – 28 Jan 1945

Dunkirk
26 May – 2 June 1940 **POLAND** Kursk
D Day Beaches **GERMANY** 4 – 20 July 1943

6 June 1944 **FRANCE**
Anzio
22 Jan – 25 May 1944
ITALY Monte Cassino
17 Jan – 18 May 1944
Crete
20 – 31 May 1941
El Alamein
23 Oct – 4 Nov 1942
EGYPT

Moscow
30 Sept – 5 Dec 1941

Stalingrad
19 Aug 1942 – 2 Feb 1943

Marco Polo Bridge
7 July 1937

JAPAN

CHINA

Midway
4 – 5 June 1942

Okinawa
14 Mar – 22 June 1945

Iwo Jima
19 Feb – 16 Mar 1945

Kohima
6 – 20 April 1944

INDIA
Imphal
29 Mar – 22 June 1944

PHILIPPINES

Leyte Gulf
17 – 25 Oct 1944

Philippine Sea
19 – 20 June 1944

Guadalcanal
7 Aug 1942 – 7 Feb 1943

Coral Sea
7 – 8 May 1942

AUSTRALIA

February. In the summer the Allies begin a two-pronged offensive to take the Philippines, cross the Pacific and invade Japan.

1944

In March Japanese troops besiege Imphal and Kohima in India. British forces relieve the towns in April and June. In May Japan mounts an offensive in China. In the Pacific Japan is defeated in the Battles of the Philippine Sea in June and Leyte Gulf in September. In October the Allies invade Burma.

1945

The Allies return to the Philippines and take Manila in March. But the conquests of Iwo Jima (February-March) and Okinawa (March-June) cost huge casualties. Japan prepares to defend the "home islands" but in August Hiroshima and Nagasaki are destroyed by atomic bombs and the USSR declares war. On August 15 Hirohito announces the Japanese surrender.

EUROPE/MEDITERRANEAN

1936–39

The early stages of German expansion. In March 1936 the Rhineland is remilitarized. In March 1938 a union with Austria is engineered. In September the UK and France agree to the transfer of German-speaking areas of Czechoslovakia to Germany. In March 1939 Germany annexes the rest of Czechoslovakia. France and the UK respond by guaranteeing Poland.

1939

On 1 September Germany invades Poland (as does the USSR on 17 September). France and the UK declare war on Germany.

1940

In April Germans invade Denmark and Norway; in May the Low Countries and France. British troops escape from the Continent in a massive evacuation from Dunkirk (May-June). The German-French armistice signed in June divides France into two zones. In

July German air attacks are launched (Battle of Britain) in preparation for an invasion of England. RAF resistance causes Hitler to postpone his planned invasion. In Africa Italians invade Egypt in September but are thrown back. Their invasion of Greece in October is also repulsed.

1941

In North Africa in March Rommel's Axis army retreats across Cyrenaica. In April Germans invade Yugoslavia and Greece and in May force the British to evacuate Crete. On 22 June Germans invade the USSR, but are halted outside Moscow in December.

1942

In North Africa the British are forced to retreat. In the USSR Germans make a major drive into the Ukraine and in August launch an attack against Stalingrad. In October, at El Alamein, British troops force the Germans into a retreat across North Africa.

1943

On 31 January the Germans at Stalingrad surrender. The Red Army counterattacks. In North Africa the Axis is defeated in May. In the USSR, in July, Germans attack the Kursk salient, and are defeated. In the Mediterranean the Allies invade Sicily in July, the Italian mainland in September.

1944

In March the Red Army crosses the Dniester. In June the Western Allies invade Normandy and the Red Army attacks Germans in central Russia. But in December the Germans launch an offensive in the Ardennes (Battle of the Bulge).

1945

After victory in the Ardennes, US troops cross the Rhine in March. The Red Army is advancing from the east. Berlin falls on 1 May; Germany surrenders on 8 May.

The social upheaval of war

World War II was a "total" war to an extent that no previous war – not even World War I – comes close to matching. By whatever measurement we use – geographic extent, the scale of military and economic mobilization in the belligerent countries, the direct impact on noncombatants in belligerent and occupied countries, the toll of casualties among both combatants and noncombatants, the disruption of civilian lives or the dislocation of the world economy – the war of 1937–45 affected more people around the world more directly than any other war before, or since. For all who lived through it, it was the overwhelming experience of the 20th century.

The actual fighting was concentrated in China, around the west and southwest Pacific, in Europe and along the Mediterranean coast of Africa. There were also occasional forays into West Africa, India and the south Atlantic. In Europe neutral countries were in a minority: in Asia an even smaller one. The United States, though itself virtually untouched by military action, was a major combatant in both Asia and Europe. Even southern Africa and Brazil supplied the Allied armies with troops. Almost every part of the world was affected, if only economically, by the reverberations of the fighting.

Five major countries were principally involved: Germany, Japan, the UK, the Soviet Union and the United States. (Among others France was knocked out in 1940, Italy in 1943; Australia and Canada played important but subordinate roles on the Allied side; and a number of other countries, like Greece and Yugoslavia, were the scene of significant guerrilla activity.) The scale of military and economic mobilization in the main countries was unprecedented – almost literally total, with virtually all industrial production and manpower, including women, conscripted to serve the needs of the war. (Hitler's reluctance to press German women into war work was a curious exception.) This human and material mobilization can be measured statistically and compared from one belligerent country to another. So, more or less, can the scale of combatant casualties: the Russians lost at least 7 million men killed, the Germans 3.5 million, the Japanese 1.2 million, the UK 250,000, and the USA 300,000. More difficult to quantify are the civilian casualties. Perhaps 300,000 died as a result of aerial bombing in Germany, 60,500 in the UK and 500,000 in Japan, including the 106,000 victims of the atomic bombs on Hiroshima and Nagasaki. But then there are the incalculable numbers of those – men, women and children – killed in the course of invasion and occupation, resistance and reprisals: those who perished in labor and concentration camps, by slave labor, forced marches, torture and all the other atrocities by which this war was so gruesomely characterized – a roll-call of bestiality led by the Nazi's systematic extermination of some 5–6 million European Jews; not forgetting those who simply died, as refugees or displaced persons, in bewildering conditions of social disruption, deprivation and distress.

The lesser effects of the social upheaval caused by the war are likewise unquantifiable. They affected, in different ways, countries far from the front line, like the United States and Canada, and even neutral countries, as well as those threatened or overrun by invasion or bombing. But they were not all bad. War shook up social rigidities in many countries, broke down sexual and moral inhibitions, gave many individuals – particularly women – opportunities of independence and self-discovery which they would not have had in peacetime. The human experience of the war, mixing excitement with tragedy, heroism with cruelty, and an intoxicating sense of purpose with long stretches of tedium and futility, was infinitely varied but, one way or another, universal.

The war was characterized, too, by new levels of mass communication: between belligerent governments and their own peoples, whose morale they were concerned to keep up; between governments and enemy populations, whose morale they hoped to break down; between Allied peoples, and even between opposed peoples, by means of the worldwide diffusion of news and popular entertainment, particularly music and film. It was a war of the air waves: it was a war of propaganda, true and false, of words and images. Like any intense, widely shared experience, it laid down a rich seedbed of memory which – for the most part after the war was over – bore a crop of powerful works of art, in all media, which are a permanent legacy of the conflict, with enduring universal resonance. In addition the war left an indelible imprint on the collective mind of all the participant countries: on the defeated Japanese and Germans a deep scar of national shame and guilt, to be expiated by hard work and exemplary devotion to the profitable pursuits of peace; on the victorious Americans and British a delusive sense of limitless power, righteousness and responsibility for protecting freedom and democracy throughout the world; on the Soviet peoples, who had suffered the heaviest casualties of all, the determination at any cost that the soil of the motherland must never be invaded again.

Above all the other consequences of the war, however – military, social, economic and political – there stand out two features in particular, immense in their implications and unique to this war: the Jewish holocaust and the American dropping of the atomic bomb. Both belong in categories already mentioned, but both events are on a scale which lifts them above generalizations about routine atrocities or conventional bombing. The discovery at the end of the war of Hitler's attempted extermination of the Jews was a shocking revelation of the depth of inhumanity to which a civilized nation could sink under a fanatical regime. It led to a widespread sense of collective guilt in Europe and America, and to the establishment in 1948 of Israel as a Jewish national home in Palestine. Sadly Hitler's monstrous example has had its imitators in the postwar world; yet the holocaust remains the benchmark against which the attempted genocide of other crazed rulers – in Cambodia, Uganda and elsewhere – is measured. More positively, the unprecedented wartime crimes against humanity have led to a worldwide awareness of human rights, enshrined and monitored – however inadequately – by the United Nations.

The mushroom cloud of the atom bombs at Hiroshima and Nagasaki has hung over the world since 1945 like a Sword of Damocles, threatening – as ever more powerful and sophisticated weapons have succeeded one another – the destruction of the world itself if they should ever be deployed. The appalling power placed in the hands of the United States and, within a few years of the war's end, of the Soviet Union as well has had the effect of making war between them unwinnable and therefore rationally unthinkable. Atomic power helped to freeze into seeming perpetuity the crude political settlement arrived at by the final position of the Allied armies in May 1945.

Nuclear weapons have not prevented smaller wars all over the world since the end of World War II. But they have placed an effective limitation on these local wars. The world since Hiroshima has been dominated by the ideological "Cold War" between the Soviet Union and the United States, but no global conflict on the scale of 1937–45. If the outcome of World War I sowed at least some of the seeds of World War II, the conclusion of the Second World War has served for nearly half a century to avert the danger of a third.

▶ **Total war: victims of bombing are pulled from the rubble.**

THE THEATERS OF WAR

Time Chart

	1936–38	1939	1940	1941
Asia/Pacific	• 7 July 1937: Marco Polo Bridge incident • 7 July–23 Nov 1937: Japanese conquest of NE and E China		• Sep 22: Japanese occupation of Indochina begins	• July 25: Occupation of Indochina complete • Dec 7: Japan bombs US naval base at Pearl Harbor • Dec 8: Japanese occupation of SE Asia begins
Europe/Med	• March 1936: Germany remilitarizes the Rhineland • 13 March 1938: Union of Germany and Austria • 12–30 Sep 1938: Czech crisis	• March 16: Germany annexes Czechoslovakia • Apr 7: Italy invades Albania • Sep 1: German invasion of Poland • Sep 17: Soviet invasion of Poland	• Apr 9–June 13: German conquest of Norway • May 10–June 22: German conquest of Low Countries and France • July 10–Nov: Battle of Britain • Sep 15: War in N Africa begins	• May 20–31: German invasion of Greece
Eastern Front		• Nov 30: Soviet–Finnish war begins	• March 12: Soviet–Finnish war ends	• June 22–Dec 5: German invasion of USSR • Dec–Mar: Soviet counteroffensive
Japan	• Oct 1937: Planning agency prepares ground for full-scale war economy • June 1938: Formation of patriotic industry association, state-sponsored • Nov 1938: "New Order in East Asia" proclaimed	• July: First labor mobilization plan • July: National conscription ordinance: workers given designated employment • Oct: "Stop Order" freezes prices and wages	• Voluntary dissolution of political parties; formation of Imperial Rule Assistance Association • Sep: US embargo on war–trade with Japan • Sep: Neighborhood associations revived	• Apr: Rice-rationing begins • Oct: Hideki Tojo becomes prime minister • Dec: Conscription expanded • Dec: Agricultural Control Law tries to check migration from farm to factory
Germany	• 13 March 1938: Union of Germany and Austria • 12–30 Sep 1938: Czech crisis • 9–10 Nov 1938: "Night of Broken Glass" – anti-Jewish pogrom	• Mar: Germany annexes Czechoslovakia • Aug 23: Soviet–German Nonaggression Pact signed • Aug 27: Food rationing introduced • Sep: Introduction of war economy regulations • Nov: Formation of war economy and armaments office of the armed forces		• Mar: "Women for Victory" campaign launched • Aug: T4 euthanasia scheme halted, after protests • Dec: Hitler assumes personal command of the German army
United Kingdom		• June: Women's Land Army formed • Aug: Emergency Powers Act passed • Sep: Internment of Nazi sympathizers and aliens begins • Sep: First wave of evacuation	• Jan: Rationing begins • May: Chamberlain resigns as prime minister; succeeded by Churchill • May: Home secretary given power of arbitrary internment • July: Local Defence Volunteers reformed as Home Guard • Sep: London Blitz begins	• Mar: Mobilization of labor by Registration and Essential Work Order • May: House of Commons destroyed by bombs • Dec: National Service Act
Soviet Union		• Apr: Third Five Year Plan approved by party congress • Aug 23: Soviet–German Nonaggression Pact signed	• June: Working day increased from seven hours to eight • July: Agricultural reforms confiscate land from farmers and impose stricter discipline • July: Large price rises introduced • Oct: Tighter regulation of industrial labor and establishment of compulsory "labor reserve schools" for the young	• June: Committee on evacuation set up • July: Stalin calls for loyalty to fatherland • July: Ration-cards introduced in Leningrad and Moscow • Aug: Emergency War Plan for economy approved • Nov: Evacuation of industrial plant completed
United States			• July: US embargo on trade with Japan • Sep: Conscription introduced	• Mar: Lend-Lease Act • June: Committee on Fair Employment Practises established to eliminate racial discrimination in labor

1942	1943	1944	1945
• May 7–8: Battle of Coral Sea • May 18: Japanese occupation of SE Asia complete • June 4–5: Battle of Midway • Aug 7: Battles of Guadalcanal begin	• Feb: Battles of Guadalcanal end • July 1: US offensives in SW Pacific begin (to March 1945) • Nov 13: US offensives in central Pacific begin (to 10 August 1945)	• Oct 17–25: Battle of Leyte Gulf	• Feb 19–Mar 16: US conquest of Iwo Jima • Mar 14–June 22: US conquest of Okinawa • Aug 6 and 9: Atom bombs dropped on Japan • Aug 15: Japan surrenders
• Oct 24–Nov 4: 2nd Battle of El Alamein	• May 7: War in N Africa ends with defeat for Germany • July 10–June 4: Main Allied campaign in Italy	• June 6–Aug 25: Allied liberation of northern France and Paris • Dec 6: Battle of the Bulge begins	• Jan 28: Battle of Bulge ends in German defeat • March 7: US forces cross Rhine • May 8: Unconditional surrender of German forces
• Soviet offensive in Ukraine • Aug 19: Battle of Stalingrad begins	• Jan 31: Germans defeated at Stalingrad • July 4–20: Battle of Kursk • July 20–Nov 30: Soviet counteroffensive • Dec 24: Soviet winter campaign begins	• May: Soviets retake Leningrad and Ukraine • June 22–Aug 23: Operation Bagration	• Jan 12–May 8: Soviet invasion of Eastern Europe • May 1: Berlin surrenders to Red Army
• Oct: Neighborhood associations take over rationing at local level	• Mar: Wartime Special Administrations Act gives Tojo supreme control over economy • Nov: Munitions ministry established	• July: Resignation of Tojo	• Mar: US B-29s begin incendiary campaign against Japanese cities • July: 10 percent cut in all staple rations imposed • Sep 2: Formal Japanese signature of surrender document
• Jan. 20: Wannsee Conference proposes extermination as the Final Solution of the "Jewish Problem" • Feb: Albert Speer becomes armaments minister • Apr: Central planning committee formed to coordinate war production • May: RAF "Thousand bomber" raid on Cologne	• Jan: Labor conscription introduced for women aged 17–45	• June: Qualitative weapons' superiority abandoned, and the economy mobilized to concentrate on quantitative production • July 20: Assassination attempt on Hitler • July: Goebbels becomes plenipotentiary-general for total war • Oct: Volkssturm created • Nov: Speer creates Ruhr staff to maintain production in the face of devastating Allied bombing raids	• Apr 30: Hitler commits suicide
• Jan: First American GIs arrive in UK • Dec: Beveridge Plan published	• Dec: Balloting for "Bevin Buys" begins		• July: Churchill resigns after electoral defeat; Attlee forms Labour government
• Apr: Nonagricultural labor conscripted for harvest • Apr: First war loan floated • May: Central partisan staff set up to organize guerrilla warfare in occupied territory	• Apr: Peak of prices on free market		
• Jan: Establishment of War Production Board • Feb: War Relocation Authority established to intern Japanese–Americans • Feb: Prohibition of non-military automobile production • June: Office of War Information established to facilitate propaganda • Nov: Secretary of Agriculture calls for 18 million "Victory Gardens"	• Smith–Connally Act • Jan: Army invites Japanese-American men in concentration camps to enlist • Feb: Allied shipping losses reach peak • May: Office of War Mobilization established to coordinate production • Nov: War production at peak	• June: Servicemen's Readjustment Act ("GI Bill of Rights")	• Apr: Death of Roosevelt; Truman becomes president

15

Datafile

Japan's invasion of China in 1937 was reckless in the extreme, for it placed enormous burdens on its empire's military resources. Japan's army was relatively small. Fewer than 1 million of the empire's 100 million served in it at any one time. Although the Japanese Empire had a population of 100 million, labor-intensive agriculture and industry, combined with a primitive conscription apparatus, meant that mobilization was inefficient. Between 1937 and 1945 7.4 million Japanese served in the armed forces, a very low proportion when compared to the UK where 6.2 million of a population of 48 million served in the armed forces between 1939 and 1945.

Japanese manpower

▲ Between 1937 and 1941 the Japanese army more than doubled in size placing enormous strains on the economy. The Japanese began the Pacific war in 1941 with armed forces which could not be expanded easily and which would consequently be very vulnerable to attritional warfare.

◄ To the Japanese army the main war was being fought in China where most of its men were deployed. The army regarded the Pacific conflict as very much the navy's war.

Deployment of Japanese divisions

China
Manchuria
Japan and Korea
SE Asia and Pacific

▶ A graphic illustration of the steadily diminishing role of the Guomindang armies after December 1941. Even before this date it is likely that some of the number are civilian rather than military casualties.

Battle casualties of Guomindang

847,000 (Japanese estimate)

In the mid 1930s the officer corps of Japan's army and navy were riven by competing factions, most of which had schemes for the expansion of Japan's empire. Within the army the *Koda ha* (Imperial Way) faction, a group of low-ranking officers allied with the extreme nationalist Black Dragon Society, pressed for expansion into Siberia. For the *Tosei ha* "control" faction (composed largely of senior officers and the general staff), invasion of China with its population of 400 million was a tempting possibility, but time was running out. Jiang Jieshi's Guomindang army seemd to be on the verge of reunifying the country after the anarchy of the 1920s.

Feuding between the *Tosei ha* and *Koda ha* came to a head in 1935. *Tosei ha* officers managed to transfer their opponents to remote and unpopular locations: but when in February 1936 the 1st Division, staffed by *Koda ha* officers, was ordered to go from Tokyo to the Mongolian–Manchurian frontier, the entire division rose in revolt, seized part of Tokyo and murdered several government members. *Tosei ha* troops suppressed the rebellion and the ringleaders were executed, but the government had a price to pay. From 1936 onward army and navy ministers had to be serving officers, subject to dismissal for behavior deemed inimical to military interests. According to the constitution of 1889, if any minister resigned the entire cabinet had to follow. Consequently even if civilian ministers united against their service colleagues, the latter could still threaten their

JAPAN'S WAR IN ASIA

resignation and bring down the entire government. The armed forces effectively held the government under their thumb.

The navy also had plans for expansion, but in yet another direction. Naval officers argued that Japan needed to secure control over supplies of raw materials – oil, rubber, tin, iron ore and bauxite – materials which the Dutch East Indies and British-ruled Malaya contained in limitless quantities. The first step would be the construction of a fleet capable of challenging Anglo-American domination of the Pacific – an aim supported by Japan's industrial combines, the *zaibatsu*, and much of Japanese society. In 1935 Admiral Yamamoto, Japan's delegate to the London Disarmament Conference, announced that Japan would no longer be bound by the Washington Treaty, which imposed limits on fleet sizes. He returned to a hero's welcome, and as vice-minister of the navy was soon overseeing a massive naval expansion program. It would be many years before Japan could challenge the British and the Americans. Domination of the Pacific could be achieved by about 1950.

Japan attempts a quick campaign in China

Japan's admirals were furious when, on 7 July 1937, large-scale fighting grew out of a minor clash between Japanese and Guomindang forces near the Marco Polo Bridge half-way between Tianjin and Beijing. The Guandong army, now firmly under the *Tosei ha*'s control, advanced

south in force and occupied the Beijing-Tianjin region as well as striking west in Outer Mongolia. For a few days in early August it looked as if the conflict might quickly be settled, but Jiang Jieshi (who a few months earlier had entered into an anti-Japanese alliance with Mao's communists) showed unexpected resolve. He concentrated his best units in the Shanghai area and on 8 August launched a heavy attack on the Japanese concession, jeopardizing Japan's Shanghai garrison. Even the most moderate civilians in the Tokyo government wanted to avoid the humiliation of evacuating the city: on 17 August general mobilization was ordered in Japan and reinforcements rushed to Shanghai. As punishment, Japan occupied territory in northern China down to the Huang (or Yellow) river – intended to be used as a bargaining counter when Jiang Jieshi was

▼ Shanghai-bound reinforcements march through Tokyo streets lined with crowds, 11 October 1937.

Emperor Hirohito 1901–89

Once portrayed as an unworldly pacifist ineffectually urging restraint on Japan's military, it is now clear that from his accession in 1926 Hirohito was more than a figurehead. He did not actively promote the military's plans2 for expansion but he did little to discourage them and took an intense interest in the conduct of the war. His power within the state system was revealed when he advised capitulation in 1945. His subsequent surrender broadcast on 15 August 1945 caused all but a few diehards to lay down their arms.

Prince Fumimaro Konoye 1891–1945

A member of the prestigious Fujiwara clan, Konoye entered Japan's house of peers in 1916, and became president of this house in 1933. Between 1937 and 1941 Konoye served three times as prime minister, but proved unable to control either the military or the naval members of his cabinets. He retired from politics in 1941 and although he remained inactive throughout the war, when he learned that the Americans were planning to place him on trial for war crimes he committed suicide.

Kanji Ishiwara 1889–1949

A pan-Asian nationalist who saw Japan's mission as the liberation of its fellow Asians from European domination, Ishiwara used his position on the staff of the Guandong army to engineer the seizure of Manchuria in 1931 and to provoke the "China incident" six years later. Though many high-ranking officers shared his views, Ishiwara fell out with Tojo and the dominant control faction, and in 1941, on the eve of Pearl Harbor, he was cashiered. He spent the rest of the war engaged in propaganda work.

forced to come to the conference table. Things worked out very differently: eight years later much of Japan's army was still tied down in China.

In early September 150,000 Japanese, organized in two mutually supporting army groups, struck south along the three main railroad lines toward the Huang. Guomindang forces, despite outnumbering their opponents three to one, lacked armor, artillery and air support, and melted away before the Japanese advance. By the first week in November some Japanese units had reached the Huang. Others drove southwest through the mountainous Shanxi province but met unexpectedly determined resistance from Mao's communists and suffered two disturbing reverses; but by November they had achieved most of their objectives.

The struggle for Shanghai was far more difficult. More than 450,000 of Jiang Jieshi's best troops assailed the Japanese: only when the landing of a fresh Japanese army group south of Shanghai in Hangzhou Bay on 5 November threatened them with envelopment did they withdraw to Nanjing. Jiang Jieshi's forces were shattered. He had lost 270,000 men. Japanese casualties, 40,000 of the 200,000 engaged, had not been light either. Tokyo thought the campaign had ended with the fall of Shanghai, but local commanders had already decided to advance on Nanjing, the Guomindang capital, unaware that Jiang Jieshi had moved his government to Hankou in the southwest. Nanjing fell on 13 December: for a month Japanese troops indulged in an orgy of looting, rape and murder. They burnt down a third of the city and butchered between 200 and 300 thousand Chinese.

Japanese atrocities failed to dent the Guomindang's resolve. In mid-December Tokyo used the German ambassador to Hankou to propose terms to Jiang Jieshi. All military activity would cease if he acknowledged the authority of the army's puppet governments in northern China and Mongolia, agreed to further the economic integration of China and Japan, accepted responsibility for the war and agreed to pay reparations. On 26 December Jiang Jieshi rejected these proposals out of hand.

Japan attempts to defeat the Chinese government
Japan's only option was to continue the war. On 16 January 1938 the prime minister, Prince Konoye, announced that Japan would have no further dealings with the Guomindang, and would instead "rely upon the establishment and growth of a new Chinese regime for cooperation" – in effect, create a new government. Two months later in a wave of patriotic zeal the diet voted a national mobilization law which extended conscription and introduced rationing: Japan settled down for a long war.

By March 1938 nearly 500,000 Japanese troops had been sent to China; the army in north China now launched a southward offensive to link up with Japanese forces in the Shanghai-Nanjing area. It went disastrously wrong. Only half of the 60,000 men who found themselves surrounded by 200,000 Chinese at Tai'erzhuang managed to fight their way back north. So one month later the

Jiang Jieshi 1887–1975
Leader of China in 1937, Jiang had established his authority in the late 1920s: in 1927 he had ousted the communists from the nationalist Guomindang party and in 1928 had established his government in Beijing. The Japanese forced him out, to Nanjing, Hankou, and finally to Chongqing in summer 1938. He rejected their terms, but in spite of receiving lavish supplies from the USA could not expel them. On Japan's surrender in 1945 he found communists embedded in former Japanese territory. Civil war followed; the Guomindang lost; Jiang fled to Formosa.

Mao Zedong 1893–1976
A member of China's communist party from its foundation in 1921, Mao became its leading figure in the late 1920s. Narrowly avoiding destruction at the hands of the Guomindang, Mao led the communists in the "Long March" of 13,000km (8,000mi) to safety in Shaanxi (1934–36). After the Japanese invasion there was a truce between the communists and the Guomindang but in practice the communists waged guerrilla war against the Guomindang as well as the invaders. By the time of the Japanese surrender they were strong enough to defeat the Guomindang in the civil war of 1946–49. Mao then dominated China for 27 years.

Japanese tried again, their reinforced armies this time advancing simultaneously from north and south; they sliced through Chinese defenses and linked up a Xuzhou on 20 May for what should have been a decisive victory. More than 100,000 Chinese were trapped between Xuzhou and the Yellow Sea, but as the Japanese closed in they melted into the countryside, merging imperceptibly with the peasantry.

Even if Japan could not destroy the Chinese armies, at least it could drive Jiang Jieshi from Hankou. Forces headed west toward the rail junction at Zhengzhou, planning to swing south down to the Guomindang's new capital. They advanced

◄ After the fighting in July 1937, Japanese troops staged a formal triumphal entrance into Beijing in early August.

▼ From August to November 1937 the Japanese attempted to capture Shanghai. Half a million troops were engaged in bloody combat. Japanese aircraft bombed the city repeatedly, and civilian casualties were heavy. This photograph was taken in the wake of a raid in early November on Shanghai's eastern (Nanjing) railroad station.

along the southern bank of the Huang; by early July they were less than 80km (50mi) from Zhengzhou when a wall of water engulfed them. Thousands drowned, most equipment was lost, and the advance halted. The Chinese, unable to stop the Japanese by military means, had broken the Huang dykes.

By September the Japanese had regrouped: reinforced to 12 divisions (about 250,000 men) they drove southwest toward Hankou. On 10 October, after heavy fighting, they entered the now-ruined city only to find that Jiang Jieshi had again moved his capital, this time to Chongqing. Although the Japanese launched limited offensives south of the Yanzi the following year, the capture of Hankou marked the limit of their territorial expansion. In 15 months and at the cost of 70,000 dead they had overrun an area of 1.8 million sq km (700,000 sq mi) with a population of 170 million, the most economically productive area of China.

By this time the Japanese, who physically occupied only the major cities and railroad lines of this vast area, faced a new threat – sporadic guerrilla activity from the communist 8th Route Army in Shaanxi which by September 1937 had started to infiltrate north China. The Japanese handled the guerrilla problem more subtly than western nations did after 1945. They realized that Mao's revolutionary war was essentially political in nature so they created a variety of civilian agencies to win the population's loyalty. After two and a half years of consolidation, while they raised and trained a pro-Japanese Chinese army, Tokyo established, on 30 March 1940, a government in Beijing under a former prominent Guomindang member, Weng Jing-wei. But the communists had also been busy and on 20 August 1940 Mao launched his "Hundred Regiments" offensive, an

intensive series of small-scale guerrilla raids all over northern China. Overnight Japanese hopes of peaceful consolidation evaporated. Their response was a program of calculated terrorism, the "Three All Policy" – take all, burn all, kill all. Japanese columns moved through the most heavily infiltrated areas creating a wasteland, but for every communist suspect killed they created ten new guerrillas. Japan was still fighting the insurgents when it was forced to surrender in 1945.

By autumn 1938 Japan had realized the painful truth that there could never be a decisive battle to end the war with China. But they could render the Guomindang forces impotent by cutting off Jiang Jieshi's supply lines from the outside world. As early as 3 May 1938 forces from Formosa, acting without authorization from Tokyo, had occupied the southern Chinese port of Xiamen. In September Tokyo ordered the systematic seizure of China's remaining ports. Guangzhou was occupied on 25 October, Fuzhou on 23 November, Hainan on 10 February 1939; nine months later a force landed at the head of the Gulf of Tongking, advanced inland and captured Nanning, thereby cutting the major rail and road link between the French Indochinese port of Haiphong and Chongqing.

But Japan could do little about the supplies which China continued to receive via the old silk route from the USSR through Xinjiang. On 11 July 1938 elements of the Guandong army, claiming that Russian forces had violated Manchurian territory, had attacked Soviet positions on Chengkaifeng Hill, where the borders of Korea, Manchuria and Siberia met. After 30 days of bitter fighting they were bloodily repulsed. Nine months later much more serious fighting had broken out between the Guandong army and Soviet forces along the Mongolian border; by September 1939, after suffering more than 18,000 casualties, the Japanese had withdrawn, defeated. Although in the summer of 1940 diplomatic efforts improved relations with the Soviet Union, until the Germans invaded the western USSR on 22 June 1941, Tokyo was acutely aware of a major threat to the northwest.

China was also receiving supplies from the south. The Haiphong–Nanning railway line was now defunct but supplies could be trucked to

▶ After their initial onslaught, the Japanese attempted to bring the Guomindang to battle by launching drives up the Huang Ho and Yangzi river valleys, and attempted to starve them of supplies by occupying ports along China's coast (1938–39). It was all to no avail. The Chinese continued to withdraw out of reach and established new supply lines via French Indochina and British Burma.

▲ The bandy-legged, buck-toothed Jap of Western cartoons of the 1930s. This German cartoon is a reminder that until Japan's entry into the Axis on 27 September 1940 relations with Germany were ambivalent.

◀ After a grueling four-month campaign, Japanese forces from northern China linked up with their forces in central China to the west of Xuzhou. This photograph, taken on 19 May 1938, the day the northern and southern thrusts met, shows troops of Japan's 2nd Army streaming westward from Xuzhou, driving the Guomindang ever deeper into south central China.

▼ In the wake of the retreating Guomindang came hordes of refugees.

The Japanese Invasion of China and Indochina 1937–41

Map labels:

USSR
MONGOLIA
MANZH-OUGUO
JAPAN
CHINA
BURMA
SIAM
FRENCH INDOCHINA
PHILIPPINE IS

SUIYUAN
CHAHAR
JEHOL
MANZHOUGUO (Jap)
Shenyang
Zhangjiakou
Baotau
Datong
Beijing
Marco Polo Bridge
Tianjin
Port Arthur (Jap)
KOREA (Jap)
Seoul
Yinchuan (Ningxia)
Zijingguan Pass
Ladies Pass
HEBEI
Bo Hai
Taiyuan
Shijiazhuang
SHANXI
Huang
Ji'nan
SHANDONG
Qingdao
Yellow Sea
Xan'an
Anyang
GANSU
SHAANXI
Kaifeng
Tai'erzhuang
Wei
Zhengzhou
Dongguan
Xuzhou
JIANGSU
Xi'an
HENAN
Huai
Grand Canal
Han
Nanjing
ANHUI
QINGHAI
Jialing
SICHUAN
HUBEI
Hankou
Shanghai
Chengdu
Yangzi
Hangzhou
CHINA
Yalong
XIKANG
Chongqing
Dongting Hu
Yuan
Nanchang
Poyang Hu
ZHEJIANG
Changsha
HUNAN
JIANGXI
Wenzhou
East China Sea
GUIZHOU
Hengyang
Yangzi
Gan
Guiyang
FUJIAN
Fuzhou
BURMA ROAD
Kunming
YUNNAN
GUANGXI
Liuzhou
Xiamen
GUANGDONG
Nanning
Xi
Guangzhou
Shantou
Formosa (Jap)
Red
Hanoi
Haiphong
Macao (Port)
Hong Kong (Br)
FRENCH INDOCHINA
Gulf of Tongking
South China Sea
Hainan
Mekong
SIAM

Legend:

- - - International boundary 1937
Chinese Communist base area 1937
Occupied by Japanese forces
before 1937
1937
1938
1939
1940
1941
Japanese attacks
✗ Japanese defeat
— Main railroad

Scale 1:15 000 000
0   600 km
0   400 mi

NORTHERN AND CENTRAL THEATERS

1937

July 28
(to Dec. 27). Following clashes at Marco Polo Bridge (July 7) the Japanese strike south into Hebei province along three main railroad lines. Beijing and Tianjin are quickly occupied: by the end of 1937 Japan controls eastern China north of Shanxi province.

August 8
(to Dec. 13) A Japanese amphibious assault against Shanghai runs into Jiang Jieshi's best armies: the city does not fall until Nov. 11. The Japanese drive west and capture Nanjing (Dec. 13).

1938

March 1
(to April 6) A Japanese army advances south along the Ji'nan–Xuzhou railroad and is surrounded by 200,000 Chinese at Tai'erzhuang (March 24). The Japanese fight their way north (April 6).

May 1
(to May 20) Reinforced, the Japanese launch converging attacks from Ji'nan in the north and Nanjing in the south and capture Xuzhou on May 20. Their northern and central forces are now linked.

June 1
(to July 1) The Japanese strike west along the Xuzhou–Xi'an railroad aiming to capture the vital Zhengzhou railway junction. Kaifeng falls on

June 6 but as the Japanese approach Zhengzhou the Chinese break the Huang dykes, engulfing the Japanese.

August 1
(to Oct. 10) Shifting their axis of advance, Japanese converge on Jiang's capital Hankou and take the city on Oct. 10. But Jiang has removed his government to Chongqing.

1939

March 27
Japanese capture Nanchang.

September 14
(to Oct. 16) Five Japanese divisions converge on Changsha, and in a month's fighting are driven northward – the end of Japanese expansion in central China until 1944.

SOUTH AND INDOCHINA

1938

May 11
(to Nov. 23) To cut off supply lines, Japan begins occupying China's ports: Xiamen on May 31, Guangzhou on Oct. 25, and Fuzhou on Nov. 23.

1939

February 10
(to Nov. 24) Still trying to isolate China, Japan lands on Hainan Island on Feb. 10 and occupies the remaining ports. A force lands on the south China coast on Nov. 15, drives north and captures Nanning, cutting the Hanoi–Changsha rail link (Nov. 24). China now has only two supply routes: the railroad from Haiphong and a road from Lashio in Burma.

1940

June 25
(to Sept. 22) After France's defeat in Europe, Japan by agreement lands forces in Indochina. Warships in Haiphong harbor effectively close the Haiphong–Kunming railroad. On Sept. 22 Japan begins a military occupation of the Haiphong-Hanoi area.

July 18
(to Oct. 18) The UK capitulates to Japan's demand to close the Burma road. Three months later, the Luftwaffe defeated, the UK reopens it (Oct. 18).

1941

July 24
Japanese forces occupy central and southern Indochina.

Chongqing via a single-track line running northwest from Hanoi to Kunming. Moreover, since early 1938 the Chinese had been constructing a road southwest of Kunming to Lashio in Burma. The Japanese army now saw a solution to the China war in a drive south to occupy French Indochina and British Burma, thereby cutting Jiang Jieshi's supply lines. Thus it was that late in 1939 army policy began to converge with the navy's long-standing plans for southern expansion. It was a dangerous move which might result in conflict with the European colonial powers; since September both army and navy had been observing the progress of war in Europe, hoping that a reverse for the western Allies would afford them an opportunity for expansion.

Friction between Japan and the USA

That opportunity came, almost miraculously, in May and June 1940: Germany's occupation of the Low Countries and France and the apparent imminence of its invasion of Britain suddenly rendered the Southeast Asian colonies vulnerable. Japan's army and navy urged action but the civilians in Yonai's cabinet, wary of US reaction, were more cautious. Relations between the two nations had been deteriorating since 1937. As early as 5 October 1937 US President Roosevelt, influenced by the powerful China lobby, had suggested a quarantine of Japan and other aggressor nations. Two months later Japanese attacks on British and American gunboats on the Yangzi prompted his proposal (which horrified the UK cabinet) for an Anglo-American blockade of Japan. Japan's abject apology on Christmas Day 1937 obviated the need for such action, but during the next 18 months the American press whipped up strong anti-Japanese sentiments within the USA. Private American citizens sent millions of dollars to the Guomindang. In July 1939, the government, responding to public and congressional pressure, gave Japan six month's notice of the termination of a commercial treaty of 1911 which had given favored status to certain categories of Japanese imports. Worse was to come after the fall of France in June 1940; the US congress rushed through an act to expand the US fleet by 17 battleships, 11 aircraft carriers, 40 cruisers, nearly 70 submarines, and over 100 destroyers. Japan's admirals were aghast. Their own naval expansion program was tiny by comparison; by 1943, with the launching of the American program's first ships, they would be consigned to inferiority for ever.

The time window was small; Japan had to act while it still dominated the Pacific. Civilians in the government prevaricated; on 16 July the navy, acting in concert with the army, engineered the fall of the Yonai government. They would only allow Prince Konoye's new cabinet to take office on the condition that Japan would commit itself to southward expansion. Negotiations would settle border differences with the USSR: US intervention would be discouraged by Japan's entry into the Axis alliance with Germany and Italy. This settled, two days later the new government secured a diplomatic triumph by persuading the

◄ After summer 1938 pitched battles were a rarity but guerrilla attacks took an increasingly heavy toll on the Japanese. This picture taken in 1939 shows the result of a guerrilla attack on the railroad system of north China and the efforts of Japanese engineers to overcome the disruption.

▲ Troops of the communist 8th Route Army pose with the Great Wall as a dramatic backdrop for a propaganda photograph. Mao's forces inflicted a humiliating defeat upon Japanese forces in the Battle of Pingdiquan in the Wutai Mountains on 25 September 1937.

UK to close the Lashio-Kunming road; on 22 September, having demanded and received from the Vichy government the right to land troops, Japan began to occupy northern Indochina.

The Americans responded with vigor. On 26 September they placed an embargo on steel and scrap-iron exports to Japan, which cut its supply of construction materials by 80 percent. The Japanese navy prepared for the worst; on 15 October it ordered full war mobilization, to be completed in 18 months. The USA also geared up. In December Roosevelt gave full approval to a scheme for supplying Jiang Jieshi with new B-17 bombers on condition they were used to attack Tokyo; but delays in their construction forced the scheme to be abandoned. In January 1941 Roosevelt ordered a large proportion of America's battle fleet to move to Pearl Harbor in Hawaii and increased the flow of supplies to General Douglas MacArthur's forces in the Philippines. On 15 April he signed an executive order authorizing American pilots to volunteer to serve in China.

By summer 1941 the Japanese military were alarmed by the strength of the American reaction; the risk of war now seemed a certainty. Though the navy wanted to continue southern expansion, it wished to do so cautiously. On 22 June they had an unpleasant surprise. Elements within the army responded to the German invasion of the USSR by demanding an end to risky southern expansion and a move against Siberia. The navy thought Japan's chance would be lost foreover; it demanded the immediate occupation of southern Indochina and on 25 July Tokyo proclaimed a joint Franco-Japanese protectorate over the whole of Indochina. The American reaction the following day was dramatic; all Japanese assets in the United States were frozen, meaning that trade between the United States and Japan, including the export of oil, ceased. Within days the UK and the Netherlands had followed suit. Although Japan had a two-year stockpile of oil, it was now left with two choices: to negotiate or to fight.

The Konoye cabinet determined to follow both courses simultaneously – to prepare for war but to hope that the Americans would agree to lift the embargo in return for Japanese concessions. But what did the Americans want? On three occasions during August and September Konoye tried to arrange a summit meeting with Roosevelt, offering to withdraw all Japanese troops from Indochina as soon as the "China Incident" had been settled, but received no reply. On 3 September an army–navy liaison conference set a deadline of 10 October (later extended to 15 October) for negotiations to be successful. If not, war was the only recourse. On 2 October the US secretary of state, Cordell Hull, finally replied. America would not resume normal relations unless Japan evacuated not only Indochina but China as well – a demand the army, after four years of war, and 185,000 ahead, could not possibly concede.

On October 15 the deadline expired. Determined not to plunge Japan into war with the USA, Konoye resigned and the war minister, General Hideki Tojo, formed a government. Although in cabinet meetings Tojo had previously argued for war, as prime minister he had grave doubts. The navy refused him assurances that victory was possible; the best they could promise was a year's domination of the Pacific after which the Americans would inevitably gain supremacy. Tojo now extended the deadline for a negotiated settlement until 1 December and on 5 November despatched Admiral Kurusu as a special envoy to Washington with a new set of proposals; Japan would withdraw immediately from southern Indochina and would agree to a phased withdrawal from China over the next 25 years. Roosevelt's administration had learnt about Japan's simultaneous military preparations via intercepted Japanese diplomatic messages and treated the proposals with contempt. On 26 November Hull again insisted that normal relations could be restored only if Japan withdrew from Indochina and China immediately, recognized no government in China other than that of Jiang Jieshi, and withdrew from the Axis alliance. When these demands were received in Tokyo on 27 November they were treated as an ultimatum. Ten days later Japan launched a new war.

Franklin Delano Roosevelt 1882–1945

President of the USA from March 1933 until his death on 12 April 1945, Roosevelt steered America through the crises of the Great Depression and World War II. He was inclined to intervene in Europe after the outbreak of war there in 1939, but isolationist sentiment prohibited it. The Japanese attack on Pearl Harbor on 7 December 1941 caught Roosevelt and the American people completely by surprise, though it should have been evident that America's economic embargos on Japan would result in conflict. Isolationist sentiment vanished overnight and though Roosevelt remained unpopular in many quarters, for the first time in history a president commanded an America united in a common purpose. Unlike Churchill or Stalin, Roosevelt made few important strategic decisions, but he did offer America inspiring and visionary leadership.

Datafile

In spring 1940 Germany invaded and conquered Norway in two months and defeated the Low Countries and France in seven weeks. These victories at unprecedented speed were achieved through the use of a new style of mobile warfare, Blitzkrieg or "lightning war". It depended for success on organization and technique rather than superiority in numbers. As these statistics show, Germany was outnumbered in manpower and tanks and had superiority only in aircraft. The French and British thought they could hold the Franco-German Front and even sent an expeditionary force to oppose the German invasion.

The most startling feature of Blitzkrieg is that dead and wounded were only a small proportion of the forces engaged. The secret lay not in killing enemies, but in confusing and demoralizing them, so that they surrendered in droves. By the standards of World War I, Germany's victories were cheap.

Balance of forces

Norwegian campaign

Invasion of Low Countries

◀ The casualty figures for the German campaign of May–June 1940 underline the lesson of Norway. France lost only 90,000 dead and 200,000 wounded, but more than 1.9 million were taken prisoner. But for the Dunkirk evacuation the British Expeditionary Force would have suffered the same fate.

▲ In the late spring of 1940 the UK and France had near parity with Germany in manpower and if Belgian and Dutch forces were included they outnumbered German forces by a healthy margin. The casualty statistics suggest a drawn battle, but this was a quirk of Blitzkrieg; the reality was a runaway German victory.

Western Front 1940

Tanks
Total 5700

47% 53%

Aircraft
Total 4200

76% 24%

British forces July 1940

14%
47%
39%

Total 778,000
Evacuated formations
Local Defence Volunteers
Regulars

Allies
Germany

◀ The outcome of the German invasion appeared extraordinary on the basis of a comparison of Allied and German armor. The Allies had more and better tanks. Germany had nearly a 2:1 superiority in aircraft but this should not in itself have been decisive. Had the Germans crossed the Channel the British could have done little to resist. Most forces consisted of untrained and ill-equipped LDVs and the remnants of the BEF which had lost all its heavy equipment (600 tanks and 2,350 guns) in France.

War broke out in Europe in September 1939 in response to Hitler's renewed attempt to establish German dominion over Europe. At first he extended German power with a series of bluffs and diplomatic triumphs. In March 1936, in defiance of the Treaty of Versailles, he successfully remilitarized the Rhineland. In April 1938 he engineered a union (*Anschluss*) between Germany and Austria. So far Britain and France stood by and did nothing. Then Hitler pressed what he claimed was his last territorial demand in Europe: for the German-speaking area of Czechoslovakia, the Sudetenland, to be transferred to the Reich. The two allies were unprepared for war and thought they could take Hitler at his word. At a conference held at Munich in September 1938, they ceded Hitler's demand and believed that the

HITLER'S WAR IN WESTERN EUROPE

Munich agreement had averted another major European war.

The ease of this success convinced Hitler that Britain and France would not resist further advances; but when he proceeded in March 1939 to annex the Czech provinces of Bohemia and Moravia they finally concluded that his word was worthless and committed themselves to defend the integrity of Poland. Without an alliance with the Soviet Union, however, the Western democracies had no means of honoring their commitment. On 23 August 1939 Hitler achieved another diplomatic coup by concluding a pact with the USSR. Eastern Europe was divided into Soviet and German spheres of influence and Poland was partitioned. Eight days later Hitler invaded Poland, and France and Britain declared war.

Hitler extends German power in Europe 1936–39

The German invasion of Norway, April 1940

The German invasion of the Low Countries and France, May–June 1940

The Battle of Britain

Churchill seeks to persuade the USA to enter the war

▼ Hitler's triumphal entry into the Sudetenland, 3 October 1938.

Adolf Hitler 1889–1945

If the blame for the outbreak of war in Europe is to be ascribed to a single man, it is to Hitler. A rootless Austrian adventurer, he had picked up in his youth a rag-bag of second-rate ideas and prejudices which had figured on the European right for a century. But through his energy and formidable gifts as an orator, he transformed them into a terrible and nihilistic philosophy. The profound error committed when he was appointed chancellor of Germany in 1933 and became *Führer* (leader) in 1934 was that nobody expected him to act upon what he believed. Racism, and antisemitism in particular, lay at the heart of his creed, and was to dominate his policy, culminating in the attempted destruction of European Jewry.

As a war leader, Hitler's greatest gift was his eagerness to take risks. He continually caught his opponents off their guard. His grasp of detail was phenomenal – he knew more about weapons than the commanders fielding them. His hypnotic hold over his subordinates ultimately worked against him.

He lived in a world of dreams, and lost all touch with reality. Believing himself to be "the greatest conqueror of all time", he refused to sanction any retreats, and the overextended Wehrmacht was overwhelmed by numbers in 1944–45. After Germany's defeat in the Battle of the Bulge, he withdrew to Berlin and committed suicide in the bunker of the chancellery on 30 April.

Wilhelm Keitel 1882–1946

Chief of the high command of the armed forces (OKW) from 1938 to 1945, Keitel was an officer of moderate ability who was completely held in thrall by Hitler. Ironically Hitler held him in low regard, and dismissed him as "a man with the brains of a cinema usher". But these were the attributes that Hitler required. He had surrounded himself with sycophants and nonentities who would not question his genius. Keitel had held no significant operational commands and his frontline service was confined to that of an artillery regiment in 1914–18. After the war he was convicted for war crimes and hanged.

▶ The Germans planned to occupy Norway by an amphibious preemptive strike. This was risky because of the inferior size of the German navy. The Germans relied on surprise, speed and ruse to land and occupy the ports before the British. Their plan worked brilliantly, except at Narvik.

▼ Below left, German troops in a Norwegian village. Movement and initiative were the keynotes of German infantry tactics. Below, ships sunk by German aircraft. Germany's losses at Narvik crippled its surface fleet.

The "phony war"

After the defeat and occupation of Poland, the war settled down to a routine of waiting. Except for the odd dramatic event at sea, like the sinking of the German pocket battleship *Graf Spee* in the Plate estuary in December 1939, little happened, though the British Expeditionary Force (BEF) was sent to France to join the considerable French forces in northern France.

This was the so-called "phony war". It suited Britain very well. The official British view was that Germany could, if necessary, be defeated in a long war: the greater economic strength of Britain and France would eventually wear Germany down, if they were only given time to mobilize it. France was confident that the Maginot Line, stretching along the French-German border from Longuyon to the Swiss frontier, was invulnerable. But the British prime minister, Neville Chamberlain, probably also hoped that stalemate would allow him to renew his efforts at appeasing Hitler, which were so rudely interrupted by Hitler's occupation of Prague in March 1939.

Thanks to the Soviet-Nazi Pact concluded in August 1939, Hitler was able to concentrate on one front at a time. The Soviet government was determined to divert German aggression away from the USSR and build up a defensive cordon around its frontiers. Stalin was not impressed by what he had seen of the Western democracies in 1939 and threw in his lot with Hitler. He invaded Poland from the east on 17 September – two weeks after Hitler had done so from the west. Two months later he invaded Finland. (See p.55.) The heroic struggle of the Finns excited Western sympathy. There were even those who wanted to send British and French troops through Norway and Sweden to aid them. This would merely have added the USSR, not to mention the neutral Scandinavian countries, to the list of Britain's enemies.

Buoyed up by his success in Poland, Hitler had planned originally to attack the west in November 1939. Severe winter weather forced the abandonment of this plan, much to the relief of the German high command.

The German campaign in the west opened on 9 April 1940, not in France but in Scandinavia. Hitler was determined to secure his right flank and supplies of bauxite ore from Sweden, which the Allies had threatened by laying minefields in Norwegian waters on 8 April.

Denmark was occupied within 24 hours. The Germans then aimed to seize the main Norwegian ports, Oslo, Bergen and Kristiansund, as rapidly as possible. German air power was crucial, and the British Home Fleet of three capital ships, six cruisers and 21 destroyers had no aircraft carrier sailing with it. The fall of these ports within hours made it difficult for the Allies to build up a base. Only at Narvik did they meet with success. Here 10 German destroyers were sunk for the loss of only two. An ill-equipped Allied expeditionary force under the British Lieutenant-General Claude Auchinleck was dispatched, and troops were withdrawn from France to reinforce it. But Auchinleck's task was hopeless and with the German attack on the Low Countries on 10 May, it was withdrawn. This evacuation was the first of a series of amphibious strategic withdrawals which were to mark the British conduct of the war in its first two years. The only major casualty was the loss of the unaccompanied aircraft carrier, *Glorious*, on 8 June. Losses on the ground were slight on both sides. The severest losses were sustained by the German Navy, whose surface fleet was crippled. But the acquisition of naval bases which threatened Britain's hold on the Northern Approaches of the Atlantic Ocean enabled the German navy to mount a much greater threat: a U-boat campaign against British sea lines of communication.

Hitler had not missed the bus, as Chamberlain had claimed. The Norwegian campaign's greatest casualty was Chamberlain's government. The irony was that it raised up in his place the man who, as first lord of the admiralty, had been most responsible for the disaster. On 10 May 1940 Winston Churchill became British prime minister, his decisive recommendation being that the Labour Party agreed to serve under him. Many, including King George VI, were sorry to see Chamberlain go. Chamberlain himself may have calculated that his surrender of power would be only temporary. Churchill had a reputation for reckless misjudgment. Chamberlain thought he would blunder; certainly he lacked a political base in the Conservative Party. But Chamberlain was

The German Invasion of Denmark and Norway 1940

● Capital city
— Main railroad

Norwegian Sea

German movements
→ Seaborne landings
▽ Airborne landings
⇒ Advances

Allied movements
➤ Seaborne landings
➤ Advances
⇢ Retreats
✈ Airfield
═ Main road

Scale 1:9 400 000
0 _____ 200 km
0 _____ 150 mi

April 9
Operation *Weserübung* ("Exercise Weser"). German troops invade Denmark: it capitulates within four hours, giving Germany control of the Skagerrak. Meanwhile German forces seize Norway's major peripheral ports and cities.

April 10–11
The Norwegian government and King Haakon VII refuse to submit to German terms. In the north a British destroyer fleet attacks German destroyers at Narvik (First Battle of Narvik).

April 12–20
Reinforced German forces push out from Oslo along the major roads. They capture Halden, Kongsberg and Hønefoss (April 13). To the north they move along the two main routes toward Trondheim. By the 20th

they are approaching Norwegian positions at Lillehammer and Rena. Meanwhile the British and French have landed troops at Namsos (April 14 and 16) and Åndalsnes (April 17) to reinforce the Norwegians. On April 13, in the Second Battle of Narvik, British destroyers again attack German ships. Meanwhile German territory around Narvik is expanded.

April 21
(to May 3) The Germans on the western road to Trondheim meet strong resistance from the Norwegians and British. They reach Otta on April 28. A final Norwegian and British action on April 30 fails to hold the Germans. British troops are evacuated from Åndalsnes on April 30 and May 1. Germans on the eastern road

reach Tynset on the 25th and meet German troops from Trondheim at Dragset on April 29. The British force at Namsos is withdrawn on May 2–3.

May 4–31
German troops advance north along the Arctic Highway. Norwegian, British and French troops attempt to stop the advance (notably at Stien on May 17) but fail. On May 31 the Germans reach Bødo and Rosvik. Meanwhile the Norwegians and their allies capture Narvik on May 28.

June 1–8
As German troops pour into France, the British and French evacuate Narvik.

June 9–13
German troops continue their advance north to Narvik.

The German Invasion of the Low Countries and France 1940

**Inset map labels:**
UK
BELGIUM
GERMANY
LUX
Cherbourg
Brest
Paris
GERMAN OCCUPIED
FRANCE
SWITZ
Bay of Biscay
Vichy
Lyons
VICHY
ITALY
Bordeaux
Marseilles
Pyrenees
Mediterranean Sea

Front lines
4 June
22 June   German advances

German deployments
Attacks
Airborne landings
Bridgeheads, 14–15 May
French deployments
British deployments
Belgian deployments

Front lines
16 May
24 May
28 May
Scale 1: 2 500 000
0 — 80 km
0 — 50 mi

**Main map labels:**
Emden
Groningen
Harlingen
Leeuwarden
Assen
Meppel
18th ARMY (B)
Ems
North Sea
Zuider Zee
Amsterdam
NETHERLANDS
Deventer
The Hague
Utrecht
Amersfoort
Apeldoorn
Arnhem
Lek
Rotterdam
Waal
Nijmegen
18th ARMY (B)
Dordrecht
s-Hertogenbosch
GERMANY
Moerdijk
Breda
Tilburg
Helmond
Essen
Roosendaal
Eindhoven
Venlo
ARMY GROUP B
Vlissingen
Peel Marshes
Maas
18th ARMY (B)
Moll
Antwerp
Roermond
Bruges
Albert Canal
Rhine
Ghent
Scheldt
Malines
Dyle
Louvain
Maastricht
Cologne
Menin
Courtrai
Brussels
6th ARMY (B)
Dunkirk
Calais
Lys
Lessines
Halle
Wavre
Fort Eben-Emael
Aachen
Boulogne
St Omer
Aire
Lille
Tournai
Nivelles
BELGIUM
Gembloux
Liège
4th ARMY (A)
Strait of Dover
Escaut
Mons
Namur
Huy
English Channel
La Bassée
Douai
Sambre
Charleroi
Houx
Arras
Maubeuge
Dinant
ARMY GROUP A
Noyelles-sur-Mer
Doullens
Cambrai
Le Cateau
Avesnes
Philippeville
12th ARMY (A)
Abbeville
Albert
Péronne
Ardennes
16th ARMY (A)
Amiens
Somme
St Quentin
Guise
Hirson
Monthermé
Bouillon
LUXEMBOURG
Trier
Mosel
Vervins
Montcornet
Sedan
Arlon
FRANCE
Marle
Crécy
Luxembourg
Oise
Laon
Longwy
Rethel
Aisne
MAGINOT LINE
Soissons
Reims

May 10
German Army Groups A and B launch a Blitzkrieg invasion of the Low Countries. The air force bombs Dutch and Belgian airfields while airborne troops land ahead of ground forces.

THE NETHERLANDS

May 10–14
Airborne troops attack The Hague and secure bridges and buildings near Rotterdam. The 18th Army drives Dutch defenders from the border and directs its main weight to Rotterdam. On May 14 the city

is heavily bombed and capitulates. The Dutch surrender the next day.

BELGIUM AND LUXEMBOURG

May 10–13
Glider-borne troops capture the Fort of Eben Emael and bridges over the Albert Canal. Armored divisions of the 6th Army cross the canal and advance (May 11). The main Belgian defenders, stationed behind the R. Dyle, begin to retreat. Liège falls on May 13. Meanwhile three armored corps of Group A

cross the Ardennes to obtain bridgeheads. German forces also invade Luxembourg.

BELGIUM AND FRANCE

May 14–23
Operation *Sickelschnitt* ("The cut of the sickle"). German forces break the French line at Sedan and the Allies retreat from the Dyle/Meuse defense line. German armored units race for the coast. Units reach the sea on May 20 and thereby split the Allied forces apart. French and British counterattacks (May 17–19

and 20 respectively) fail to reestablish contact between the two halves. German units then swing north, isolating Boulogne and Calais (May 22–23). The French 1st Army, the Belgian army and the British Expeditionary Force (BEF) are trapped between Group A and Group B advancing from the north. On May 23 Hitler and von Rundstedt order units to halt.

May 25
(to June 5) The Allies fall back around Dunkirk and are withdrawn in a large-scale evacuation (May 26–June 2).

The German advance continues. Calais falls on May 27; Belgium surrenders on May 28; Dunkirk is occupied on June 5. German forces then regroup.

FRANCE

June 5–27
German armored units pour into France. June 16, French premier Reynaud resigns; his successor, Pétain, seeks an armistice. It is signed on June 22. France is divided into an occupied zone and an autonomous state. German forces reach the Pyrenees on June 27.

Henri Philippe Pétain 1856–1951

The savior of France at Verdun in 1916–17, Pétain lived too long for the benefit of his historical reputation. The colossal casualty lists inflicted on France in 1914–18 shocked him and he was determined that it should never again endure that experience. Between the wars he became increasingly pessimistic and defeatist. He believed that "To make union with England was fusion with a corpse". He sued for peace with Germany and Italy in June 1940. He presided over the "unoccupied" Vichy zone as chief of state, a position he held until 1945. He was an elderly self-centered man who took most notice of the last person he had spoken to. After the Liberation he was tried and condemned to death. De Gaulle commuted the sentence.

struck down by cancer and was dead by the end of the year. Churchill immediately had himself elected leader of the Conservative Party and easily routed the appeasers. Though he had some difficult moments in 1941–42, he was not seriously challenged for the remainder of the war.

The fall of France

The campaign to the west of Germany began with a shattering air attack followed by parachute landings in the Netherlands and Belgium. They immediately appealed for Allied help. Plan "D", the Allied advance into Belgium to the River Dyle, was put into operation. But within five days the Dutch army had laid down its arms. Rotterdam was devastated by massive air attacks. The Belgian bastion at Eben Emael on the Albert Canal fell within hours. The Belgian army withdrew to the line Antwerp–Louvain and linked up with the BEF.

Once the Allies were committed in Belgium,

the German advance through the Ardennes began. By 14 May Army Group A, moving behind a screen of Stuka dive bombers, crossed the Meuse at Sedan. The French 9th Army, covering this sector of the front, was of poor quality and dissolved before the German assault. Paul von Kleist, commander of the Panzer groups, now wanted to halt and regroup. Guderian was furious. "I neither would nor could agree to these orders", he wrote later, "which would involve the sacrifice of surprise we had gained and of the whole initial success that we have achieved". He was given permission to continue the advance for a further 24 hours, and Guderian advanced 90km (55mi) beyond Sedan. By 17 May a bridgehead had been secured at St Quentin. The French army was paralyzed by this blow.

On 16 May Churchill visited Paris. In conference with the French prime minister, Paul Reynaud, he turned and asked Gamelin, the French commander in chief, "Where are the mobile reserves?" Gamelin replied, "There are none."

On 18 May Gamelin was sacked and replaced by Maxime Weygand who had a formidable reputation dating from his service as chief of staff to Marshal Foch in 1918. But his appointment came too late. Amiens fell on 20 May. Weygand hoped to organize a two pronged counterattack. On 21 May only the northern thrust toward Amiens could be mounted. It caught the Germans off-guard but was too weak for decisive effect.

The German advance on the English Channel continued the next day. May 23 was the critical day for the survival of the BEF. Its commander, Gort, was a courageous and determined fighting soldier. Though not the most intelligent of British generals, he was decisive. On hearing that the Belgian army had capitulated, he gave orders

▶ A staged humiliation, Hitler and his generals after the signing of the French surrender of 22 June 1940. Hitler was determined to avenge the signing of the Armistice in 1918. In the Compiègne forest the railroad car in which Marshal Foch had forced the Germans to surrender was installed, and every effort was made to rub salt into the French wounds.

◀ The original German plan was a repeat performance of the Schlieffen Plan of 1914. But an officer was captured carrying the plans. General von Manstein had developed an alternative. In Guderian's words, this "involved a strong tank thrust through Southern Belgium and Luxembourg towards Sedan, a break through of the prolongation of the Maginot line... and a consequent splitting in two of the whole French front". The success of this strategy was accentuated by the French plan to advance into Belgium.

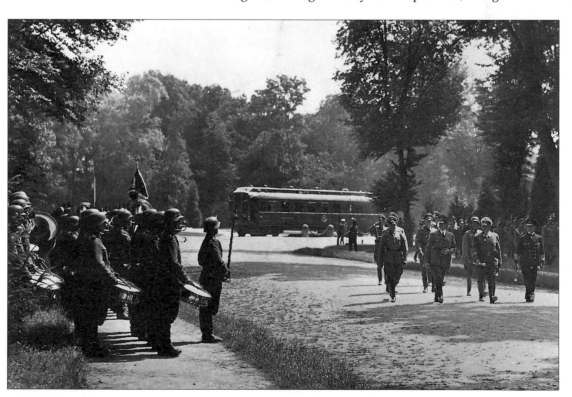

(fortified by Ultra intelligence) that the BEF should retire to the Channel ports, toward a perimeter around Dunkirk. There was not a moment to be lost, for Calais fell on 26 May.

That day the British admiralty issued orders for the commencement of Operation "Dynamo", the evacuation of the BEF from Dunkirk. This was made possible by the issue of the "halt order" by von Rundstedt, with Hitler's agreement, on 24 May. It was rescinded the following day but 24 vital hours were lost. "Dynamo" lasted nine days: it was hoped that 35,000 might be saved; in the event ten times that number were rescued.

The Battle of France now moved rapidly toward its climax. Weygand intended to organize another defensive line along the Somme. But with the Maginot Line outflanked and the morale of the French army shattered this was an empty hope. Although individual fighting units showed courage, defeatism had rotted the morale of the French army and prolonged resistance was impossible. The Germans crossed the Seine on 10 June, and two days later the French government declared Paris an open city. Churchill's offer of a complete Anglo-French Union was ignored. Reynaud resigned and was succeeded by the aged and pessimistic Marshal Philippe Pétain. He asked for an armistice and accepted German terms on 22 June. In Churchill's pithy phrase, the Battle of France was over, the Battle of Britain was about to begin. France was divided into two zones, the occupied north and west and the unoccupied south and east. France was to bear the cost of the German occupation; Pétain set up a puppet capital at Vichy. Fearful that the French navy would be seized by the Germans, the Royal Navy attacked a French squadron at Oran. For a few days it appeared possible that Vichy France would declare war on Britain.

The Battle of Britain

The most celebrated aspect of the Battle of Britain was the war in the air, which is described in another chapter. (See p.102.) But in its entirety the Battle of Britain was the last moment when the British held the destiny of Europe in its hands. A heady spirit of defiance characterized British thought and deed. Despite defeats, Churchill demanded from Germany nothing less than unconditional surrender – or, as he put it, he offered nothing but "blood, toil, tears and sweat". There would be no negotiations with the Axis powers, no compromise peace. After the fall of France, Hitler offered peace terms which were discussed seriously by the British Cabinet: some of the appeasers thought that they should be pursued. In private Churchill was less dismissive than he was in public. He was still in a weak political position. But Churchill not only sensed the public mood, he embodied it, and Hitler's terms were rejected.

Hitler's directive for the invasion of Britain, Operation "Sealion", was issued on 16 July 1940. The main thrust of the invasion would be delivered by Army Group A, which would cross from the Pas de Calais with six divisions. Another thrust based on Le Havre, would move on the

▶ German bombers over London 1940; impressive but not decisive. In reality German bombers were designed for air–ground cooperation and not strategic bombing.

▼ A miracle of deliverance, the British army escapes at Dunkirk the humiliation heaped on the French army. But in France it was regarded as a betrayal.

Winston Churchill 1874–1965

Churchill had earned the reputation before 1934 as a man of great ability, but also of romantic inclinations and reckless misjudgment. On being appointed prime minister and minister of defence in May 1940, Chamberlain thought he would blunder. Certainly he lacked a political base in the Conservative Party. But Churchill routed his opponents. He was probably the most gifted politician produced by Britain. In the range of his gifts he has been compared with Caesar. Like Caesar he could be wilful, brutal and impulsive. Yet he displayed a streak of noble romanticism that matched the exigencies of the hour. During the war he was able to bolster domestic morale, win American support for the British cause and contribute imaginatively to the formulation of strategy. In A.J.P Taylor's view, Churchill was "the saviour of his country". It is difficult to think of anyone remotely qualified to take his place.

Isle of Wight, Portsmouth and Brighton. A secondary force would land at Lyme Bay and advance on Bristol. But this plan demanded control of the English Channel, and thus air superiority. Also, the German armed forces not only lacked a tradition of carrying out amphibious operations, but lacked specialized equipment.

The commander of the German air force, Hermann Goering, boasted that he could achieve victory over British skies. But Hitler was impatient and his heart was not wholly in the operation. On 15 August came *Adler Tag*, Eagle Day, in which the air force made an all-out assault on the RAF's airfields. Air chief marshal Sir Hugh Dowding, furnished with Ultra intelligence, knew the pattern of the raids in advance. The RAF remained in being; German air superiority was not achieved. The air battle continued for another month, until on 17 September Hitler issued instructions for "Sealion's" indefinite postponement. The air war now changed character. Provoked by an RAF raid on Berlin, the German air force concentrated on the bombing of British cities.

How was Britain to survive, let alone defeat Germany? The clue was provided in Churchill's "we will fight them on the beaches" speech. Here, he explained, Britain would "carry on the struggle, until, in God's good time, the New World, with all its power and might, steps forth to the rescue and liberation of the old". Since his accession to the premiership, Churchill had cultivated the president of the USA, Franklin D. Roosevelt. In December 1940 Churchill visited Washington and the basis for future wartime collaboration with the United States was laid. Though bound by election promises to keep the USA out of the war, Roosevelt was conscious of the threat posed to American security by a Nazi superstate controlling the resources of Europe. On 10 January 1941 the president placed a Bill before the US Congress which permitted the handing over to states at war with the Axis weapons which need not be bought with dollars – "lend-lease". The bill was passed. Thus the first major step was taken toward ultimate Allied victory.

Hermann Goering 1893–1946

On the strength of his reputation as an air ace in World War I, Goering was given responsibility for the conduct of the German aerial war. A man of ability, unlike many of Hitler's Nazi cronies, Goering was also flabby and corrupt – his real political gifts canceled out by a penchant for good living, over-eating and the consolation of drugs. The longer the war went on, the less weight (figuratively speaking) he carried in the inner circles of the *Führer*. He was convicted at Nuremberg but committed suicide on the eve of execution.

Hugh Dowding 1882–1968

Dowding had been an advocate of fighter defense before 1939, and was never persuaded by the "bomber will always get through" school. He had supported the decision to deploy radar in 1935. He resisted Churchill's desire to send Fighter Command piecemeal to France during the crisis in May and June 1940. In summer and fall 1940 he won the Battle of Britain. This was a major achievement, but Dowding was aloof and morose and had many enemies. In 1940 he was dismissed as the result of a shabby cabal.

Datafile

The expansion of the US navy authorized in June 1940 threatened the predominance of the Japanese navy in the Pacific. It attempted to preempt the challenge by eliminating the US Pacific fleet. On 7 December 1941 it bombed the fleet's base at Pearl Harbor: battleships were destroyed but the US carriers were elsewhere. Thereafter Admiral Yamamoto sought to destroy the US fleet in a climactic battle, for fear of a war of attrition. But when engaged in the Battles of the Coral Sea and Midway in 1942 the Japanese suffered irreplaceable losses. The decision to challenge the US landing on Guadalcanal in August 1942 involved them in exactly the kind of conflict they feared.

Forces at Guadalcanal

36% / 64%
Japan Total 36,000

3% / 97%
USA Total 60,000

[ ] Casualties

▲◄ **The comparison of US and Japanese forces on Guadalcanal and the number of casualties (above) graphically illustrates the superior ability of the US navy to keep supplies moving to the island, while denying supplies to the enemy. In the naval campaign (left) the Japanese did better, their losses being less than those they inflicted on the Americans. But the United States' losses were being rapidly replaced.**

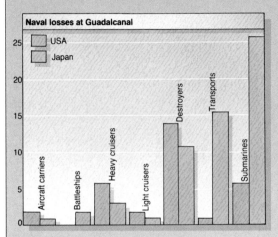

Naval losses at Guadalcanal

[ ] USA
[ ] Japan

(bar chart with categories: Aircraft carriers, Battleships, Heavy cruisers, Light cruisers, Destroyers, Transports, Submarines; y-axis 0 to 25)

▼► **The Japanese began with a slight numerical advantage over the fleets of the USA, UK and the Netherlands (below), but in reality the advantage was much greater, the Japanese having a common system of training and communication. This advantage disappeared as the USA set in motion a construction program the like of which the world had never seen (right). New American ships were better constructed and fitted with sophisticated equipment.**

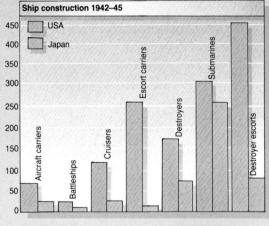

Ship construction 1942–45

[ ] USA
[ ] Japan

(bar chart with categories: Aircraft carriers, Battleships, Cruisers, Escort carriers, Destroyers, Submarines, Destroyer escorts; y-axis 0 to 450)

Pacific navies 1941

7% / 53% / 35% / 5%
Total ships 487

[ ] Japan
[ ] USA
[ ] UK
[ ] Netherlands

Airpower 1942–45

21% / 79%
Aircraft built Total 95,000

14% / 86%
Aircraft lost Total 19,700

[ ] USA
[ ] Japan

◄ **The United States outbuilt Japan in warplanes by a factor of 4:1. Although the Japanese had a marked qualitative advantage at first, by the summer of 1943, the Americans were introducing machines of greater speed, endurance, maneuverability, robustness and firepower than Japanese models. America's quantitative and qualitative superiority was reflected in the comparative air losses.**

Since the 1920s the Japanese navy had been preparing for battle with the American fleet. It assumed that the American Pacific fleet would strike against the Japanese mandates. By the summer of 1940, with war now a real possibility, the newly appointed commander of the Combined Fleet, Admiral Yamamoto, began a systematic revision of the navy's plans. The decisive action strategy now seemed very risky: if it failed the American fleet could cut the supply lines of Japanese forces in Malaya and the Indies. Far better, Yamamoto reasoned, to destroy the American fleet before it had time to put to sea. Japan would then have about two years in which to consolidate its conquests and construct a defensive perimeter in the central and south Pacific.

The problem was finding a means of destroying the American fleet in harbor. Midget submarines seemed to be the only means, yet Yamamoto, as one of the few senior officers to have qualified as a pilot, argued vigorously for a simultaneous aerial attack launched from Japan's six fleet carriers. Many officers thought this absurd. No capital ship had been sunk by aerial attack and the US base at Pearl Harbor was too shallow and too narrow for the use of air-dropped torpedoes.

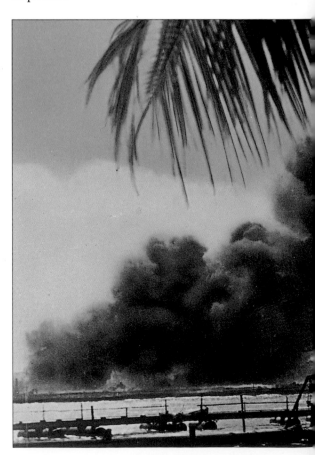

JAPAN'S WAR IN THE PACIFIC

The bombing of Pearl Harbor

On 11 November 1940 attitudes changed. That morning 21 obsolete Swordfish torpedo bombers launched from the British carrier HMS *Illustrious* sank three Italian battleships within Taranto harbor – both shallower and smaller than Pearl Harbor. The Japanese navy quickly obtained a full report and began planning a similar but large-scale attack. Technical problems were systematically overcome; by the summer of 1941 new quick-fusing shallow-run torpedoes and massive armor-piercing bombs were being manufactured. Japanese agents in Hawaii had by now given an accurate picture of the operations of the American fleet. The naval commander who planned the attack, Minoru Genda, decided that the best time to attack would be early on a Sunday morning, when the ships would be in harbor and many of the crews on leave in Honolulu. Sunday 7 December was selected: six carriers would launch 360 planes while midget submarines would penetrate the base.

In the early hours of 7 December US anti-submarine patrols reported several contacts with unidentified craft off the entrance to Pearl Harbor and at 7.00 am a radar station on the north coast of Oahu detected the approach of a large

flight of aircraft. These reports were ignored. Shortly before 8.00 am the first of 360 torpedo and dive-bombers and fighters swept down on Pearl and adjacent airbases, taking the Americans completely by surprise. During the next two hours all eight battleships in harbor and more than 300 aircraft were either destroyed or badly damaged. Exultant pilots, returning to the carriers, urged the carrier fleet commander, Nagumo, to renew the assault; harbor installations and oil storage tanks were still largely undamaged and the American carriers had still to be located. Nagumo, however, felt he had pushed his luck far enough and turned for home. It was a grievous misjudgment: Pearl Harbor was left sufficiently unscathed to continue functioning as a major base.

The consequences of the attack were ironic. Intended to destroy the fighting capacity of America's Pacific fleet, the loss of the battleships forced the Americans to rely on their carriers and to evolve a new and much more effective means of naval warfare. Moreover Japan's envoys in Washington did not deliver their country's ultimatum until 2.20 pm Washington time, about 50 minutes after the attack had started. As America's radio networks broadcast the news during the afternoon, a wave of rage swept across

▼ Pearl Harbor, 8.40 am, 7 December 1941. Hit by bombs from Japanese "Vals", a fireball shoots hundreds of meters into the air from USS *Shaw* against the backdrop of the vast cloud of smoke arising from the shambles of "Battleship Row". The destruction at Pearl Harbor initially led both the Japanese and Americans to believe that the power of the US Pacific fleet had been broken.

Hideki Tojo 1884–1948

Japan's war minister and a leading member of the army's "control faction" in the 1930s, Tojo urged expansion on the Asian continent. He became premier in October 1941 and sought at the eleventh hour to avert what his policies had done so much to bring about: war with the USA and the European colonial powers. As a soldier Tojo paid more attention to the war on the Asian mainland and at times seemed almost to enjoy the discomforture of the navy at the hands of the Americans. The fall of Saipan in summer 1944, which brought Tokyo into US bombing range, led to Tojo's resignation. After Japan's surrender he was tried for war crimes and hanged.

Isorouko Yamamoto 1884–1943

Appointed commander in chief of the Japanese Combined Fleet in 1939, Yamamoto was the architect of the Pearl Harbor attack, though he had severe misgivings about a war with the USA. He was depicted as the "Japanese Nelson" by both the American and Japanese press but his ability was not great and he committed his fleet to the disastrous Midway and Guadalcanal operations. In spring 1943 a now deeply depressed Yamamoto went on tour of forward bases in the Solomons to boost morale, but his aircraft was intercepted and shot down by American fighters, and the admiral was killed.

The War in the Pacific 1941–43

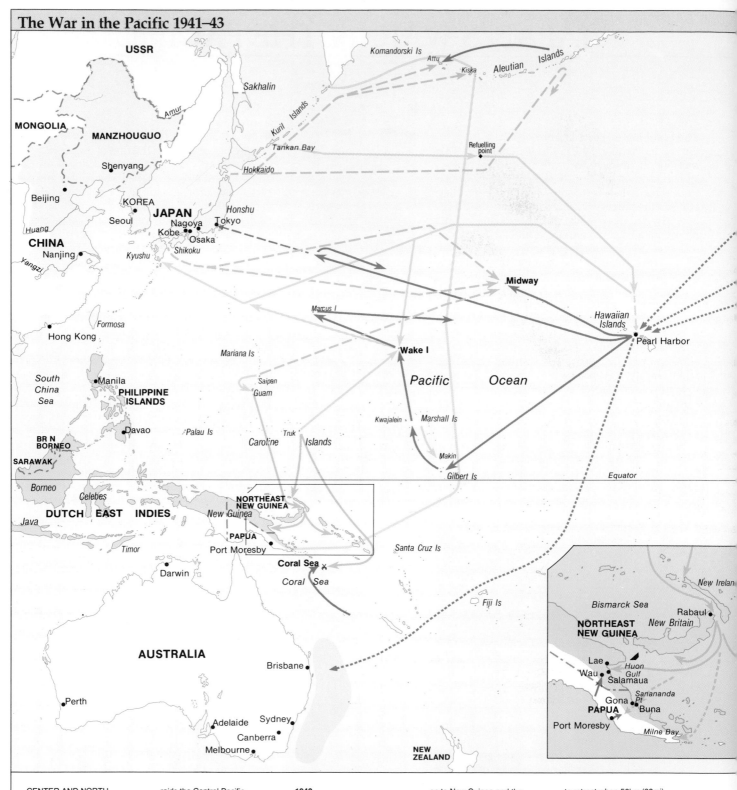

CENTER AND NORTH

1941

December 7
Japanese carrier aircraft attack the US naval base at Pearl Harbor, Hawaii.

December 8
(to Dec. 23) Japanese attack and eventually capture Wake Island (US possession). Japanese landings secure Guam and Makin (Dec. 10).

1942

February 1
(to March 4) A US task force raids the Central Pacific, attacking Japanese bases on the Gilberts, Marshalls and Marcus and Wake Islands.

April 18
B-25 bombers from USS *Hornet* bomb Japan ("Doolittle raid").

June 3
(to June 7) The Japanese seize Kiska (June 6) and Attu (June 7) while the main fleet closes on the US island of Midway; but in the Battle of Midway (June 4–5) US planes sink four Japanese carriers.

1943

March 26
(to Aug. 15) A US naval squadron drives Japanese from the Komandorskis (March 26). Americans retake Attu (May 11–29) and the Japanese evacuate Kiska (July 29).

SOUTHWEST AND SOUTH

1942

January 23
Japan's South Seas force captures Rabaul in New Britain.

March 8
(to July 7) The Japanese move on to New Guinea and the Solomons: they occupy Lae and Salamaua, Tulagi (May 3) and Guadalcanal (July 7).

May 7–8
Battle of the Coral Sea. Both sides withdraw.

July 21
(to Jan. 22, 1943) Japanese troops land on the north Papua coast and advance toward Port Moresby. A subsidiary force lands at Milne Bay but is repulsed by Australians (Aug. 25–Sept.5). Meanwhile Australians force the Japanese

to retreat when 50km (30mi) from Port Moresby and then annihilate them (Nov. 20–Jan. 22, 1943).

August 7
(to Feb. 7, 1943) US marines seize Tulagi on Guadalcanal (Henderson Airfield). The Japanese navy counterattacks, sinking US ships off Savo Island (Aug. 9). The next five months see a series of naval battles. On Guadalcanal the Japanese launch unsuccessful attacks (Sept. 12–14, Oct. 23–25, Jan. 10–Feb. 7) and withdraw.

CANADA

UNITED STATES

Seattle

San Francisco

Los Angeles
San Diego

Area occupied by Japanese forces

    to 7 Dec 1941

    to 6 Aug 1942

Japanese movements 1941

    7-23 Dec

    Airstrike 7 Dec

Japanese movements 1942

    20 Jan-7 May

    3-7 June

    6 July- 26 Sept

Allied movements 1942

    Airstrike 18 Apr

    Attacks

    Supply route

    Japanese submarine activity 1943

    Location of sinking 2-3 March 1943

Equatorial scale 1: 62 800 000

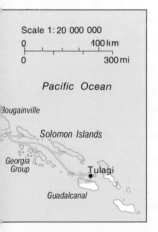

Scale 1: 20 000 000

0   100 km

0   300 mi

Pacific Ocean

Bougainville

Solomon Islands

Georgia Group

Tulagi

Guadalcanal

1943

January 18
Japan deploys submarines off the east coast of Australia.

January 20–30
The Japanese reinforce Lae and Salamaua.

March 2–3
The Japanese send a convoy from Rabaul to Lae. But it is destroyed by 200 US planes.

June 16
Japan withdraws its submarines from Australia.

◄ Manila, 31 December 1941. MacArthur declared it an "open city" on 27 December 1941. Four days later it was bombed by the Japanese.

◄◄ After the bombing of Pearl Harbor and the conquest of Southeast Asia, Japan launched a two-pronged offensive. A task force attempted to expand the perimeter in the Southwest Pacific, but was turned back in the Battle of the Coral Sea. A little later the bulk of the Imperial Navy thrust into the Central and North Pacific in an attempt to bring the remnants of the US navy to battle. This operation ended in the disastrous Battle of Midway.

Douglas MacArthur 1880–1964

As US army commander in Southeast Asia in 1941, MacArthur was responsible for a faulty defense of Luzon which led to rapid enemy advance. But his defense of the Bataan Peninsula turned him from a failure into a hero. He escaped to Australia in March 1942. Thereafter he sought to return to the Philippines as soon as possible, an aim that brought him into bitter conflict with the US navy, especially with admirals Nimitz and King. He returned in October 1944 and was preparing for the invasion of Japan when it capitulated in August 1945. He took the formal surrender on 2 September aboard USS *Missouri* in Tokyo Bay..

the country. Overnight isolationist sentiment vanished and when Roosevelt asked Congress for a declaration of war the following day he addressed a nation united as never before. Japan could scarcely have engineered a worse result.

American and Japanese responses

For the moment, however, it seemed in Tokyo that a mighty victory had been won. Japan's conquest of the British and Dutch Empires could now proceed unhindered (see pp. 42–43) and a defensive perimeter could be established in the Pacific. Within the area enclosed by the perimeter the American bases of Guam and Wake were quickly overrun, and the American-protected Philippines isolated. America's commander in the Philippines, General Douglas MacArthur, had long expected a Japanese attack, and had at his disposal 30,000 American and 100,000 Filipino troops, supported by the United States' small Asiatic fleet, and about 200 modern fighters and bombers. Yet although MacArthur learned of the Pearl Harbor attack at 3.00 am Manila time, when Japanese bombers from Taiwan swept over Luzon's airbases at midday they found the American squadrons still sitting on the runways. It was a second Pearl Harbor: within 30 minutes more than half MacArthur's air force had been destroyed. Over the next few days unopposed Japanese air attacks forced the Asiatic fleet to withdraw to Java and on 22 December large

Japanese forces landed at Lingayen Gulf on the western coast of Luzon, followed two days later by another landing at Limon Bay in the south of the island. MacArthur's inadequately trained Filipino divisions soon crumbled, and as Japanese columns closed on Manila from north and south, MacArthur withdrew his forces northwest to the rugged Bataan Peninsula which, with the island fortress of Corregidor off its tip, controlled the entrance to Manila Bay. American forces in the Manila Bay area did not surrender until 6 May, and those still at large in the southern Philippines continued organized resistance until 18 May, when many melted into the jungles and started guerrilla campaigns.

The prolonged resistance of MacArthur's forces was embarrassing for the Japanese but even more embarrassing for the Roosevelt administration. Since the first assault MacArthur had kept up a barrage of demands for reinforcements, demands which could not be entirely ignored because he was fast becoming a national hero. His presence in the Philippines was particularly irritating to Admiral King, chairman of the joint chiefs of staff (JCS), and Admiral Nimitz, the commander in chief in the Pacific (Cincpac). After Pearl Harbor, US admirals concentrated on defending Hawaii and maintaining communications with Australia.

MacArthur's position posed a problem. Roosevelt solved it in early March by ordering MacArthur and some of his senior staff to escape

▲ The flight deck of the carrier USS *Yorktown* during the Battle of the Coral Sea (7–8 May 1942): a Douglas Dauntless dive bomber followed by a row of Douglas Devastator torpedo-bombers. Coral Sea was the first battle in which opposing fleets did not come into direct conflict.

to Australia, where, shortly after his arrival on 17 March, MacArthur was placed in command of the newly created Southwest Pacific Area. Like Nimitz, MacArthur found he had few forces at his disposal, and would have to remain on the defensive for some months to come. However, without consulting either the president or the JCS MacArthur had already announced his policy to the Australian press:– "I came through and I shall return". For MacArthur the only road to Tokyo ran through the Phillipines; for King and Nimitz it ran through the islands of the Central Pacific. Herein lay the genesis of the bitter disputes over strategy which were to bedevil the conduct of

America's war in the Pacific in the years to come.

The Japanese, too, were now having problems deciding on a strategy. With the capture of Rabaul on 21 January, and the occupation of Lae and Salamaua on the north coast of New Guinea in early March, the southeastern part of their Pacific perimeter had been secured. One faction within the army, whose most vociferous spokesman was General Yamashita, the conqueror of Malaya, wanted to invade Australia immediately. The predominant China faction within the army and Yamamoto's "combined fleet" faction within the navy united to oppose this scheme and gradually Yamamoto's plans were accepted by imperial headquarters. The admiral devised two complimentary strategies: the isolation of Australia by the capture of Port Moresby, followed by a drive southeast through the Solomons, the New Hebrides, New Caledonia and Fiji; and a combined fleet offensive into the central Pacific to take the island of Midway and bring the remnants of the American fleet to battle. Japan thus embarked on two enterprises which divided its forces and placed an enormous strain on its already overloaded merchant marine. The astounding successes of the first four months of the war had created an atmosphere in which anything seemed possible and the meticulous planning which preceded the Pearl Harbor attack was now very much less in evidence. Senior officers had been infected with

Ernest Joseph King 1878–1956

King became chief of naval operations in March 1942 and was also a member of the US joint chiefs of staff and the Allied combined chiefs of staff. While agreeing in principle to a "Germany first" strategy, he resisted British pressure for a purely defensive stance against Japan. He also sought to relegate MacArthur's Southwest Pacific Area to the status of a backwater and to keep Britain's navy out of the Pacific. Though unsuccessful in both endeavors, King had engineered the growth of the US navy into the most powerful naval force in the world history.

what Japanese historians would later call the "victory disease", the major symptom of which was continued attempts to achieve difficult objectives with slender resources.

The Battles of Coral Sea and Midway

The American fleet was still very much smaller than Japan's – as yet Nimitz had only four carriers – but intelligence had now broken Japan's naval codes. This coup gave Nimitz an inestimable advantage, for by gaining advance warning of Japan's moves he could concentrate his forces and achieve at least local equality. By 17 April intelligence had discovered Yamamoto's plans to take Port Moresby, and Nimitz concentrated a task force in the south Pacific built around the carriers *Lexington* and *Yorktown*. The three task forces Yamamoto sent south outnumbered the Allied fleet but contained only three carriers, the *Shoho*, *Shokaku* and *Zuikaku*, which together could launch some 140 aircraft, about the same number as the *Yorktown* and *Lexington*. The ensuing Battle of the Coral Sea was the first in history in which warships of the opposing fleets did not come into direct conflict. It was carrier aircraft against carrier aircraft, a weapon in which the Americans had parity with the Japanese. On 7 May American divebombers scored their first major success of the war by sinking the *Shoho*. The following day Japanese aircraft sank the *Lexington* and damaged the *Yorktown*, but not before American machines had hit and badly damaged the *Shokaku*. Alarmed by the loss of two carriers the Japanese withdrew north, temporarily abandoning their plans to take Port Moresby. It was their first strategic reverse.

The Coral Sea action convinced Yamamoto that the decisive battle had to be fought before the Americans became any stronger. Japan had already suffered a rude shock on 18 April when a flight of B 25 medium bombers raided Tokyo. It had been a morale boosting stunt – the bombers had been launched 1,300km (800mi) off the coast of Japan from the carrier *Hornet* – but many Japanese were convinced that they had flown from Midway. Yamamoto, anxious to press ahead with his Combined Fleet offensive, decided not to wait for the *Shokuku* to be repaired or for the *Zuikaku* to have its severely depleted squadrons rebuilt. His 165 ships, including four large and four light carriers, seemed more than sufficient to deal with the Americans. His plan was complex, the fleet being divided into four widely separated task forces.

Once again naval intelligence had kept Nimitz apprised of Japanese intentions. The damaged *Yorktown* sped back from the south Pacific and was repaired in an astonishing 48 hours (her captain had thought she would be in dry dock for at least three months) then sailed for Midway to rendezvous with the *Enterprise* and *Hornet*. The fleet commander, Admiral Spruance, had some 50 ships in all, and was outnumbered three to one by Yamamoto. But the Coral Sea battle had shown that what now mattered was aircraft, and the 250 aboard his three carriers, supported by 109 machines based on Midway, gave Spruance a slight superiority over the Japanese. Early on 4 June Nagumo's carriers came within air range of

▲◄ At 14.30 on 4 June 1942 "Kate" torpedo bombers from Vice-Admiral Chuichi Nagumo's sole surviving carrier *Hiryu* score a torpedo strike against the damaged USS *Yorktown* (above). At the same time 100km (60mi) to the west Midway-based B-17s make an ineffectual high-level attack on *Hiryu* (left). Within hours of these photos being taken both carriers had been mortally wounded, the *Hiryu* by dive bombers from USS *Enterprise*, and *Yorktown* by torpedoes from the Japanese submarine I-168.

Midway and, unaware of the proximity of the American carriers, launched strikes against the island. Convinced they had destroyed American airpower on Midway the aircraft returned to their carriers around 9.00 am and began the lengthy procedure of refuelling and rearming. The decks of the carriers were covered with fuel lines and bombs when American torpedo-bombers, followed by waves of dive-bombers, struck the Japanese. By 10.30 am *Akagi*, *Kaga*, and *Soryu* were flaming wrecks. Nagumo's surviving carrier, the *Hiryu*, managed to launch an airstrike which located and crippled *Yorktown* (she was later sunk by a Japanese submarine) but the *Hiryu* was in turn discovered by the *Enterprise*'s aircraft and sent to the bottom.

Having failed to secure a decisive victory Yamamoto knew that the navy faced the prospect of unremitting warfare with an enemy whose power was increasing daily. But within imperial headquarters the attitude was less gloomy. Midway had been a setback but the "victory disease" still gripped many planners. Japan still dominated the Pacific and headquarters decreed that operations to isolate Australia (suspended since the Coral Sea) should now proceed. As a first step the perimeter in New Guinea and the Solomons was to be expanded by two concurrent operations. In June 1942 engineers began constructing an airfield on the island of Guadalcanal in the southeast

Five minutes! Who would have dreamed that the tide of battle would shift completely in that brief interval? Visibility was good. Clouds were gathering at about three thousand meters, however, and though there were occasional breaks, they afforded good concealment for approaching enemy planes. At 10.24 the order to start launching came from the bridge by voice-tube. The air officer flapped a white flag, and the first Zero fighter gathered speed and whizzed off the deck. At that instant a lookout screamed: "Hell-divers!" I looked up to see black enemy planes plummeting toward our ship.

MITSUO FUCHIDA
MIDWAY, 4 JUNE 1942

Solomons; six weeks later, on 21 July, a division-sized force landed at Buna on the northern coast of Papua. When completed the Guadalcanal airfield was to provide aircover for operations against the New Hebrides. By this time the landing force in Papua would have advanced across the rugged Owen Stanley range via the Kokoda Trail and taken Port Moresby from the north.

But the period of Japan's easy victories was already past. Midway had removed the threat to Hawaii and substantial American forces had been added to those already despatched to the South Pacific. By early July a naval task force, including three carriers and a new battleship, and an army division had arrived in New Caledonia, and the 1st Marine Division had landed in New Zealand. MacArthur's forces in SWPA had also increased substantially. With large forces now available in the Southwest and South Pacific, on 2 July the joint chiefs of staff ordered an Allied offensive – a parallel advance on Rabaul. When the Japanese landed at Buna, MacArthur had been on the point of carrying out the first stage of his part in the operation – the occupation of Papua's north coast – and to this end had already reinforced Port Moresby and established a powerful base at Milne Bay on Papua's eastern tip. South Pacific forces too had been preparing to advance into the Solomons when on 5 July Nimitz received word that the Japanese were constructing an airfield on Guadalcanal, which, if completed, would pose a major threat to American operations. Nimitz responded with characteristic energy. On 7 August 1st Marine Division, transported in a heavily protected convoy, landed on the northern coast of Guadalcanal and the nearby island of Tulagi. They drove surprised Japanese construction troops into the jungle and seized and dug in around the airstrip, renaming it Henderson Field after a hero of Midway.

Reversals for Japan on land and sea

Japanese headquarters in Rabaul now faced a difficult situation. What should they do: close down the Papuan operation and concentrate on the new threat or attempt to contain the marines until Port Moresby had been taken? Either decision would have been sensible. Instead Rabaul HQ decided to continue the advance on Port Moresby and to rush forces to Gaudalcanal to eject the Americans.

The Papuan operation was the first to run into trouble. On 25 August, endeavoring to speed up the capture of Port Moresby, a regiment landed at Milne Bay and, unaware of the strength of the Australian garrison, launched a frontal attack. In ten days of bitter fighting the Japanese lost more than 1,000 dead and by 5 September had been pushed into the sea. Their Guadalcanal counteroffensive became bogged down at the same time. Contrary to Rabaul's expectations, the marines fought tenaciously and in what became known as the Battle of Bloody Ridge killed more than 600 Japanese and smashed their attack.

Having suffered two serious reverses within a week, Rabaul finally accepted the impossibility of simultaneously taking Port Moresby and driving the marines from Guadalcanal. As the marines

seemed to represent the greater threat, on 25 September Rabaul ordered the Papuan expeditionary force, which had by then pushed to within 46km (29mi) of Port Moresby, to withdraw to the northern slopes of the Owen Stanleys, and dig in.

It was a decision which should have been made six weeks earlier. Denied adequate supplies, the retreat across the Owen Stanleys quickly turned into a shambles. Veteran Australian brigades pursued them closely, wiped out the Japanese rearguard at Templeton's Crossing near the crest of the range on 16 October, and encircled and annihilated the main body at Gorari on the northern slopes of the range three weeks later. Now only the Buna beachhead remained. By the third week of November the Australians, assisted by the American 32nd Division which had landed on Papua's northern coast a few kilometers east of Buna, closed on the Japanese beachhead. With Japanese airpower completely absorbed by the struggle then raging on Gaudalcanal, Allied aircraft dominated the skies of northern Papua and made resupply and reinforcement of the beachhead virtually impossible. The Japanese fought stubbornly from heavily bunkered positions for nearly eight weeks but on 22 January 1943 the last pockets of resistance were exterminated. It was Japan's first major defeat on land.

Meanwhile the Imperial Japanese Navy had made an all-out effort to destroy Henderson. On the nights of 14 and 15 October two strongly escorted battleships, *Kongo* and *Haruna*, swept down on the beachhead and bombarded the airfield, temporarily putting it out of action. The Japanese had at last reasserted control of the waters around Guadalcanal, an achievement which had far-reaching consequences. Ever since landing on Guadalcanal the marine commander, Major-General Vandegrift, had been complaining bitterly to Cincpac about the relatively poor performance of the navy in supporting his beleagured troops. The fact that Japanese battleships were operating off Guadalcanal was taken as evidence that his complaints were justified and on 18 October Nimitz gave the South Pacific a new commander, Rear Admiral William H. Halsey.

▼ Immaculately clad in their white tropical uniforms, Japanese sailors pose carefully for a photographer on Guadalcanal in August 1942. A few weeks later these men looked very different – filthy, emaciated, with their uniforms in tatters.

Capitalizing on the success of the battleship raid on 25 October, Yamamoto at last committed a large carrier task force to the Solomons. As it plowed south toward the Santa Cruz Islands to the east of the Solomons, Halsey's carriers moved north. The ensuing action was a virtual replay of the Coral Sea, the Americans and Japanese launching simultaneous air strikes. The Japanese sank *Hornet* and badly damaged *Enterprise* but American air strikes also hit home, badly damaged *Zuiho* and *Shokaku*, and forced the Japanese to turn about. Yamamoto was furious. Believing that more aggressive leadership would have produced a major victory he dismissed carrier force commander Nagumo and ordered yet another battleship bombardment of Henderson to cover large-scale landings at Cape Esperance. On the night of 12 November, 18 Japanese warships, including the battleships *Hiei* and *Kirishima*, swept down the northern coast of the island and collided with an American force of 5 cruisers and 8 destroyers. In pitch darkness the fleets opened fire at point-blank range and in the bloody melee which followed all 18 Japanese ships were extensively damaged and the *Hiei* and two cruisers were sunk. Two nights later the *Kirishima* with 4 cruisers and 9 destroyers again raced toward Henderson and this time was intercepted by a

powerful American force. Failing to spot the battleship *Washington* the Japanese concentrated their fire on the destroyers and *South Dakota* and within minutes had sunk or disabled the destroyers and silenced the battleship. Meanwhile *Washington* had closed to within 6.5km (4mi) of *Kirishima* and a devastating broadside sank the Japanese battleship. The fighting on 12 and 14 November (Naval Battle of Guadalcanal) gave the Americans control over the waters of the southern Solomons.

The fighting on the island had not gone well. On the night of 23 October the 20,000 Japanese then on Guadalcanal had stormed the American perimeter and had been repulsed with heavy casualties. As American control of the waters of the southern Solomons became tighter their strength on Guadalcanal grew – 58,000 men by December – while that of the Japanese diminished. On 10 January 1943 the Americans attacked and drove the Japanese toward the western end of the island from where the Imperial Navy managed to evacuate 12,000 survivors during the first week in February. The campaign had cost the Japanese 25,000 dead, the Americans fewer than 3,000 casualties. More importantly, Japan had lost 600 aircraft and 24 warships. American aircraft and shipping losses were similar but were being easily replaced – those of Japan were not.

▲ 5 October 1942, Port Moresby-based B-17s hit the Japanese airfield at Buna. By the end of the month such raids had given the Allies control of the air over northern Papua.

How splendid the first stage of our operations was! But how unsuccessfully we have fought since the defeat at Midway! Our strategy, aimed at invasion of Hawaii, Fiji, Samoa, and New Caledonia... has dissipated like a dream. In addition, the occupation of Port Moresby and Guadalcanal has been frustrated... In war things often do not turn out as we wish. Nevertheless, I cannot stem my feeling of mortification.

ADMIRAL UGAKI
31 DECEMBER 1942

Datafile

World War I had seen the end of European world dominance, as markets were lost to America and Japan and as New York took over from London as the world's financial capital. By the end of World War II the USA had fully realized its potential for world hegemony. In the early years of the war Japan had clearly been boxing above its true weight. In 1942 it conquered a vast area with 200,000 men – yet by the end of that year the USA had 346,000 troops in the Pacific theater. United States gross national product increased from 88.6 billion dollars in 1939 to 198.7 in 1945 and, between 1940 and 1944, US output of manufactured goods grew by 300 percent.

Manufacturing output 1937

- 5%
- 4%
- 35%
- 22%
- 14%
- 11%
- 9%

- USA
- Others
- USSR
- Germany
- Britain
- France
- Japan

▶ **The staggering growth of the US share of world merchant shipping was matched in the military sphere. The UK had abandoned the naval equality with the US established by treaty in 1922. By 1944 the US Navy was roughly three times the size of the British Royal Navy. American submarines destroyed almost 90 percent of the shipping Japan had possessed in 1941.**

- Rest of world (tons)
- US fleet (tons)

World merchant fleet

17% / 83%
1939

52% / 48%
1947

▲ **H.C. Hillman's figures for manufacturing output closely match, in the ratios shown, those for arms production in 1942 (below center) which were compiled by a different scholar, Dieter Penzina. The rashness of the Japanese attack on the USA is evident. Even with the UK committed on other fronts, and France and the Netherlands impotent, Japan stood no long-term chance in the Pacific. Meanwhile, Australia industrialized rapidly: machine tool factories rose from 3 prewar to over 100.**

▶ **These figures for arms production underestimate US dominance – US war industry reached top gear only in 1944. Between 1941 and 1944 the rate of Japanese aircraft production increased nearly sixfold to 2,348 per month. But Japanese arms were made by harshly exploited labor at the expense of consumer goods.**

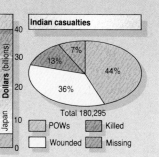

Arms production 1942

USA / USSR / Germany / Britain / Japan
Dollars (billions)

Indian casualties

- 7%
- 44%
- 13%
- 36%

Total 180,295

- POWs
- Wounded
- Killed
- Missing

▲ **India contributed at peak 2.5 million servicemen to the Allies' war effort – roughly as many as the rest of the British Empire and Commonwealth, bar the UK itself, combined. Indian troops fought bravely in North Africa and Europe, while of 27 Victoria Crosses awarded for the Burma campaign, 20 went to Indians. Among Indians captured, about 4,000 out of 12,000 held in Germany and at most 13,000 out of 60,000 in Malaya-Singapore, joined the Indian National Army formed by Subhas Chandra Bose to fight alongside Japan. INA men went into the Imphal offensive; 400 were killed, 715 deserted and 1,500 died of disease and starvation.**

Battle of Imphal

British IV Corps / British XXXI Corps / Japanese 15th Army / Indians / Japanese reinforcements
Thousands

◀▼ **In the Battle of Imphal from 29 March to 22 June 1944, the Japanese were aiming to strike into India from Burma. But they were always at a numerical disadvantage (left). British forces were heavily hit by disease. The Japanese fared worse: malnutrition accounted for many of their deaths from disease.**

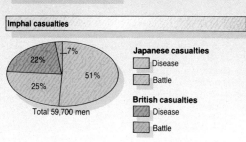

Imphal casualties

- 7%
- 22%
- 51%
- 25%

Total 59,700 men

Japanese casualties
- Disease
- Battle

British casualties
- Disease
- Battle

The world's longest-lived empire was the Chinese. Since the 3rd century BC one dynasty of emperors had succeeded another. But by the beginning of the 20th century the Manchu dynasty was in decay, undermined by the economic "opening up" of China by the European powers. When it fell in 1911, civil war ensued. The dynamic Japanese, who had proved by their defeat of Russia in 1905 that they could confront a mighty European empire and win, were irresistibly drawn into the vacuum. By the 1930s two leaders had emerged to contend for the honor of restoring the integrity of the empire: Jiang Jieshi, leader of the Nationalist Guomindang, and the communist Mao Zedong. By 1937 Jiang had asserted his authority over the provincial warlords and was presiding over rapid modernization. The communists were reduced to a small rump living in caves at Yan'an in a remote part of northwest China. But Mao was a shrewder strategist than Jiang.

Younger empires from the "barbarian" European world had seized control of Southeast Asia. Three centuries of Spanish rule in the Philippines had ended in 1898, when the USA had taken over. The Portuguese retained only tiny enclaves. But the Dutch had come to govern most of Indonesia. The British, from the 1750s, had acquired piecemeal power over the whole subcontinent of India and moved on in the later 19th century to conquer Burma and control Malaya. Over the same period the French had taken over "Indochina" – Vietnam, Laos and Cambodia.

Contradictions of imperial rule

Briefly these empires had been imposing and profitable, but they were essentially short-lived, based on an anomaly. Four hundred million Indians and 60 million Indonesians outnumbered British and Dutch home populations by eight to one. To govern in the East, thin-spread Europeans had to recruit and train "native" clerks and other subordinates. While Hindu, Buddhist and Islamic traditionalists resented rule by white Christians, young "natives" educated in Western ways acquired ideas which they turned against their white masters. Thus Pandit Nehru welcomed "the Western gift of science" but campaigned against British rule in India, while the Indonesian nationalist Sutan Sjahrir announced that it was only by using "the dynamism of the West" that the East could be released from subjugation. European liberal ideas were in contradiction with colonial tyranny. Nationalism itself was the most potent import, though Europeans often professed to be baffled by Asian adaptations of the idea. How could there be an Indian "nationalism" embracing Hindu, Sikh, Bengali and Punjabi? How could "Indonesia" ever have existed without the

EMPIRES AT BAY

Dutch? Whites failed to understand that the agrarian and urban industries they had introduced had created new social classes detached from tradition, while their roads, telegraphs and railroads had linked hitherto separate communities.

Nevertheless the Dutch, and still more the British, had moved, during World War I and after, to appease nationalism. But every concession of a share of authority to "natives" had reinforced the demand for full independence. The French did not escape by being less generous and eventually reaped the fiercest nationalist whirlwind of all in Vietnam.

During the 1930s the European powers were weakened by economic depression. Imperialist ideology and considerations of prestige, rather than rationality, preserved the European will to dominate politically areas whose assets they could not monopolize.

It was true that the native troops of the Indian army gave the British a reserve of manpower which could be deployed in other parts of the world, but it required 50,000 white soldiers to hold down the country. British exports to India had fallen from 1,175 million rupees in 1914 to 480 million in 1937, and the balance of trade favored India. Britain had lost control of the Indian domestic market to "native" competition. The Dutch East Indies likewise had come to import more from Japan and export more to Europe. The French in Indochina were superficially the most successful. But people in France paid no less for Michelin tyres than the Swiss who had no colonies.

The motor car was becoming a modern necessity. Southeast Asia produced practically all the world's rubber and nearly half its tin. The USA was the chief buyer, Malaya the chief producer, of both commodities. Over the dying empires Japan hovered like a predatory kite, watched from afar by a mighty eagle. The Japanese, modernizing violently and committed to the conquest of China, needed rubber and tin, and the oil and bauxite of the Dutch East Indies, and the rice of Burma and Thailand. In 1942 they showed that they could impose their claim.

▼ A rubber factory in British Malaya before World War II. The fact of white domination is plain enough. Not so clearly disclosed are the evil conditions suffered by "coolie" workers.

▶ In their conquest of Southeast Asia the Japanese advanced over a tenth of the world's surface at an amazing speed. The story of this campaign, however, masks the divisions and dilemmas of the Japanese command. Should India be invaded? Australia? Should resources be held back for a strike against the USSR? As it happened, the Japanese tide flowed thinly over precisely the area known as "Southeast Asia" before meeting its limit in New Guinea and Melanesia. With the Battle of Midway, June 1942, its ebb in effect began.

▼ Japanese troops hail yet another victory in early 1942. It was a triumph to transform into victorious warriors such bespectacled persons as seen here. An Australian soldier who became their prisoner said later: "Whatever their other qualities might be, to me they are – with envy – the brave Japanese."

But a glance at the datafile shows at once how hopeless the Japanese cause was if the eagle of America moved. The British and Dutch had not believed that the Japanese would dare to take on the USA. Nor did the Americans themselves. Americans professed to be anti-imperialist. The Philippines since 1916 had been governed by reliable Filipinos. In 1935, as if to upstage developments in British India, the USA had promised full independence in 14 years' time.

Yet Churchill, who had proclaimed in 1940 that the British Empire should survive another thousand years, signed in August 1941 the Atlantic Charter which declared the "right of all peoples" to choose the form of government under which they lived. An official information handout for British troops in 1943 announced self-righteously, in line with government professions: "To demands from other Powers that we should 'hand over the colonies' we reply that we are already in the process of handing them over to their only true owners, the Colonial peoples themselves.... Self-government is better than good government."

The British had long before developed the "Dominion" model, by which colonies could become self-governing under the British throne. This made it easier to contemplate decolonization than in France or Holland, where the communists were at one with the political right in believing that their empires must be regained.

The defeat of the Europeans
On 8 December 1941, the day after Japan bombed the US naval base at Pearl Harbor, Japanese forces attacked Hong Kong, Thailand, Malaya and Burma. A series of devastating and rapid advances followed. Four months later the Japanese were masters of Southeast Asia. Organized US resistance in the Philippines continued until May 18 but proved fruitless. Economic ties between European possessions in Southeast Asia and their respective "motherlands" were completely cut, even in those which remained nominally under European rule, such as the possessions of Portugal and Vichy France, which were not at war with Japan. But the Portuguese enclave at Macao on the Chinese coast was dominated by Japanese "advisers", and the Portuguese part of the island of Timor shared the same fate as the Dutch section. In French Indochina the Japanese did what they liked.

They stationed troops in Tongking (North Vietnam) in September 1940 after a Franco-Japanese Treaty acknowledged their "preeminent position in the Far East". The first of a series of commercial treaties the following May provided that all Vietnamese rice, corn, coal, rubber and minerals available for export should go to Japan, and in November all Vietnamese enterprises were ordered to work for the Japanese. Meanwhile Japanese troops had spread through the country. The French lost their last leverage in Vietnam when their troops and administrators were attacked by the Japanese in April 1945. Covertly the Japanese had encouraged local nationalism. Communists led by Ho Chi Minh dominated the Vietminh popular front formed in 1941, built up under Vo Nguyen Giap (a guerrilla leader in the north), and were poised to dominate the whole country when war ended.

The twilight of the British Raj
Part of the mystique surrounding British rule in India was dissipated when thousands of US servicemen arrived in the subcontinent during the war and astonished whites and natives alike by surviving without sun helmets. In sterner ways the war also hastened recognition by Britons that they must go. Denouncing Japanese cruelty implied support for the softer values of liberalism and humanitarianism against the credo that might was right. If Japanese expansionism, like that of Germany and Italy, was to be seen as immoral, where did that leave British imperialism? The UK's allies the USA and the USSR were both professedly anti-imperialist. Under any leader other than Churchill, the British might have conceded Indian independence during the war.

Churchill detested the nationalist Congress Party and its venerated leader Mahatma Gandhi. He would have agreed with Lord Linlithgow, the Viceroy who wrote early in 1939 that British "evacuation in any measurable period of time" was "unthinkable."

Linlithgow personally declared war on behalf of all India in the September of that year. The response of Indians was very varied. Millions volunteered for the Indian army (troops from which could still be reliably used after the war to

The Japanese Conquest of Southeast Asia 1941–42

Japanese carrier route/air strike

Possessions 1940

British
French
Dutch
United States
Portuguese

Occupied by Japanese forces before Dec 1941
Japanese attacks
Major naval battle
Location of sinking

Scale 1:27 000 000

0 — 800km
0 — 500mi

1941

HONG KONG
December 8
Japanese bombard Victoria and land on Dec. 19. The British surrender on Dec. 25.

MALAYA
December 8
Japanese capture Victoria Point airfield in southern Burma (Dec. 16). The main army breaks the British line at Jitra (Dec. 13). The British retreat to Singapore island.

PHILLIPINES
December 10
Conquest of Luzon. Japanese land at Aparri, Vigan (Dec. 10)

and Legaspi (Dec. 12). The main force lands at Lingayen Gulf on Dec. 22.

BRITISH NORTH BORNEO, SARAWAK, BORNEO, CELEBES AND AMBOINA
December 16
Units land at Miri and expand along the coast. Others seize Davao in Mindanao (Dec. 20) and Jolo island (Dec. 25). Two forces capture main towns of Borneo and the Celebes. Amboina falls on Jan. 30, 1942.

1942

SINGAPORE
February 1
After an intensive bombardment Japanese land

on Feb. 7. The British surrender on Feb. 15.

SOUTHERN SUMATRA, TIMOR AND BALI
February 14
The Japanese isolate Java. On southeast Sumatra they seize airfields and refineries near Palembang (Feb. 16) and occupy Oosthaven (Feb. 20). They bomb Darwin (Feb. 19), and land on Bali (Feb. 18) and Timor (Feb. 19).

JAVA
February 26
Two task forces converge on Java. One defeats an Allied fleet in the Battle of the Java Sea (Feb. 27) and lands troops at Kragan (March 1). The other

lands troops near Batavia and sinks two Allied cruisers (Battle of the Sunda Straits March 1.) Bandung surrenders on March 9.

SOUTHERN BURMA
January 20
Japanese cross Thailand and take Moulmein (Jan. 31). Rangoon is occupied on March 8. Meanwhile British troops have withdrawn.

NORTHERN SUMATRA, ANDAMAN AND CEYLON
March 23
Japanese forces occupy northern Sumatra and the Nicobar and Andaman Islands (March 23). They bomb

Colombo (April 5) and Trincomalee (April 9).

BURMA
March 30
A Japanese force advances along the Sittang and defeats Chinese at Toungoo (March 30). A second takes Lashio (April 29), then Mandalay. The third follows the Irrawaddy takes Prome (April 2) and the Yenangyaung oilfields (April 19). Chinese and British abandon Burma (April 30).

THE PHILIPPINES
January 1
US and Filipino forces on the Bataan Peninsula surrender on April 9. Corregidor falls on May 6.

help restore the French and Dutch briefly to rule in Vietnam and the East Indies). India, thanks to "native" enterprise, was the world's sixth largest steel producer. Its industry came to supply three-quarters of the needs of British troops in the Middle Eastern theater as well as all its own army's requirements, save tanks and big guns. More than half of the 950 men in the elite Indian civil service were now "natives". Constitutional advance before the war had put 11 huge provinces under the control of elected cabinets of Indian ministers.

But in protest at Linlithgow's unilateral declaration of war, Congress ministers, who controlled 6 of the 11 provinces, resigned. Nor was Congress impressed by Linlithgow's "August Offer" of

1940 when Britain's position in the war against Germany was dire. Indians would be allowed to devise their own constitution when the war ended, and meanwhile Indian politicians would be invited to join the Viceroy's Executive and Defence Councils. The campaign of civil disobedience which Gandhi launched in October led to 14,000 going to jail.

American pressure on Churchill to decolonize merely made him privately more stubborn. The Japanese advance in 1942 made conciliation of Congress seem urgent, but when Churchill sent Sir Stafford Cripps, a member of his war cabinet, to India in March, there is every reason to believe that he wanted the mission to fail. Cripps' offer was to be of Dominion status (equal to Canada's

Australia and New Zealand at War

▲ Australian troops: from a population of 7 million, 550,000 served in the forces overseas. Over 23,000 were killed in action; 8,000 died in Japanese prisoner of war camps. Volunteer soldiers fought bravely and widely. Australian tradition forbade conscription for overseas fighting, but Curtin managed to get a compromise through parliament – conscripts could be sent to a restricted "Southwest Pacific Zone" which did at least include all of New Guinea.

On the face of it Australia was the most loyal of Dominions. Prime minister Robert Menzies declared war without consulting his Parliament, announcing on radio, "Britain is at war, therefore Australia is at war." But even he found Churchill's hauteur toward Australia hard to stomach, and after he fell in 1941 a Labour prime minister of working-class Irish Catholic origins succeeded him ("bad stock", Churchill muttered privately). Australians had long feared Japan. Yet after Pearl Harbor, Churchill treated John Curtin and his colleagues as if they were panicky children. He was furious when Curtin signed a newspaper article declaring, "Australia looks to America, free of any pangs as to our traditional links with the United Kingdom." But Labour was reelected in 1943.

Australia faced real peril. Towns in the North were bombed. Papua, governed from Australia, was invaded. Nineteen Australians died when Japanese submarines appeared in Sydney Harbor in May 1942.

Meanwhile, Australia was the only possible base for US operations in the Southwest Pacific. Nearly a million US servicemen sojourned in the country. The USA in its turn seemed prone to treat Australian views too lightly. Even Curtin, close to MacArthur, worried about the danger of US domination. On their side, US diplomats continually complained about "Digger" addiction to class struggle and strikes.

New Zealand, on the other hand, remained besottedly loyal to King and Empire. More than a year before Pearl Harbor a Home Guard was created on the British model. New Zealanders deprived themselves, even of potatoes, to send the UK all the food they could. Despite calling up a quarter of all males for military service (who incurred the Commonwealth's highest casualty rate), New Zealand achieved the highest agricultural productivity of any combatant nation. Women were heavily mobilized. For instance, "Women Herd Testers" replaced men, with equal pay.

or Australia's), but only after the Japanese were defeated. Gandhi reportedly called this a "post-dated cheque on a failing bank". Cripps, a peacetime friend of Nehru, exceeded his remit in suggesting that the viceroy's Executive Council with its Indian preponderance might act as a genuine cabinet. But Churchill would not permit this offer to stand. Congress leaders felt cheated. Gandhi called on the British to "Quit India". The Congress leaders were imprisoned. A wave of popular protest swept the country, in which the railway line between Delhi and Calcutta was blown up so that supplies could not reach the Burma front; police stations were sacked; policemen killed; telephone wires cut. About 1,000 people, almost all Indians, died. The British did not "quit", but they were shaken.

A new viceroy, Sir Archibald Wavell, arrived in September 1943, personally determined to press ahead with rapid constitutional advance. But though he released Gandhi the following May, Churchill would not allow him to meet the Mahatma. Not until May 1945 would Wavell get permission to bring into his Executive Council members of Congress and of the Muslim League, which had won less than 5 percent of the Muslim vote in 1937.

The League, led by Mohammed Ali Jinnah, had made much capital out of the situation created by British and Congress intransigence. Committed to establishing a separate Pakistan ("land of the pure") for the 100 million Muslims who formed a quarter of India's population, it had been gratified by Cripps' pledge that any province could opt out of the proposed Indian Union. Churchill had allowed this because he wanted to upset Congress and cement the loyalty of the Muslims who were disproportionately numerous in the Indian army. His refusal to move decisively towards the Dominion status for India which had been clearly foreshadowed in 1935 helped to ensure that when independence finally came, the subcontinent would be divided.

Meanwhile the war brought horror to Bengal. Matters had been so organized that this province had been spared famine for 60 years. But the Japanese occupation of Burma cut off supplies of rice. The pressure of military demands on the rail road system made Punjab rice hard to bring in. Nehru claimed that distribution problems had been exacerbated by the panicky destruction of

thousands of river craft lest these should fall into Japanese hands. The famine killed 3.4 million people. Such a disaster struck at the claim that the British deserved credit for governing wisely in the natives' interests.

Japan renews the conquest of China

The oldest empire would prove unconquerable. The Chinese people would eventually sort out their own destiny. Meanwhile the Japanese invasion led to a three-way division of the country. The Japanese controlled the seacoast and the great cities on or near it; but Jiang could not be dislodged from his southwestern capital, Chongqing: Mao's communists made steady gains from their northern base in Yan'an.

American liberals liked to imagine that Mao's Red Army were not real communists, merely "agrarian democrats". In fact they were pursuing a brilliant, ruthless strategy on behalf of a version of Marxism and they also recognized the authority of Moscow – though the USSR was never able to enforce it.

Mao believed that the people were to revolutionaries what water was to fish – the element in which they moved. The Japanese raped and murdered: Jiang's conscripts looted and bullied: Mao's men paid their way, helped with the harvest, respected women and property. This created safe bases. Whoever attacked the Reds attacked the people. The Japanese, pushing forward, left large areas to their rear thinly garrisoned. The Reds moved in their troops and political organizers, set up self-governing authorities and organized militias. Grateful peasants were given the holdings of landlords who had fled or collaborated.

The second phase was "strategic stalemate". The Reds wore down Japanese strength by guerrilla action. In 1937 Mao's forces had been confined to some 90,000sq km (35,000sq mi) of arid and poor land in northern Shaanxi, with a population of 1.5 million. By the end of 1943 they effectively controlled 570,000sq km (220,000sq mi) with a population of 94 million. Since the Red Army was waging revolutionary war, clashes

◄ India contributed at peak over 2 million servicemen – roughly as many as the rest of the British Empire and Commonwealth combined. Of these 24,338 were killed, 11,754 declared "missing", and 64,354 were wounded. Among nearly 80,000 captured, perhaps 17,000 joined the Indian National Army formed by Subhas Chandra Bose to fight alongside Japan. Of 6,000 INA men sent to the front, nearly one third died and a quarter surrendered or deserted.

▼ A Japanese poster for Indian consumption. The text, in Hindu and Bengali, reads: "Don't follow the English blindly. Forget the differences in religion and be united to bring about the independence of India." Addressing white opponents, Japanese propagandists were hampered by idiomatic difficulties. (One line read: "The remaining British planes took to their heels.") Their attempts to play on soldiers' sexual neuroses produced unintentionally hilarious results, as in a leaflet which showed a "Slick Yank" fornicating with a Melbourne girl and exclaiming, "Take your sweet time at the front Aussie – I got my hands full right now with your sweet tootsy at home."

with Jiang's troops were not ruled out and did occur. Mao and Jiang watched each other as closely as either did the common enemy. By February 1944 Jiang was deploying up to half a million of his best troops against communist-held areas in the northwest.

The Americans tried to convince themselves that Jiang was a liberal democrat. US General "Vinegar Joe" Stilwell was installed as his chief of staff. The Allies wished to make China a base for offensive operations against Japan, preferably with active help from Jiang's forces. But the Japanese advance into Burma blocked the route *via* Mandalay, the "Burma Road", by which supplies had reached Jiang. The only alternative was an airlift over the Himalayas. It was attempted but not till December 1943 did the monthly tonnage of supplies reach five figures.

Neither the British, preoccupied in Europe, nor the USA, fighting back in the Pacific, would release the forces required to clear the Japanese off the "Burma Road". A three-pronged attack on Burma agreed by combined chiefs of staff in 1943 was abandoned. Instead a more limited operation was devised to drive a new road south from Assam to join the northern section of the old one. In August 1944 Stilwell, with two American-trained Chinese divisions based in Assam, succeeded in establishing the new "Ledo Road". Overland traffic to China by this route began in January 1945.

Japan's last campaign in China

In April 1944 the Japanese had begun a huge campaign in China. By now their aim was essentially defensive, to remove China as a base from the Americans. "Operation Ichi-Go" committed 1.8 million Japanese troops against Jiang's 6 million. It showed up in a devastating light the corruption and ineptitude of the Nationalists. Henan was a province ravaged by famine due to a long drought after Jiangs's government had commandeered most of the 1942 grain crop for taxes. Millions had died of hunger and disease. When

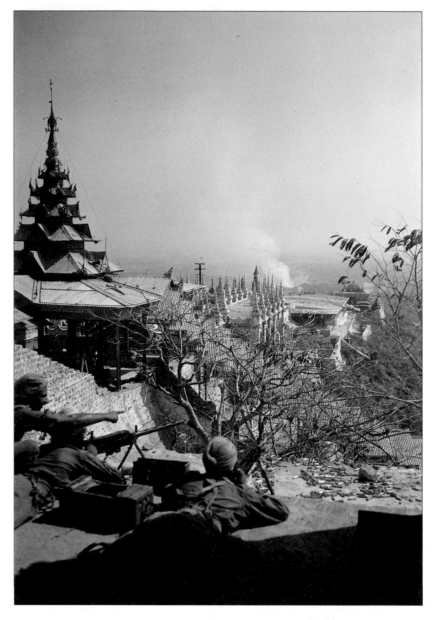

the Japanese struck, Chinese units in Henan were under strength, so that officers could pocket pay for nonexistent soldiers. The commander and his men had been heavily involved in black market trade with the Japanese. The Chinese 12th and 13th armies fought each other as they fled. Local peasants with pitchforks disarmed 50,000 Chinese troops. In three weeks 60,000 Japanese smashed a Chinese force of 300,000 and reached their objective, the northern section of the railroad. By late November the US 14th Air Force had been deprived of six bases and the Japanese were within 320km (200mi) of Chongqing. Jiang, however, was still no pushover. He gathered all the troops he could, including some flown from the Burma front, halted the Japanese at Kuizhou and managed to drive them back.

Chongqing, its population swollen from 200,000 to over a million, was a theater of intrigue and graft. US Lend-Lease became a basis for rampant corruption. Inflation soared to astronomic levels. The peasantry had been taxed to the limit, so the government simply printed more notes. The peasants, salaried classes and intellectuals

◄ Indian machine gunners on Pagoda Hill during the battle for Fort Dufferin in Mandalay, March 1945. The city was taken by the British after a fierce 12-day siege. The British campaign in Burma aimed to restore British prestige in Asia.

◄▼ At a base in China (bottom left) one of Jiang's soldiers guards US fighter planes. The "Flying Tigers", commanded by General C. L. Chennault, were flamboyantly successful against the Japanese.

► A confident Guomindang poster: "The more we fight, the stronger we get. The more the enemy fights, the weaker he gets".

▼ Chongqing in 1941, damaged by Japanese air raids. In this formerly quiet trading town at the confluence of the Yangzi and Jialin rivers, "Vinegar Joe" Stillwell would seethe over the behavior of Jiang Jieshi, whom he privately dubbed "the Peanut Dictator".

were all alike alienated from Jiang's regime. However, 27 Japanese divisions – a third of the whole army – were tied up in China in 1943 and 1944. In this way Jiang served the Allied cause.

US policy toward China was based on misapprehensions. Traditionally the USA favored what was called the "Open Door" policy – all nations should have equal economic opportunity within China and the territorial and administrative integrity of the country should be respected. In 1943 the USA relinquished "extraterritorial" rights which had given its citizens special privileges in China. The desire to see Jiang and Mao as Jeffersonian democrats was a reflection of this idealism. Roosevelt strove to bestow "Great Power" status on China. Jiang was one of the "Big Four" at the Cairo conference in November 1943 where Roosevelt committed himself to returning Formosa (Taiwan) to China and preventing any Soviet seizure of Chinese territory in the north. In return he got Jiang's promise that he would reach a settlement with Mao. Roosevelt did not keep America's side of the bargain, nor Jiang his. Nevertheless in 1945 China became one of the five permanent members of the Security Council of the new United Nations.

我愈戰愈強
敵愈戰愈弱

國際反侵略運動中國分會製

Datafile

The German invasion of the Soviet Union, launched the greatest land war in world history, involving the Red Army in 1,418 days of war on battlefronts which varied from 3,000 to 6,200km (1,860–3,900mi). Red Army campaigns destroyed, captured, or disabled 607 enemy divisions, more than three times the total of German and satellite divisions destroyed in North Africa, Italy and western Europe.

Soviet losses

▲ The Red Army suffered horrendous casualties in the course of the Soviet-German War. During the very first three weeks of war the Red Army lost 98 divisions, destroyed or disabled. The German army took over 3 million prisoners, many destined to die from starvation or execution, by the end of 1941.

Deployment of multiple rocket launchers

497 (Kiev)

62 (Stalingrad)

▲ The Red Army's "wonder weapon" was first used in July 1941 with devastating effect upon unsuspecting German troops. The BM-13 MRL (Multiple Rocket Launcher, popularly known as "Katyusha") fired 16 132mm caliber missiles, each weighing 42.5kg with a range of 8,470m, in 7–10 seconds.

▶ The initial Soviet numerical superiority in tanks was restored slowly after the devastating losses of the 1941 battles. At Stalingrad in November 1942 the odds shifted in Soviet favor as new tanks rolled out of the Urals factories, while at Kursk in July 1943 growing Soviet strength brought new "tank armies" into the field.

▶ German forces in the East reached their peak in winter 1942 at the giant Battle of Stalingrad. There were constant Soviet complaints that in the absence of a "Second Front" in the west the German command was free at critical moments to transfer divisions from western Europe to bolster the Eastern Front.

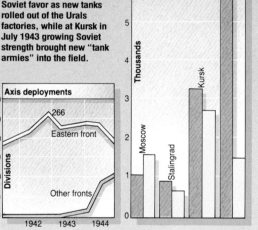

Axis deployments

266

Eastern front

Other fronts

Tank forces

USSR

Germany 6,250

Moscow
Stalingrad
Kursk
Berlin

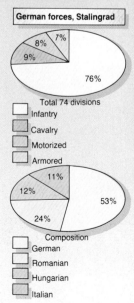

German forces, Stalingrad

7%
8%
9%
76%

Total 74 divisions
- Infantry
- Cavalry
- Motorized
- Armored

11%
12%
24%
53%

Composition
- German
- Romanian
- Hungarian
- Italian

◀▶ In the critical battle for Moscow at the end of 1941, neither side enjoyed any great superiority in manpower, the German forces near to exhaustion and the Red Army drawing on very limited reserves. Both sides were fighting near to the limits. The same condition prevailed at Stalingrad on 19 November 1942 when the Red Army launched its counter-offensive, 1,000,500 Soviet troops opposed to 1,011,500 German and Axis troops, though the 28 Axis divisions (Italian, Romanian and Hungarian) were militarily inferior to Soviet and German forces. These supporting divisions could not protect the German flanks and it was here that the Red Army struck first.

Battle forces

USSR
Germany

Moscow
Stalingrad
Kursk
Berlin

At 0300 hours on Sunday 22 June 1941 Adolf Hitler unleashed 3.5 million German soldiers, supported by 3,680 tanks and 2,770 combat aircraft, to execute Operation "Barbarossa" – the code name for the massive surprise attack on the Soviet Union. He initiated nothing less than the greatest land campaign in the history of the world.

Planning for the invasion of the USSR had begun shortly after the collapse of France in June 1940, the Soviet-German Nonaggression Pact signed in August 1939 presenting no obstacle whatsoever. On 5 December 1940, in the wake of foreign minister Vyacheslav Molotov's ill-starred November visit to Berlin, Hitler issued "Directive 21", "Case Barbarossa", deliberately invoking a medieval memory (the nickname of the 12th-century emperor Frederick I) for a war to be waged with deliberate medieval cruelty. Early in 1941, to those who even hinted at the magnitude and the risks involved, Hitler implacably declared his intention to fight and "to flatten them [the Russians] like a hailstorm".

Hitler's attitude to Stalin and the USSR

Hitler had long regarded Bolshevism not only as an ideological enemy but as a deadly physical menace from which Germany and indeed the whole of Europe must be saved, by ruthless eradication of the whole system and its Stalinist satraps. Barbarossa embodied not only a military campaign but an ideological crusade given added ferocity by the infusion of Nazi racist creeds, seeking the extermination of the Slav *Untermensch*, the Slav "subhuman", whose fate was determined by the "special guidelines" developed side by side with the military plans. The ideological struggle must proceed at the same time as "the clash of arms". Heinrich Himmler's SS would undertake "certain special duties" including the annihilation of Bolshevik commissars and the Communist intelligentsia". Hitler personally commanded that his senior officers put any ideas of "soldierly comradeship" out of their minds in this war.

For Hitler Stalin represented only a "cold-blooded blackmailer" with whom he intended to finish. Soviet policy, ie Stalin's attitude, bespoke menace, as he invested eastern Poland as his "share" of the Soviet-German Pact, moved into the Baltic states (Estonia, Latvia, Lithuania) with more attendant cruelties in June 1940 and in the spring of 1941 resisted German policies and actions in the Balkans. Worse, in late March and early April 1941 Stalin appeared to be carrying through a covert mobilization of his Red Army on the western frontiers of the USSR.

In the three years before the invasion Stalin had attempted to prevent isolation. To make an alliance, however, was a difficult proposition. In

THE EASTERN FRONT

1938 British and French appeasement of German ambitions had aroused Stalin's suspicion. In August 1939 Soviet negotiations with the British and French for military cooperation against Germany collapsed. Stalin feared that the USSR might be left to fight Germany alone. So when Nazi Germany offered Stalin a nonaggression pact he could scarcely refuse, especially as the agreement also gave the USSR a free hand in eastern Europe and Finland. In 1941, while German troops pushed into the Balkans, Stalin carefully insured himself against a two-front war by concluding the Soviet-Japanese Neutrality Pact on 13 April 1941. Both dictators played games of the utmost perfidy, Hitler out of manic hostility, Stalin from arrogance, conceit and misjudgment. Though he received multiple warnings of a German attack, Stalin persuaded himself that Hitler would never embark on a two-front war. In the west the UK remained undefeated. Hitler suspected an Anglo-Soviet "plot". Stalin feared British intrigues either to entangle him in war with Germany or else to agree on an Anglo-German separate peace, leaving Hitler a free hand in the east. The flight of Rudolf Hess to Scotland (10 May 1941) only intensified this particular paranoia. The warnings went unheeded.

▼ Motorized German troops in Russia, 1941. The 148 invading German divisions inflicted massive defeats on the Red Army. The German Panzer divisions hopelessly outclassed the Soviet tank forces. German infantry accomplished prodigies of fighting and marching.

The Soviet-Finnish War

The Soviet-Finnish War, also known as the "Winter War", lasted from 30 November 1939 to 13 March 1940. Four Soviet armies attacked Finland. Soviet troops advanced to the defensive positions of the Finnish "Mannerheim Line" on the Karelian isthmus but were unable to reduce the Finns. A second phase, from the end of December 1939 to 12 March 1940, culminated in a massive but costly Soviet effort to smash through the "Mannerheim Line". The Finns had to sue for peace, but Soviet aims could not be realized in full.

The war cost the Soviet Red Army 200,000 dead, the loss of 1,600 tanks and 634 aircraft. No less than 1.2 million Soviet troops were employed in what General Zhukov later called the "acid test", a test which both the Soviet leadership and German intelligence believed the USSR had failed. In mid-April 1940, on the orders of the Politburo, the Main Military Soviet met to discuss the lessons of the Winter War and the serious shortcomings in Soviet performance. An immediate consequence was the removal of Voroshilov as defense commissar and his replacement by Timoshenko whose Order No. 120 of 16 May 1940 listed Soviet failures. Officer training, especially that of junior officers, needed drastic improvement, as did that of general troop training for hard fighting. Timoshenko wanted an army realistically trained and better equipped, able to fight like the Finns. Iron discipline must also go hand in hand with intensive training.

Based on Soviet performance against the Finns, German intelligence concluded that the Red Army was simply not capable of fighting a modern war. In particular, the damage inflicted in 1937–38, when Stalin purged the Soviet command, could now be seen and (in one view) could take 20 years to repair. This gigantic military machine simply operated in the mass: organization, leadership and equipment were unsatisfactory. The principles of leadership were sound, but the commanders inexperienced. The communications system and troop transportation were bad, the fighting quality of Soviet troops in heavy combat doubtful. Russian tanks were badly armored, the Red Army "leaderless".

To some degree the views of both sides, Soviet and German, coincided. Both, however, drew different disastrous conclusions: the Soviet side that the damage could be quickly repaired, the German that it would never be. German perceptions of Soviet weakness added to the case for invading the USSR. Soviet actions to improve the Red Army subsequently contributed to holding and defeating the German army.

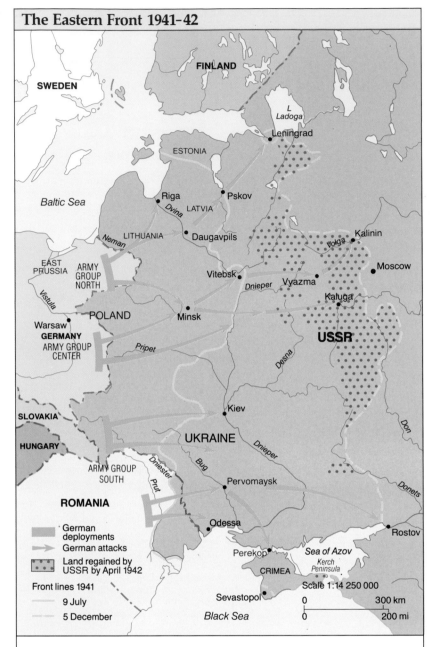

The Eastern Front 1941–42

Legend:

- German deployments
- German attacks
- Land regained by USSR by April 1942

Front lines 1941
- 9 July
- 5 December

Scale 1:14 250 000

0   300 km
0   200 mi

Josef Stalin 1879–1953

Secretary-general of the Soviet communist party from 1922, Stalin ran the Soviet war effort as an extension of his personal dictatorship through a centralized machine. The state defense committee, established on 30 June 1941, under Stalin's direction forced through the total mobilization of the country, while the *Stavka* (high command) and the general staff with the Front commands under his control ran military operations. After the resounding Soviet victory at Stalingrad Stalin assumed the title of marshal of the Soviet Union but took greater account of military advice. As a military commander he was mediocre, even less than competent; as a war leader, associated with Churchill and Roosevelt, he showed qualities of determination, clear-sightedness and a stubborn defense of Soviet interests.

Germany's threefold drive into the USSR

For the attack in the east the German command mustered 153 divisions (including 19 Panzer divisions) divided into three main Army Groups, North and Center deployed north of the Pripet Marches, and South, aimed at Kiev. Additional support came from Romanians, Italians, Slovaks, Hungarians and latterly the Spanish. Lined up along the huge front, half mobilized, imprisoned within Stalin's orders to avoid "provocations", the Red Army deployed 170 divisions supported by a huge tank park of 17,000 machines, many of them aging or unworkable, and 8,000 antiquated aircraft. The battle-tested German divisions tore through these badly deployed and poorly commanded Soviet forces. In the north Leningrad was closely invested, to suffer 900 days of ghastly siege conditions. At the center the Soviet Western Front caved in: only in the south did Army Group South have to fight its way through Soviet armor, which was trying to hold the Germans from Kiev.

The German offensive inflicted vast losses on the Red Army – 98 of the original force of 170 Soviet divisions disappeared from the order of battle, destroyed or savagely mauled. Corps vanished, divisions shrank to brigades. With millions made prisoner by the Germans, Stalin's own son among them, Red Army strength plummeted to its lowest wartime strength in November 1941. Poorly trained, barely armed "worker-militias" took up positions to face crack German units. Leningrad and Murmansk were under constant threat and fire. Army Group Center had smashed through Soviet reserves in October and was driving for Moscow, which was in the grip of evacuation. Stalin, now self-appointed supreme commander, stayed, charging General Georgii Zhukov with the defense of the capital. In the south Kiev had fallen and with it much of the Ukraine, the huge Soviet "breadbasket". Industrial production dipped disastrously with plants either lost to the Germans or dismantled in a gigantic improvised industrial evacuation to the deep interior, which put 80 percent of Soviet equipment *"na kolesakh"*, "on wheels".

By the beginning of December 1941 the Red

1941

June 22
(to July 9) The first phase of Barbarossa, the German invasion of the USSR. Hitler launches three army groups on a Blitzkrieg offensive: Army Group North, toward Leningrad; Army Group Center, toward Moscow; Army Group South toward Kiev and the Ukraine. Group North captures Daugavpils on June 26, Riga on June 30 and Pskov on July 9. Group Center encircles Soviet troops west of Minsk and captures Vitebsk on July 9. Less progress is made in the south.

July 9
(to Dec. 5) The German attack on the cities and advance into the Ukraine. In the north, German armies advance quickly toward Leningrad which they reach on Sept. 8, but they cannot breach the city's defenses and are forced to begin a siege. In the center, armies approach Moscow from the west and southwest. The

Germans take Vyazma on Oct. 7, Kaluga on Oct. 12 and Kalinin on Oct. 14. But they have not progressed fast enough: Moscow's defenses are being strengthened and the Russian winter has begun. In the south German forces capture Kiev (Aug. 14) and sweep through the Ukraine and into the Crimea (though Sevastopol holds out). They capture Rostov at the mouth of the Don on Nov. 21, but are forced out eight days later.

December 5
(to Jan. 5 1942) The Soviet counteroffensive. To relieve pressure on Moscow, Soviet forces attack on the Kalinin Front (north of Moscow) and on the West and Southwest Fronts (south of Moscow). Army Group Centre is forced back. The Red Army retakes Kalinin on Dec. 16 and Kaluga on Dec. 30. In the Crimea Soviet troops begin to land on the Kerch Peninsula (Dec. 26) to relieve Sevastopol.

1942

January 5
(to March 31) The Soviet Winter offensive. Following the success of the initial counterattacks Stalin decides to launch an offensive on all Fronts. The Red Army makes gains in the north and central areas but is stalled in the south. Eventually the offensive peters out. (Kerch is held until May 1942, after the loss of which Sevastopol falls to the Germans, in June.)

▶ Soviet troops on the Volkhov Front, about 400km (250mi) northwest of Moscow. On 5 December 1941 the Red Army attacked the flanks of the German armies pressing on Moscow.

◀ On 22 June 1941 three huge German Army Groups with four tank armies in the lead invaded the Soviet Union, advancing several hundred kilometers within weeks, blockading Leningrad, occupying the Ukraine and closing in on Moscow itself. The Soviet counterblow at Moscow in early December 1941 developed into a major counteroffensive which continued until the spring of 1942.

Army was again filling out with men and even machines. Red Army manpower had climbed back to a figure of 4,196,000. The recovery from the frightful losses had been made possible largely by the mobilization of fresh reserves from the interior and the reorganization of existing armies, from which specialist troops and particularly artillery assets were withdrawn to build yet more reserves. Already 124 divisions had been disbanded due to heavy losses and reformed, in many instances as rifle brigades. The formation of 286 new rifle divisions proceeded apace, while in deepest secrecy special reserve armies were carefully husbanded in and around Moscow. At the beginning of November 1941 Soviet reserves consisted of three armies; at the beginning of

December that figure rose to eight armies with 44 rifle divisions and 14 cavalry divisions, plus a further 13 rifle brigades. And the first tanks were coming from the relocated factories. Already two limited counterstrokes, at Tikhvin in the north and Rostov in the south, had registered some success. Stalin literally hoarded reserves in the Moscow area, 30 brigades with 9 reserve armies forming. The "Battle for Moscow" now took a new turn, even as some German scouts could see the Kremlin towers. During December 5–6 a limited counterstroke from the Kalinin and Western Fronts designed to fend off an immediate threat to Moscow suddenly rolled against weakened and extended German forces and continued to roll. The Russian recovery had begun, assuming the form of a counteroffensive and resulting by 13 December 1941 in a Soviet communiqué announcing the repulse of the German attempt to encircle the capital.

Now Soviet ambitions, in particular those of Stalin, overreached themselves. On 17–18 December Stalin ordered the Volkhov and Northwestern Fronts to strike against Army Group North; and amphibious landings on the Kerch peninsula aimed to relieve Sevastopol. Against the advice of General Zhukov and Marshal Shaposhnikov, Stalin contemplated a vast multifront counteroffensive against all three German Army Groups. Rather than concentrating on Army Group Center, Stalin planned a great "war-winning" attack to recover all he had lost. War production, not yet fully recovered, could not sustain such a scale of operations, but Stalin brooked no argument. Late in January 1942 Soviet armies made deep penetrations but lacked the resources to strike for distant objectives. German resistance increased. In the south the Soviet offensive stalled. In March 1942 Soviet offensive operations ceased, Soviet forces having in the previous three months attacked

Heinz Guderian 1888–1954

A German pioneer of armored warfare, Guderian commanded the 2nd Panzer Group and the 2nd Panzer Army in the invasion of the USSR. For an unauthorized withdrawal in December 1941 Hitler retired him. He was recalled as inspector general of Panzer troops in 1943. Guderian opposed the German offensive against the Kursk salient in order to conserve German tanks but was overruled. Hitler dismissed him in March 1945.

Aleksandr Vasilevskii 1895–1977

The "brains" behind most of the successful Soviet operations, Vasilevskii began the war as deputy chief of the general staff and head of operations. He became chief of the general staff in June 1942. However, much of his time was spent at the Front as a "*Stavka* representative", planning and coordinating operations. In February 1945 he took over a direct front command and was made a member of the *Stavka*.

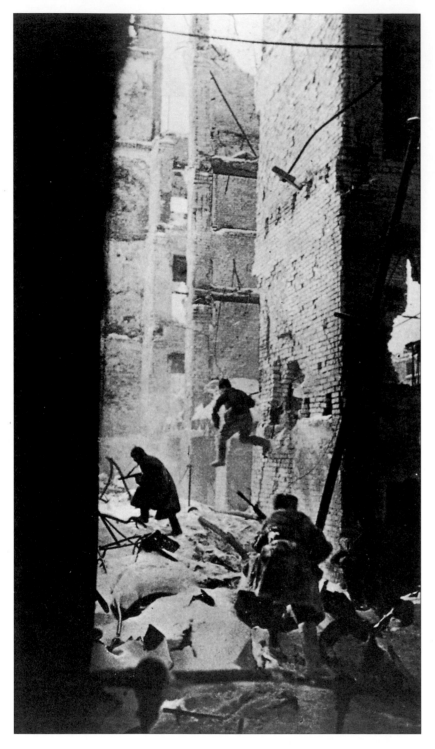

▲ The epic battle of Stalingrad engulfed more than 2 million men, trapping the German 6th Army in ferocious fighting inside the ruined city. Day and night battles raged for single houses, cellars and factory floors. Chuikov's 62nd Army clung on desperately to tiny bridgeheads on the western bank of the Volga, denying the Germans full control of the city. On 19 December 1942 the Soviet counteroffensive opened, finally trapping the 6th Army.

for the UK, which had gone to war against Hitler because of his violation of Poland. Stalin also demanded a "Second Front", a cross-Channel attack against German forces in western Europe, but Allied strength was insufficient. Stalin repeated his demand in 1942 and 1943, but his pressure was resisted and rebuffed. He took this as almost a breach of faith and his innate suspiciousness was heightened.

Hitler changes direction

By November 1941 it was clear that the German Blitzkrieg had failed. German planners now worked on the details for an offensive in summer 1942. Hitler now decided to go for the economic jugular rather than the political heart. A southern campaign would trap Soviet forces and be followed by a drive into the Caucasus and an assault on Leningrad. The main objective was the Volga river, to cut a Soviet lifeline, but it was the oil of the Caucasus which drew Hitler on and he intended the "Stalingrad operations" merely to protect the deep drive to the oil. German armies would make the main attack, the Axis "satellite" armies would hold the flanks. In spring 1942, as the armies of both sides released themselves from the clinging spring mud, the *rasputitsa*, Stalin also contemplated offensive operations, with the object of recapturing Kharkov. Marshal Timoshenko would strike from the Izyum salient won in January, but it would be a risky move and was criticized by Marshal Shaposhnikov.

Here was a prelude to further disaster. German infantry held the front while a Panzer group attacked the flank and encircled Timoshenko's forces, losing a quarter of a million men taken prisoner, plus more than 1,000 tanks. On 18 May 1942 the German Spring offensive opened and carved its way into the eastern Ukraine and on to the upper Don. Soviet defenses, weakened by such loss, fell apart. The crisis which produced Stalin's draconian order No. 227 of 28 July 1942: "Not a step back". Persuaded now that the German attack in the south was not a feint to draw Soviet forces away from Moscow, Stalin ordered his best commanders – Zhukov, Vasilevskii and Voronov – southward. For all of Stalin's alarm and resort to "the discipline of the revolver", the Red Army was neither finished nor in hopeless flight, a view entertained quite mistakenly by Hitler. On the contrary, it was the German 6th Army under von Paulus which was marching to its doom, toward Stalingrad. At this juncture, in mid-July 1942, Hitler split his forces, dividing Army Group South in Group "A" and Group "B", the former to drive into the Caucasus, the latter with the 6th Army to invest Stalingrad. After an agonizing siege Sevastopol fell to von Manstein's 11th Army on 3 July whereupon Hitler transferred the 11th Army to Leningrad. The scene was almost set for the terrible drama of Stalingrad.

German attempts to capture the city began on 19 August, 1942. Four days later German troops reached the Volga north of the city. Luftwaffe bombing set the city ablaze only to have the defenders set up defensive positions in the ruins. Hand-to-hand fighting ensued for the major buildings and installations – the Tractor Factory, Red

across 1,600km (1,000 mi) of front, destroyed or damaged 50 German divisions, cleared the Moscow and Tula regions and in places penetrated to a depth of 320km (200mi).

After the German invasion of the USSR the British prime minister, Winston Churchill, had offered British assistance for the USSR, which was confirmed in an agreement signed on 12 July 1941. Additional support was provided by the USA, especially after Hitler declared war on the USA on 11 December 1941. From the outset Stalin adopted a peremptory tone with his new-found allies. His stated war aims included the recovery of the USSR's frontiers of 1941, which included eastern Poland. This demand caused difficulties

The Eastern Front 1942–43

1942

May 18
(to July 29) The German Spring offensive. Aiming to capture the oil fields of the Caucasus, German forces make a drive into the eastern Ukraine. They capture Rostov and approach Stalingrad.

August 19
(to Feb. 28, 1943) The Germans begin their attack on Stalingrad but meet determined resistance. For over five months German and Soviet forces vie for the city. Meanwhile the German drive to the southeast continues and reaches its furthest extent on Nov. 18. Soviet resistance causes the Germans to withdraw. The German army attacking Stalingrad is isolated and eventually surrenders (Jan. 31). Soviet counterattacks force the Germans back to their positions of summer 1942.

1943

July 4–20
German forces launch a major attack on the "Kursk salient", which protrudes from the Soviet line. Soviet armored forces hold the salient and Hitler calls off the attack.

July 20
(to Nov. 30) After their victory at Kursk, Soviet forces break out south of the salient. By the end of November they have reached or crossed the Dnieper and retaken Kiev (Nov. 6).

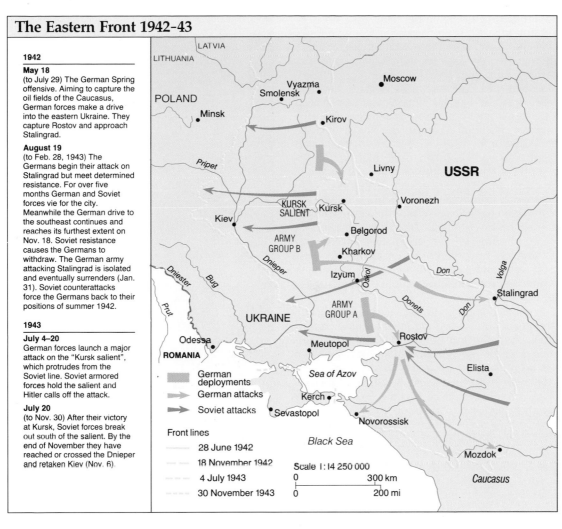

German deployments
German attacks
Soviet attacks
Front lines
28 June 1942
18 November 1942
4 July 1943
30 November 1943
Scale 1:14 250 000
0   300 km
0   200 mi

◀ The Soviet victory at Stalingrad was the turning-point of the Soviet–German war. The quantity of Soviet arms and men now gained the advantage over the Germans' superiority in skill and equipment.

▼ In the early morning of 1 February 1943 Radio Moscow announced the German surrender at Stalingrad. The newly promoted Field Marshal von Paulus and his staff were taken prisoner. Twenty German and two Romanian divisions had been destroyed; the Soviet command claimed 91,000 prisoners.

Barricades factory, Red October Foundry, the "commanding height" of Mamayev Kurgan – followed by close-quarter combat for rooms, cellars, even sections of wall. The vital ferries chugged across the Volga, bombed and shelled but never stopped. Gradually the Soviet positions shrank. Vasili Chuikov took command of 62nd Army and stayed put himself, virtually clinging to the river bank. During the first half of November 1942 ice clogged the Volga, the ferries stopped, all that was left to the Soviet defenders was to "stick it out". Both sides felt the crisis. Von Paulus, for his part, understood the significance of Soviet forces massing on his flank and sought permission from Hitler to pull back to a winter line. Hitler refused: von Paulus was categorically forbidden to abandon Stalingrad. A final German attack was planned for November 18. The next day, in morning fog, Soviet tanks crashed into the two Romanian armies and then the Italian army holding 6th Army's northern and southern flanks. Within four days, on 23 November, 6th Army was encircled.

The 6th Army suffered death by slow starvation. Almost 300,000 soldiers were trapped and 30,000 wounded were entombed, cut off from care, in ruined cellars. Malnutrition increased the ravages of disease. But the fate of Stalingrad was linked to the possible doom facing German armies deep in the Caucasus. There had been a Soviet breakthrough against the Italian 8th Army south of Stalingrad. Coupled with a German sur-render at Stalingrad, the way would be open to cut off German Army Group A and close its escape route at Rostov. At the end of December 1942 Hitler authorized withdrawal from the Caucasus and the "race for Rostov", full of fateful implications, was on. The German 6th Army at Stalingrad, palsied and dying, fought on, tying down Soviet forces needed to seal the German escape route from the Caucasus. In the event, amidst fierce battles, German 1st Panzer Army moved the 650km (400mi) to Rostov and safety, leaving 17th Army in the western Caucasus to hole up in the Kuban. Von Paulus, newly promoted field marshal, played out the final act with his surrender on 31 January 1943.

Erich von Manstein 1887–1973

A soldier since 1906, Manstein, was given command of 11th Army in the Crimea. In July 1942 it captured Sevastopol, and was moved northward to assault Leningrad. But soon Manstein's "fire brigade" was rushed south again and Manstein took over Army Group Don to check the Soviet advance westward from Stalingrad. Manstein failed to relieve the encircled Germans at Stalingrad but stabilized the Front. In March 1943 he retook Kharkov, and attacked the Kursk salient but on 30 March 1944, with Army Group South under threat, Hitler dismissed his "master tactician".

I will cite only one example to illustrate the intensity of this battle (during Kursk). Nearly thirty tanks were advancing on a battery commanded by Captain G.I. Igishev. The gunners engaged them in unequal combat. Their four guns let the enemy approach to within 600–700 metres before opening fire. They destroyed 17 tanks, but by this time only one gun was left of the battery, with three men to serve it. They continued to fire, putting two more heavy tanks out of action. The enemy was forced to retire. Thanks to the heroic combined operations by all arms the attack was repulsed.

K.K. ROKOSSOVSKII

Soviet forces gain the upper hand

The full fury of the Soviet counteroffensive broke over the German southern wing, though Stalin's attempt to break into the Kuban defensive perimeter and trap 400,000 German troops failed. Manstein held Rostov until 14 February 1943 and redeployed 1st Panzer, while Soviet plans called for a drive on Kharkov to thrust deep into the German rear and complete the Soviet encirclement east of the river Dnieper. In a series of parrying blows and counterstrikes, Manstein chopped off the Soviet spearheads and planned late in February to retake Kharkov, abandoned temporarily on 15 February. One month later the Germans again held Kharkov and could even think of driving north on Kursk. Manstein proposed an attack to eliminate the salient just formed and holding six unprepared Soviet armies. But the mud came and indecision overcame the German command. The Kursk salient jutted out intact, the next German target.

In the late spring and early summer of 1943 a strange, unaccustomed lull settled on the Eastern Front. At Stalingrad the German army had suffered a grave psychological blow but it had not yet been defeated decisively in the field. Both sides now fixed their eyes on the Kursk salient. Hitler intended to attack it as the first step in his summer offensive. Zhukov at the beginning of 1943 advised Stalin that there would be no further drive to the Volga, rather an attack toward Moscow taking the most immediate route – striking first through the Kursk salient. For once Stalin listened and agreed in spite of misgivings to delay his own offensive and build a formidable defense in the salient. The Soviet defense in depth ran for more than 160km (100mi), built around six zones and massively mined.

For his planned attack Hitler demanded more mighty Tiger tanks, and so constantly delayed his offensive, thus allowing the Red Army more time to prepare. When the blow came on 4 July 1943 the German army pitted 42 divisions and the cream of the Panzer arm against 54 Soviet divisions with 12 tank corps. Striking from the northern and southern faces German armor chewed its way through Soviet defenses, bringing about the greatest tank battles in history and culminating in the enormous armored joust at Prokhorovka on 12 July 1943. The next day Hitler called off the attack, transferring a Panzer corps to

Italy on July 17 and ordering two Panzer divisions north to stave off a Soviet threat to Army Group Center. As Hitler "temporarily" canceled his attack on the salient, the Red Army loosed its own considerable forces in the south, making for the river Dnieper on a front constantly broadening, dropping a large airborne force on the Bukhrin bridgehead on 24 September 1943. But it was left to General N.F. Vatutin to strike out for Kiev, which fell early in November 1943. The Soviet offensive slowed but German forces had been pushed back to the Dnieper and the German Panzer arm gravely mangled as a result of Kursk. The stalemate had been broken. From now on the German army was condemned only to retreat.

Stalin now demanded the liberation of the Ukraine and the smashing in of the entire German southern wing. In January 1944 Koniev carried through the "Korsun encirclement", a "touch of the Stalingrad whip" and the continuation of his "mud offensive". After the reduction of the Korsun "pocket" in late February, Zhukov at the beginning of March took over 1st Ukrainian Front and speedily sliced 4th Panzer Army in two; on 17 March Koniev was over the river Dniester and moving to encircle 1st Panzer Army. In the

▼ Soviet mounted troops pull a gun through the spring mud. Both the Red Army and the German army had to battle the mud brought annually in the spring thaw, though Soviet tanks, with their broad tracks, found it easier to sail these glutinous seas. Usually the *rasputitsa*, the thaw, brought an enforced lull on the main battlefronts but in the late winter of 1944–45 General Koniev launched his "mud offensive" in the Ukraine. Exploiting his wide-tracked tanks and American-supplied 4-wheel and 6-wheel trucks, as well as sturdy peasant carts, he carried out a major encirclement, while German tanks and motor vehicles, road-bound as they were, struggled against the mud.

Crimea the 17th Army, withdrawn from the Kuban bridgehead, was another Soviet target, in an attack begun on 7 April 1944. At the northern extremity of the Eastern Front at long last, after months of innumerable horrors, in January 1944, a major Soviet offensive rammed the Germans away from Leningrad.

The Soviet defeat of Nazi Germany

With Army Group North pushed back and Army Group South in tatters only Army Group Center remained relatively inviolate, the Red Army's oldest and most formidable enemy. Stalin now planned its complete destruction. His Operation Bagration was timed to open on a memorable date: 22 June. By now the Second Front had materialized, but Stalin's plans were his own. Four Soviet Fronts with more than 2.5 million men attacked German positions headon; one by one, the German armies splintered and broke, 3rd Panzer at Vitebsk, 4th Army on the Dnieper, 9th Army at Bobruisk. By mid-July German forces had been swept from Belorussia and the Red Army had moved into northeast Poland.

In late August 1944 a strategic earthquake boiled up in the Balkans completely destroying the

▲ On 5 July 1943, after a hesitation which proved well-nigh fatal, Hitler launched the German armies in the attack on the massively fortified Kursk salient. In what became known as the "death ride" of the 4th Panzer Army, German and Soviet armor clashed in the greatest tank battle of World War II. The nimble but outgunned Soviet T-34 medium tanks, as seen here, literally charged into the ranks of the mighty German Tiger tanks. Such ferocious engagements, made at the cost of great Soviet losses, finally broke the power of the German Panzer troops.

◀ *Za Stalina, Za Rodinu!* – "For Stalin, For the Motherland!" Red Army troops, like the civilian population, fought under this slogan: Red Armymen used it as a battle-cry, soldiers scrawled it on tank turrets. Here Stalin rides high over Soviet tank-borne infantry symbolically pressing westward.

The Eastern Front 1944–45

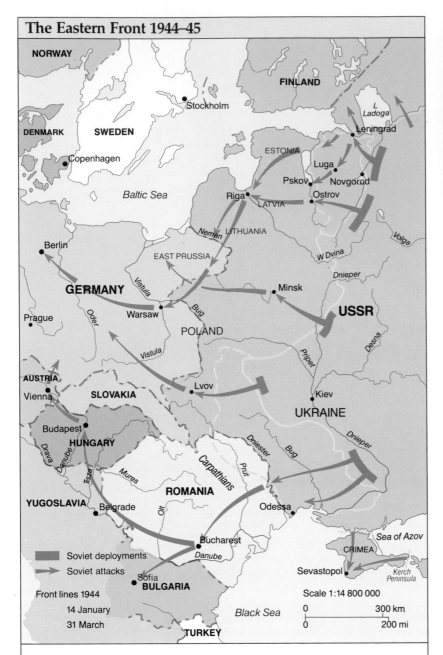

Soviet deployments
Soviet attacks
Front lines 1944
14 January
31 March

Scale 1:14 800 000

0   300 km
0   200 mi

1943–44

December 24
(to mid May 1944) The Soviet winter campaign, consisting of three major offensives: in the Ukraine, the Crimea and in the north. The main offensive is the Soviet bid to regain the Ukraine. Despite fierce German resistance, Soviet forces push forward and on March 17 General Koniev and Soviet troops cross the Dniester. By mid April they are approaching the Carpathians. The northern offensive begins on Jan. 14. Soviet forces attack near Leningrad and then near Novgorod. Leningrad is freed from siege on Jan. 26. Soviet forces advance south to Luga, but are unable to capture Pskov and Ostrov. In April Soviet forces attack Germans sealed in the Crimean Peninsula. Sevastopol is recaptured on May 12.

June 22
(to Aug. 23) Operation Bagration, the Soviet offensive

in the central part of the Front. The offensive breaks up the German Army Group Center. On July 26 Soviet troops reach the Vistula in Poland and then move toward Germany. Further south Soviet forces take Lvov and push toward the Vistula.

August 20
(to Sept. 8) A Soviet attack on Romania causes the country to change sides. Soviet troops enter Bucharest on Aug. 31. On Sept. 8, Bulgaria declares war on Germany and places its troops under the command of the Red Army.

October
Soviet forces move into Slovakia, Hungary, and Yugoslavia. Soviet forces and Tito's partisans clear Belgrade on Oct. 19. Soviet forces attack Budapest on Oct. 30 but the city resists until February 1945.

1945

January 12
(to Feb. 24) Soviet troops advance in Poland and move into East Prussia. Warsaw falls on Jan. 17. By the end of Feb. Soviet troops are on the Oder, only 60km (37mi) from Berlin.

February 24
(to May 8) The fall of the major cities. A Soviet invasion of Austria leads to the fall of Vienna on April 7. An offensive launched against Germany on April 16 takes the Red Army to Berlin: the city is encircled on April 25 (the same day as Soviet and US troops meet at Torgau on the Elbe) and surrenders on May 1. On May 8 Prague capitulates.

German southeastern theater. A Soviet offensive into Romania, beginning on 20 August, trapped 16 German divisions in the Jassy-Kishinev operation. Romania capitulated without delay and promptly changed sides, perfidy which doomed more Germans. Bulgaria followed suit; Soviet units moved into Yugoslavia to operate with Tito's partisans; and plans were afoot to drive into Hungary. Malinovskii reached Budapest on 30 October 1944 with no less than 64 divisions, completing the encirclement by the end of December but initiating yet another ghastly siege. In the north Finland had also surrendered.

The Red Army was now poised to advance into the Reich itself, the "lair of the Fascist beast". Already in November 1944 Stalin had nominated the commander to capture Berlin, Marshal Zhukov. Halted since July 1944 on the Vistula, staring at a Warsaw in the flames of revolt but rendering no assistance, the Red Army now mustered five Fronts for the grand assault on the Reich. The "Vistula-Oder operations", launched on 12 January 1945, brought Zhukov to the River Oder at the end of January, to Küstrin, a mere 60km (37mi) from Berlin. Koniev had invested most of Silesia. Despite this immediate threat Hitler insisted on sending 6th Panzer Army to Hungary for an offensive designed to win his way back to the Danube.

In the south the German offensive in Hungary failed. The way lay open to Vienna which fell to Tolbukhin on 7 April. Now it wanted little more than a week for the gigantic Soviet offensive aimed at Berlin, which Stalin knew would not be an Anglo-American objective. Three Soviet Fronts – 2nd Belorussian, 1st Belorussian and 1st Ukrainian – stood ready on the Oder-Neisse river line, a mass of 2.5 million men, more than 6,000 tanks, 41,000 guns and 7,500 aircraft. Zhukov opened his attack on 16 April with a gigantic cannonade which could be heard in Berlin itself. Koniev crossed the Neisse and raced from the south for Berlin. Zhukov, his mass of men and armor stumbling over themselves, fought to break through from the east while Rokossovskii to the north blocked 3rd Panzer Army. The encirclement of Berlin was complete on 25 April 1945, while on the River Elbe Soviet and American troops linked up, cutting the Reich in half. After days of bitter and often bloody street fighting, on 30 April the

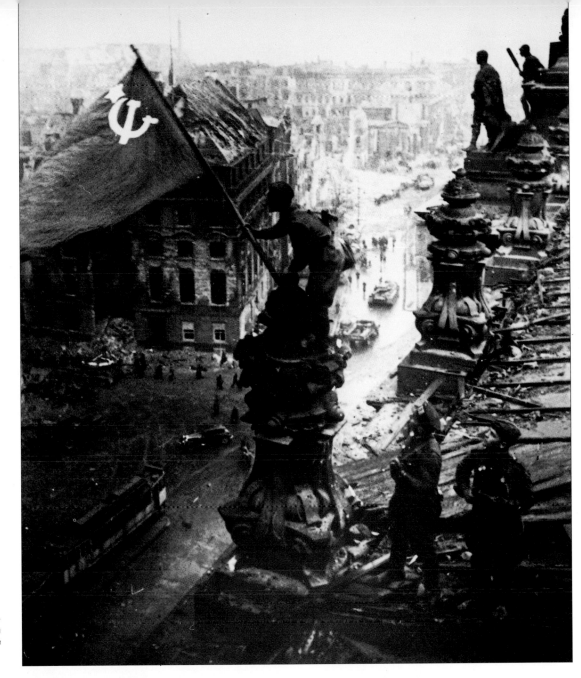

◄ Bulgarians greet units of the Soviet 3rd Ukrainian Army Group. At the end of August 1944, with Soviet armies flooding through Romania, Bulgaria faced the prospect of a Soviet invasion. Never an ardent ally of Hitler and his campaigns in Russia, Bulgaria proceeded to disarm Germans withdrawing from Romania, and, on 8 September 1944, declared war on Germany. Bulgarian troops were placed under Soviet command. Marshal Fedor Tolbukhin's 3rd Ukrainian Group crossed the frontier between the lower Danube and the Black Sea, and occupied the whole country without resistance.

◄◄ 1944 was the year of the Red Army's "ten decisive blows", launched initially on the flanks. In the north Leningrad was freed from blockade; in the south, large-scale operations recovered much of the Ukraine. In the center, in June 1944, the Red Army smashed Army Group Centre, and struck westward toward Poland.

► Toward noon on 30 April 1945 Soviet regiments took up positions for the final assault on the Reichstag in the heart of Berlin. After a day of heavy fighting and bombardment, two sergeants, Yegorov and Kantariya, succeeded in planting the red victory banner high over the building at 22.50 hours. It was the symbol of the Soviet triumph over Nazi Germany.

Walter Model 1891–1945

One of Hitler's "ruthless generals", Field Marshal Model took over the 9th Army on the Eastern Front in January 1942 and led it in the massive 1943 German operation against the Kursk salient, unsuccessfully as it proved. After holding commands in the north and the Ukraine, Model joined Army Group Center in April 1944 but he was unable to halt the massive Soviet offensive of summer 1944. He committed suicide in 1945.

Georgii Zhukov 1896–1974

The "general who never lost a battle", Zhukov joined the *Stavka* (GHQ) on 23 June 1941 and remained a member throughout the war. In spring 1944 he controlled the operations that smashed German Army Group South. At the beginning of 1945 he planned and directed the mighty Vistula-Oder operations, driving into Germany, and then, in the final assault on Berlin, commanded the 1st Belorussian Front.

Reichstag itself was stormed and the red "Victory banner" hoisted over it. With Hitler dead, the city surrendered on 1 May.

It remained only to race for Prague. Koniev's tank armies wheeled away from Berlin and sped into Czechoslovakia from the east. On 8 May 1945 Marshal Koniev transmitted a capitulation order to all German units in western Czechoslovakia, accompanying it with a massive artillery barrage. On 9 May Soviet units linked up in Prague.

Stalin frequently reminded his wartime allies that the Red Army and the Soviet people were carrying the heaviest (and the bloodiest) burden of the fighting against Nazi Germany. In 47 months of fighting the Red Army inflicted more than 70 percent of the total losses in men and weapons suffered by the German army, destroying in the process 214 divisions, capturing 56, disabling 143 divisions and accepting the surrender of 93.5, making a grand total of 607 divisions. The corresponding tally for Anglo-American forces amounted to 176 enemy divisions.

Datafile

Compared to the fighting in France in 1940 or 1944 or on the Eastern Front (1941–45) the statistics for the Mediterranean theater seem unimpressive. Germany and the USA regarded the area as a sideshow and only Italy and the UK committed substantial forces. But the campaign did serve as a testing ground where British forces could develop new techniques and regain confidence after the debacle of 1940.

Libyan campaign

- ☐ Italy
- ☐ UK

(bar chart, vertical axis labelled "Hundreds", bars for Guns, Tanks, Fighters, Bombers)

El Alamein campaign

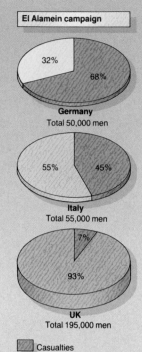

32% / 68%
Germany
Total 50,000 men

55% / 45%
Italy
Total 55,000 men

7% / 93%
UK
Total 195,000 men

▨ Casualties

◀ In December 1940 the numerical superiority of Italian over British forces in North Africa was crushing. However, organization and technique were more important than numbers. Most of the 320 British tanks were concentrated in the highly trained 7th Armoured Division; Italian tanks were distributed among infantry units.

▶ Montgomery did not attack at El Alamein (23 October 1942) until he had achieved nearly a 2:1 numerical superiority. Unlike the highly mobile actions which had thus far characterized the desert war, El Alamein was an attritional battle: over 50 percent of Axis forces became casualties, most as prisoners.

▼ The North African campaign was very important in restoring British confidence but its effect on the outcome of the war was marginal. Germany lost nearly as many men (800,000) in Russia in the first six months of Operation Barbarossa as all the combatants did in nearly three years in North Africa.

Losses in North Africa

Axis
- ☐ Germany
- ☐ Italy

Allies
- ▨ UK
- ☐ USA
- ☐ France

(bar chart, vertical axis labelled "Hundred thousands")

Invasion of Sicily

8% / 92%
Germany
Total 65,000 men

5% / 95%
Allies
Total 160,000 men

1% / 99%
Italy
Total 230,000 men

4·5% / 0·5% / 95%
Prisoners
Total 150,600

▨ Casualties

El Alamein forces

- ☐ UK
- ☐ Axis

(bar chart, vertical axis labelled "Thousands", bars for Guns, Tanks, Aircraft)

▲ Material deployed at El Alamein. As with manpower, British preponderance in materiel was crushing: 400 of the 600 Axis tanks were Italian and incapable of meeting the more heavily armored and gunned British tanks with any hope of success. Similarly the majority of the 675 Axis aircraft were Italian and inferior.

◀ In the invasion of Sicily (July–August 1942) Axis defenders outnumbered the Allies by nearly 2:1, but the reluctance of the Italian forces to fight was reflected in the small number of battle casualties as opposed to the vast number of prisoners taken by the Allies (143,500 of the 230,000 strong Italian garrison).

War came to the Mediterranean basin on 10 June 1940, when Italy declared war on the Allies. Italy's dictator, Benito Mussolini, was jealous of Hitler's spectacular successes and hoped that Italy, too, could achieve massive and glorious victories that would mark a revival of the "New Roman Empire". For Mussolini his decision was disastrous. Only crushing defeat, humiliation and political nemesis followed. For Hitler the decision was distracting and he too paid a heavy price for Mussolini's impulsive act. Italy was wholly unprepared for war.

The first British advance and retreat

The war in the Mediterranean followed the same pattern as that in western Europe. A period of inactivity was followed by rapid and crushing movement. The Italian army in Libya appeared very imposing – on paper: 250,000 men. The British commander-in-chief Middle East, General Sir Archibald Wavell, had only 36,000 men in Egypt. In September 1940 the Italians began a timid invasion of Egypt, halting after only 80km (50mi) at Sidi Barrani.

Wavell believed that the Italian 10th Army should be attacked at Sidi Barrani and driven

THE WAR IN THE MEDITERRANEAN

back to Libya. The results of this audacious decision were momentous. Within two days five Italian divisions had been destroyed. He reached the coastal hamlet of Beda Fomm and cut off the Italians. In 62 days the Western Desert Force had annihilated 10 divisions, capturing 130 prisoners, 380 tanks and 845 guns. It was a great feat of arms, but incomplete. O'Connor urged that he be allowed to press the advance and seize Tripoli. Wavell refused: the Germans were menacing Greece.

Wavell's forces were spread very thinly. Not only was he advancing in Libya, but since January he had also been attempting to reconquer Italian Abyssinia. Now he was required to send troops to aid the Greeks. In 1939 the British government had guaranteed Greek independence along with that of the ill-fated Poles. The Greeks were reluctant allies. The Greek dictator, General Ioannis Metaxas, refused to do anything that might antagonize the Germans. British help had to be covert. On 29 January 1941 Metaxas died and within a month the Greek government at last acknowledged that it needed British troops to counterbalance the growing German threat. These could only come from one source: O'Connor's Western Desert Force.

The British-supported Greek campaign (March–April 1941) was a disaster, mitigated only by another naval victory over the Italians, at Cape Matapan on 28 March. The Germans invaded Greece and Yugoslavia on 6 April. The Greek army of 14 divisions refused to give up its gains in Albania. The British and three Greek divisions took up position on the incomplete Aliakmon Line. A gap emerged between this position and the main Greek army through which the Germans surged and within two days Salonika had fallen. The British then withdrew to Thermopylae and thence to Piraeus. Evacuation – a repeat of Dunkirk – was the only option. The Royal Navy

▼ Heirs to the Roman Legions? The abysmal performance of Italian troops in the opening campaigns of the desert war forced German intervention. These members of the Afrika Korps were captured at Tobruk in November 1941. In the later campaigns the Italians fought bravely, though their equipment was poor. But relations with the Germans were always tense.

Benito Mussolini 1883–1945

Dictator, or *Il Duce*, of Italy. He had seized power in 1922 during the "March on Rome." Always inclined to swagger and boast, he degenerated from being a dominating figure on the international scene to a buffoon and helpless puppet. The Italian declaration of war (10 June 1940) was followed by a string of humiliating defeats. But Mussolini's own position was not threatened until 1943. In July, after the Allied invasion of Sicily, at a meeting of the fascist grand council, a motion was passed (19–7) depriving him of power. Imprisoned, Mussolini, was rescued only to preside over a German puppet government in the north. With the collapse of German authority, he was captured and executed unceremoniously.

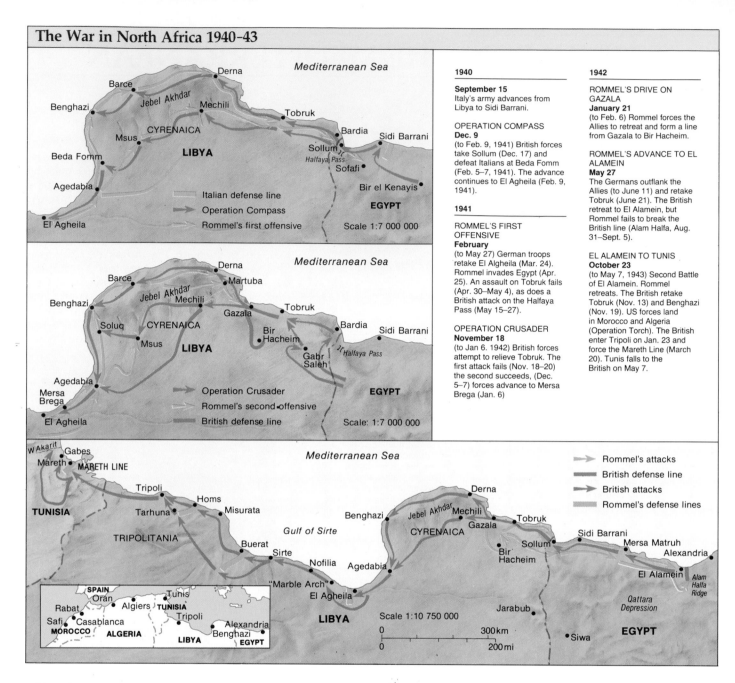

The War in North Africa 1940–43

Mediterranean Sea

Derna · Barce · Jebel Akhdar · Mechili · Benghazi · Tobruk · Msus · CYRENAICA · Bardia · Sidi Barrani · Beda Fomm · **LIBYA** · Sollum · *Halfaya Pass* · Sofafi · Agedabia · Bir el Kenayis · **EGYPT** · El Agheila

Italian defense line
Operation Compass
Rommel's first offensive
Scale 1:7 000 000

Mediterranean Sea

Derna · Barce · Martuba · Jebel Akhdar · Mechili · Benghazi · Gazala · Tobruk · Soluq · CYRENAICA · Bir Hacheim · Bardia · Sidi Barrani · Msus · **LIBYA** · Gabr Saleh · *Halfaya Pass* · Agedabia · Mersa Brega · **EGYPT** · El Agheila

Operation Crusader
Rommel's second offensive
British defense line
Scale: 1:7 000 000

Mediterranean Sea

W Akarit · Gabes · Mareth · MARETH LINE · Tripoli · Homs · **TUNISIA** · Tarhuna · Misurata · TRIPOLITANIA · *Gulf of Sirte* · Buerat · Sirte · Nofilia · "Marble Arch" · El Agheila · Benghazi · Jebel Akhdar · Mechili · Derna · Tobruk · CYRENAICA · Gazala · Sollum · Sidi Barrani · Mersa Matruh · Bir Hacheim · Alexandria · El Alamein · *Alam Halfa Ridge* · Agedabia · Jarabub · *Qattara Depression* · **LIBYA** · Siwa · **EGYPT**

Rommel's attacks
British defense line
British attacks
Rommel's defense lines

SPAIN · Oran · Tunis · Rabat · Algiers · **TUNISIA** · Safi · Casablanca · Tripoli · **MOROCCO** · **ALGERIA** · Alexandria · Benghazi · **LIBYA** · **EGYPT**

Scale 1:10 750 000
0 — 300km
0 — 200mi

1940

September 15
Italy's army advances from Libya to Sidi Barrani.

OPERATION COMPASS
Dec. 9
(to Feb. 9, 1941) British forces take Sollum (Dec. 17) and defeat Italians at Beda Fomm (Feb. 5–7, 1941). The advance continues to El Agheila (Feb. 9, 1941).

1941

ROMMEL'S FIRST OFFENSIVE
February
(to May 27) German troops retake El Algheila (Mar. 24). Rommel invades Egypt (Apr. 25). An assault on Tobruk fails (Apr. 30–May 4), as does a British attack on the Halfaya Pass (May 15–27).

OPERATION CRUSADER
November 18
(to Jan 6. 1942) British forces attempt to relieve Tobruk. The first attack fails (Nov. 18–20) the second succeeds, (Dec. 5–7) forces advance to Mersa Brega (Jan. 6)

1942

ROMMEL'S DRIVE ON GAZALA
January 21
(to Feb. 6) Rommel forces the Allies to retreat and form a line from Gazala to Bir Hacheim.

ROMMEL'S ADVANCE TO EL ALAMEIN
May 27
The Germans outflank the Allies (to June 11) and retake Tobruk (June 21). The British retreat to El Alamein, but Rommel fails to break the British line (Alam Halfa, Aug. 31–Sept. 5).

EL ALAMEIN TO TUNIS
October 23
(to May 7, 1943) Second Battle of El Alamein. Rommel retreats. The British retake Tobruk (Nov. 13) and Benghazi (Nov. 19). US forces land in Morocco and Algeria (Operation Torch). The British enter Tripoli on Jan. 23 and force the Mareth Line (March 20). Tunis falls to the British on May 7.

achieved a second "miracle" in getting the troops away in face of German air superiority. The same exercise was to be repeated once Crete had been lost the following month.

The easy victories of O'Connor had been transformed into bitter defeat once the overwhelming might of the Germans had been brought in to redress the balance. The British had been driven from the northern shores of the Mediterranean. Yet worse was to follow. In February 1942 German troops arrived in Tripoli.

There can be little doubt that if the full might of the Wehrmacht had been deployed in the Mediterranean then British power in this region would have been destroyed in the autumn of 1941. British forces were too weak and poorly equipped to withstand German professionalism. The following years were to show that Britain's commanders had quite enough difficulty coping with the forces that were reluctantly dispatched by the German army high command (OKH). It

considered North Africa a "side show", a tiresome distraction from the main objective – the invasion of Soviet Russia. Before December 1942 German forces in North Africa never amounted to more than three divisions. But they were commanded by a redoubtable officer and a master of mobile warfare: Erwin Rommel.

Rommel seizes the initiative

Within six weeks "this obscure general", as British Intelligence referred to him, had launched a counteroffensive. The British were caught flatfooted. Their best troops had been sent to Greece, and so had their commanders. Lieutenant-General Philip Neame was brought in to take command. His troops were inexperienced at armored warfare and so was he. He was not only intellectually ill-equipped but psychologically unprepared for the challenge he would face. He established an unimaginative HQ kilometers behind the frontline. Rommel undertook O'Connor's advance

▲ The "pendulum war" in North Africa. Both the Allied and Axis armies were small by the standards of the Eastern Front. For the first two years of the campaign neither side could secure a decisive victory as their offensives lost momentum when they advanced further from their bases and drove the enemy back on his. It was only after summer 1942, when American equipment began to arrive in abundance, that the margin of quantitative superiority swung decisively in the Allies' favor.

▶ Rommel's precarious supply lines – stretching from Tripoli to the Egyptian frontier – forced him to rely heavily on airpower. The aircraft shown here are mainly JU52s – slow but reliable "work horse" transport aircraft.

in reverse. Benghazi fell on 4 April and Derna three days later. Wavell was unhappy with Neame's performance and sent O'Connor to "advise" him, a most unhappy compromise as it turned out. Going up to Derna both Neame and O'Connor were captured. The loss of O'Connor was a disaster. He had shown himself to be one of the very few British commanders who were equal to the demands of mobile warfare: perhaps the only senior British general who would have been a match for Rommel.

The only glimmer of hope for Wavell was that Tobruk continued to hold out. All that he had achieved in four months had been cancelled in one. The rout in North Africa could have been greater had Rommel not been obsessed with taking Tobruk. He refused to consider anything else. On 23 April 1941 General Franz Halder, chief of staff to OKH, wrote in his diary that "things are in a mess... Rommel is in no way equal to the task. He rushes about the whole day between his widely scattered units... and fritters away his resources". General Friedrich von Paulus was dispatched to report on the desirability of continuing the siege. Von Paulus advised that no more troops should be sent to Rommel until the situation improved.

This message was decoded by Ultra and sent to Wavell by Churchill. The "Tiger" convoy carrying 300 new tanks had also arrived in Alexandria. Churchill, conscious of growing British strength and Rommel's weakness, pushed Wavell into a premature offensive. The result was Operation Battleaxe. Wavell launched his armor up the Halfaya Pass in a vain effort to destroy the German armor and break through to Tobruk. Rommel preferred to hold his armor in reserve and repel the British attack with his antitank guns – especially the deadly 88mm antiaircraft gun which he used in an antitank role. The British armor was devastated – over half of it was lost in the battle. Rommel then launched his own armor in a counterattack at Sidi Omar but the Western Desert Force withdrew before the jaws of Rommel's trap slammed shut.

The first British victory

After this defeat Wavell was replaced by the commander-in-chief India, General Sir Claude Auchinleck, a commander of fine character and high reputation, but a complete stranger to GHQ Cairo. The British forces were reorganized as the 8th Army, and Lieutenant General Sir Alan Cunningham was brought fresh from his triumphs in Abyssinia to take command. Cunningham was a tactician of some ability, but like so many British generals, quite inexperienced in the techniques of armored warfare. He was ordered by Auchinleck to plan Operation Crusader to occupy Cyrenaica and relieve Tobruk.

This operation, more than any other, illustrates the interdependent character of the North African campaign. By the autumn of 1941 the plight of the British island of Malta, lying astride Rommel's lines of communication, and the only British outpost remaining in the central Mediterranean, was becoming desperate. Its relief also had to be considered. This could be aided by seizing the

Claude Auchinleck 1884–1980

A product of the Indian (not British) army, after service in Norway and India, Auchinleck was appointed commander-in-chief Middle East, on 22 June 1941. He was a general of first-rate tactical flair, but was a poor judge of character. He led the 8th Army to the first British victory over a German-commanded force in Operation "Crusader". But he was held responsible for the defeats of 1942, and his victory at First Alamein was not acknowledged. He was sacked in August 1942 and returned to India.

Archibald Wavell 1883–1950

A cultivated man and well-read , Wavell was forced to make war pulled in opposite directions, and yet he succeeded. Apart from Operation "Compass," he put down a pro-fascist coup in Iraq. Just as O'Connor was poised to make a move on Tripoli, Wavell participated rather more readily than was later acknowledged in the ill-fated intervention in Greece. "Things fell apart", Rommel counterattacked, and Wavell's response "Battleaxe", was unsuccessful. He was moved to India and rose to the viceroyalty.

▲ Although Rommel operated in oil-rich areas, throughout his campaigns in North Africa his fuel supply operated on a shoestring. Operating from Italy, Axis oil tankers put in to Tripoli, unloaded their precious cargoes and the oil was then moved to the front by road. The Allies tightened their stranglehold during 1943.

Libyan ports and assisting the Royal Navy in their capture. But the British army could only move on these ports under the cover of air power, and to guarantee that cover more airfields in Cyrenaica had to be captured. Yet the desert air force could not use these until the 8th Army had driven Rommel from Cyrenaica. Consequently, the operations in this campaign revolved around the northern communication centers.

The burden of responsibility lying on Cunningham's shoulders was so great that he decided to give up smoking, and this put his nerves on edge. The plan he evolved for Crusader was highly unsatisfactory. He intended to destroy Rommel's armor in a great tank battle. The lessons of Operation Battleaxe had not been learnt. The 8th Army was to advance rapidly, taking Rommel by surprise, and then halt and wait for the German armor to deploy. To surrender the initiative on the first day of an offensive was foolish in the extreme, and so it was to prove.

Although Cunningham had 455 tanks to Rommel's 412, he only had 72 antitank guns to Rommel's 192. This equation had great importance, and Cunningham should have paid more attention to it. He was successful in achieving surprise but not in gaining a decisive victory over the enemy's armor. A chaotic battle of attrition developed around Sidi Rezegh. Rommel made a "dash for the wire" deep into Cunningham's rear. "It was the contagion of bewilderment and fear and ignorance", wrote the war correspondent, Alan Moorehead. "Rumors spread at every halt, no man had orders". Cunningham seemed to lose his nerve and counseled retreat. Auchinleck relieved him, replacing him with his chief of staff, Neil Ritchie.

The crisis of the battle passed. Rommel's thrust was too weak and he was forced to retreat. Tobruk was relieved and the 8th Army arrived triumphantly at El Agheila. The scale of the victory was substantial. Rommel had suffered 24,500 casualties and lost almost 400 tanks. Operation Crusader was the first major British victory over a German-commanded force in World War II. It was sorely needed but of short duration. The opening of the war against Japan deprived Auchinleck of badly needed reinforcements and

Rommel launched a counterattack which drove 8th Army back to the line Bir Hacheim-Gazala.

Rommel enters Egypt

The desert war now entered its period of crisis. The British and their allies had built a large fortified line, based on minefields and several strong points or "boxes". These appeared to enjoy no relationship with the armored, mobile forces. Rommel determined to break through this line before it grew too strong. On 26 May he attempted to outflank the Gazala Line from the south. The Free French forces resisted gallantly at Bir Hacheim but were overwhelmed. Rommel advanced into the British rear and "dug in" in the "cauldron". This amounted to a "bridgehead" out of which Rommel intended to advance once he had refuelled and worn down the British armor in a series of defensive actions. On 4–5 June British armor was indeed dissipated in a number of uncoordinated piecemeal attacks; by 12 June only 70 British tanks survived. With massive air support Rommel struck towards Tobruk. Its capture on 21 June was a severe moral blow for Churchill's government. Rommel was promoted to field marshal and his troops celebrated "with captured tinned fruit, Irish potatoes, cigarettes and canned beer". On 23 June Rommel crossed the Egyptian frontier. Two days later Auchinleck relieved Ritchie

Erwin Rommel 1891–1944

A man who had no other interest but soldiering, Rommel was a brilliant cavalry general, tactician, and exponent of armored warfare. He took over the Deutsche Afrika Korps (DAK) in 1941. The skill he exhibited in commanding this outnumbered force earned him the admiration of his adversaries, and Auchinleck was forced to issue a general order deprecating this tendency. His success was owed to his eye for ground, his personal style of command, leading "from the front", and the important realization that armored warfare revolved around the antitank gun just as much as around the tank. Temperamentally inclined to neglect matters such as logistics, his formula was much less successful against a prudent general like Montgomery. He committed suicide in 1944.

It was a battle of attrition. Its main aim was to contain the enemy's armor and wear down Rommel's infantry by a process of "crumbling". Once these had been destroyed, Rommel's defensive line would collapse and the armor could break out. The plan ran into difficulties and Montgomery was forced to modify it. The Australians launched a diversionary attack to distract Rommel's reserves. Once these had been committed the armor broke through and the pursuit began on 1–2 November. In Britain El Alamein was hailed as a great victory. But its results were disappointing. Rommel escaped and the long battle exhausted the victors almost as much as the vanquished.

On 8 November 1942 the Anglo-American 1st Army landed in North Africa – Operation "Torch". Rommel was forced to withdraw back to Tunisia. Montgomery advanced cautiously and on 23 January 1943 occupied Tripoli. The 1st Army became bogged down in the Tunisian mountains. Rommel succeeded in routing the Americans, but Montgomery, forewarned by Ultra intelligence, was well prepared. For no loss the 8th Army destroyed 50 of Rommel's precious tanks and then closed up to the Mareth Line. After an imprudent frontal assault, Montgomery traversed this with a classic "left hook" which saw the 8th Army safely into the Tunisian mountains above Gabes.

The noose was tightening around the Axis forces in North Africa. Rommel left Africa on 9 March 1943 and was succeeded by General Hans-Jürgen von Arnim. Alexander now commanded the 1st and 8th Armies of the 15th Army Group. The Cape Bon peninsula was a great natural fortress. Alexander gave the Germans no respite to build up their defenses, and following a great

▲ US infantry advancing through the Tunisian hills, 20 January 1943. American standards of training and tactics in North Africa were initially very poor and shocked visiting British officers. Some claimed that the Americans "were our Italians". After their defeat at Kasserine Pass, the US 2nd Corps was transformed by Patton and Bradley into a first-rate fighting force.

▶ Crowds celebrate the liberation of Tunis in May 1943. A French colony, Tunisia had been spared the horrors of war until the German occupation in response to the "Torch" landings in November 1942. By the standards of Western Europe, their ordeal had been mercifully short.

and took personal command of 8th Army. He withdrew to the El Alamein position. There in July he fought a confused action called First Alamein. Rommel was halted but not defeated. "It is unlikely", Auchinleck telegraphed London, "that an opportunity will arise for resumption of offensive operations before mid-September". This was not good enough for Churchill and he determined to go to Cairo and sort out affairs there personally, accompanied by the chief of the imperial general staff, General Sir Alan Brooke. Auchinleck was dismissed and returned to India as commander in chief. He was replaced by General Sir Harold Alexander; a few days later – after Churchill's first choice had been killed in an air accident – Lieutenant-General Bernard Montgomery was appointed to command the 8th Army.

Montgomery and El Alamein

Montgomery's first aim was the restoration of the 8th Army's morale. He succeeded brilliantly. A man of pronounced individuality, he exuded confidence, and at El Alam Halfa he fought a model defensive battle in which, for once, German armor attacked British antitank guns and was repulsed. Still, Montgomery would not be hurried into launching his own offensive. A thorough and prudent general, he began his attack on 23 October 1942: the Second Battle of El Alamein.

offensive down the Merjerda Valley, Tunis fell on 7 May. Alexander signalled to Churchill: "Sir, it is my duty to report that the Tunisian Campaign is over. All enemy resistance has ceased. We are masters of the North African shores."

From Africa to Italy

From North Africa the war now spread once more to the northern shores of the Mediterranean with the invasion of Sicily, which was agreed to by Churchill and Roosevelt at the Casablanca conference in January 1943. The amphibious landing operation went well, but was followed by bitter fighting in the mountains north of Catania. Patton advanced westward to Palermo and arrived in Messina a few hours before Montgomery. The fall

of Sicily led also to the fall of Mussolini. Churchill and Brooke argued that this victory should be exploited by an invasion of the Italian mainland to knock Italy completely out of the war. The idea of Italy as a "soft underbelly" did not appeal to the Americans, but they agreed reluctantly to the continuance of the war in the Mediterranean so long as it remained subordinate to Operation "Overlord", the invasion of France. General Mark Clark would land with the US 5th Army at Salerno in September; Montgomery would cross the straits of Messina and advance up the Italian "toe".

Everything that could go wrong at Salerno did go wrong and the Allies were almost driven back into the sea. Montgomery, who was sulking because 8th Army had been denied the Salerno

The Allied Invasion of Italy 1943-45

1943

July 10
(to Aug. 17) Operation Husky: the British and US invasion of Sicily. The British objective is Messina, but they are checked south of Catania (July 18). They attempt to go west of Mt. Etna but move slowly: Catania is captured on Aug. 5. The Americans meet fierce resistance but as German units withdraw they take Palermo (July 22) and then reach Messina first (Aug. 17).

September 3–20
Operation Baytown. As a diversionary strike, British forces advance up the "toe". Auletta is reached on Sept. 19, Potenza on Sept. 20.

September 9–19
Operation Avalanche. A British-American force lands in the gulf of Salerno. It meets fierce German resistance. Heavy bombardment forces the Germans to withdraw to the Gustav line.

September 9
(to Nov. 30) Operation Slapstick. British forces land at Taranto and move quickly to Foggia (Sept. 27). Thereafter progress is slow. They cross the Sangro river at the end of Nov. (28–30) but have insufficient strength to attack the Gustav Line.

September 12
(to Dec. 31) Allied forces advance from the Salerno area. British forces enter Naples (Oct. 1), US troops Benevento (Oct. 2). The Germans withdraw in stages and holed the Bernhard Line (Nov. 5–15). The Allies cross the Garigliano (Dec. 2–6) but exhaustion keeps them south of the Rapido.

1944

January 17
(to June 4) The Allies attempt to break the Gustav Line at Monte Cassino. Three attacks fail (Jan. 17, Feb. 15–18, March). Meanwhile an attempt is made to outflank it with landings at Anzio (Jan. 22), but the Allies are besieged there until late May. The Gustav Line is finally broken 30km (20mi) east of Cassino on May 11 and Poles storm Cassino on May 18. This success enables troops from Anzio and Cassino to break out: they enter Rome on June 4.

mission, did not hurry to Clark's aid. The US 5th Army survived; Naples fell in October 1943. Thereafter the pace of operations slowed down.

Stalemate and Allied success

The Italian peninsula was ideal country for defensive operations: narrow, mountainous, with rivers running from west to east. The Germans, commanded by Field Marshal Albert Kesselring (a former airman), constructed defenses to protect Rome, the Gustav Line. The result was stalemate. Alexander fought four great battles below Monte Cassino. He used massive artillery bombardments and strategic bombers in a ground-support role, but could not break through. The Italian mountains were among the worst terrains the Al-

lies fought over. The slogging match at Cassino resembled the Somme, though the casualty bill was somewhat shorter. Another amphibious effort, at Anzio, almost ended in catastrophe.

Alexander's greatest victory, Operation Diadem, opened on 11 May 1944. A greatly strengthened 8th Army smashed through the center of the Gustav Line. The left-hand thrust, Clark's 5th Army, should have wheeled behind the rear of the Germans and enveloped them, but Clark let the Germans escape, preferring the glory of the capture of Rome, which fell on 4 June. Kesselring withdrew with his army intact to a new defensive line south of Bologna, the Gothic Line. Alexander was determined to continue the offensive and advance on Vienna. The Americans were adamantly opposed to this scheme.

After the Yalta conference in February 1945, Alexander was instructed to seize any opportunities that presented themselves. He acted decisively and secured the complete military victory that had eluded him the year before. A fine deception scheme persuaded the Germans to expect an amphibious scheme on the Adriatic coast. The 5th Army in fact struck west of Bologna and the 8th Army through the Argenta Gap. The Germans were encircled south of the River Po, the armies linking up appropriately at a town called Finale. The war in the Mediterranean was at an end. It had been a major contribution to the Allied victory, providing that badly needed front behind which to build up strength and experience for the decisive battle in the West. Thereafter it distracted some 25 German divisions. The campaigns in Italy and North Africa were the decisive proving grounds for the Allied armies.

▲ Partisans in Bologna in May 1945. Most were leftwing and so were suppressed by the British, who remembered their experience in Greece in 1944 when a communist coup had followed liberation.

◀▲ In terms of ships and troops employed the invasion of Sicily was the largest amphibious operation in history — even larger than Overlord. Other amphibious operations — Salerno and Anzio — were not to go so smoothly.

◀ The great abbey of Cassino in ruins after its capture in May 1944. Its majestic presence looming over the junction of 5th and 8th Armies exerted an eerie psychological hold over Allied troops who felt that they could not move unobserved. Whether the aerial bombing was justified is controversial. What was certainly not justified was that the bombing should be uncoordinated with the ground attacks — allowing time for the Germans to recover.

ALLIANCES AND VICTORY IN WORLD WAR II

The USA, USSR and UK defeated the Axis powers for three main reasons: first, because their strategic and military cooperation was closer and more effective than the enemy's; secondly, because the Soviet armies and people fought with such persistent courage while the West was mobilizing its forces; and thirdly, because the Axis powers made avoidable political and military blunders.

The broad success of Anglo-American cooperation owed much to General George Marshall, the US army chief of staff. From the bombing of Pearl Harbor onward, Marshall insisted on two principles: that a combined Anglo-American chiefs of staff organization should plan strategy, and that in each major theater all Allied forces and all three services should operate under a supreme Allied commander. In addition Roosevelt and Churchill, the heads of government, met frequently for personal conferences.

In Europe and the Mediterranean both the USA and UK contributed substantial forces and cooperation was close if not always harmonious. In the war against Japan, however, the US Central Pacific and Southwest Pacific Commands conducted largely American campaigns (with help from Australia and New Zealand), separate from the British Southeast Asia Command.

The positions in regard to Anglo-American cooperation with the USSR and China were different, partly for political, partly for geographical reasons. Stalin in the USSR and Jiang Jieshi in China were political and military dictators who would not brook the loss of sovereignty which effective military integration requires. Moreover, the Eastern and Chinese fronts were separated from contact with the Western Allies by enemy-controlled territories and Chinese forces could only hold defensive lines.

So far as Stalin was concerned, however, Allied cooperation meant simply that the Western Allies should supply as much material and arms as they could, and invade Western Europe as soon as possible. For the West it meant that the Red Army should hold the bulk of Germany's armies until the Allies were ready to strike in the West.

The position on the Axis side was totally different. Neither of the two dictators, Hitler and Mussolini, were natural cooperators. They frequently disagreed on political and military objectives and several times launched important strategic or political initiatives without consulting each other. Liaison officers were exchanged and there were occasional meetings between heads of state or senior ministers or officers, but little coordination of strategy or real cooperation.

With Japan, too, there was a lack of genuine consultation; which makes it all the more surprising that Hitler allowed himself to be dragged into open war with the USA at a moment chosen by the Japanese. There were no joint war plans with Japan, and a total absence of strategic cooperation. The Japanese and the European Axis fought their widely-separated campaigns with little regard for each other.

- • Allied leaders' conference

Country declaring war against European Axis power

- 1939–40
- 1941–42
- 1943–45

Country declaring war against Japan

- ○ 1937–38
- ○ 1939–40
- ○ 1941–42
- ◉ 1943–45

- Axis or associated power

CONFERENCES OF ALLIED LEADERS

1941

OFF NEWFOUNDLAND August 9–12
Churchill (UK), Roosevelt (USA)

WASHINGTON Dec. 22–Jan. 14, 1942
Arcadia conference. Churchill (UK), Roosevelt (USA)

1942

WASHINGTON June 17–21
Churchill (UK), Roosevelt (USA)

LONDON July
Churchill (UK), H.L. Hopkins (USA, Roosevelt's envoy), G.C. Marshall (US chief of staff), E.J. King (US chief of naval staff)

1943

CASABLANCA Jan. 12–23
Symbol conference. Churchill (UK), Roosevelt (USA)

WASHINGTON May 11–25
Trident conference. Churchill (UK), Roosevelt (USA)

QUEBEC Aug. 11–24
Quadrant conference. Churchill (UK), Roosevelt (USA)

MOSCOW Oct. 18–30
Foreign ministers: V. Molotov (USSR), C. Hull (USA), A. Eden (UK)

CAIRO Nov. 23–27; Dec. 2–7
Churchill (UK), Roosevelt (USA), Jiang Jieshi (China)

TEHRAN Nov. 28–Dec. 1
Churchill (UK), Roosevelt (USA), Stalin (USSR)

1944

QUEBEC Sept. 10–17
Octagon conference. Churchill (UK), Roosevelt (USA)

1945

YALTA Feb. 4–11
Argonaut conference. Churchill (UK), Roosevelt (USA), Stalin (USSR)

POTSDAM July 14–Aug. 2
Terminal conference. Stalin (USSR), H. Truman (USA), Churchill replaced by C. Attlee (UK)

▲ The two dictators, Hitler and Mussolini, together. Hitler was grateful to Mussolini for his support of German seizure of Austria in 1938 and respected him as a colleague and senior statesman. Mussolini, however, was jealous of his more powerful partner. Consequently, Axis consultation and cooperation tended to be irregular.

◄▲▼ Cooperation between the Allies occurred at all levels. Below, Stalin, Roosevelt and Churchill meet at Tehran; left, Eisenhower, Montgomery and their staff plan for D Day; above, Soviet and US troops meet in defeated Germany.

Datafile

At dawn on 6 June 1944 British and American forces began to land on five beaches in Normandy, in a colossal amphibious operation. It was the culmination of a year's planning and the start of Operation Overlord.

The success of Overlord depended above all on three key factors. First, Operation Fortitude, the elaborate deception plan which convinced the Germans that Normandy was not the objective. Secondly, the achievement of aerial supremacy over northern France, which meant that the invasion fleet could put the troops ashore without interference from the Luftwaffe. And thirdly, the ability of the Allied navies to move and keep supplied a force which was the equivalent of the British city of Birmingham. If in the first six weeks any one of these operations had gone wrong the Germans would have pushed the Allies back into the Channel, with consequences which are incalculable.

Invasion of Normandy

- Frontline
- Reinforcements

Invasion of Normandy

8%

92%

Total 11,891 aircraft

- Allies
- Germany

◀ **The elimination of the Luftwaffe.** In the spring of 1944 the Allies shifted their aerial offensive from Germany to northern France and after a three-month battle of attrition achieved a crushing superiority. Allied air forces could then provide aerial defense and hamper German efforts at resupply and redeployment.

▲ **A graphic illustration of Overlord's dependence on Operation Fortitude.** The comparatively small number of men the Allies were able to land in the first few days would have been pushed into sea had the Germans concentrated their forces against them. Fortunately Hitler was convinced that Normandy was a feint.

Normandy losses

27%

46%

27%

Aircraft
Total 7,616

21%

47%

32%

Dead and wounded
Total 425,000

- Germany
- USA
- UK

◀ **The Normandy fighting** was a bloody attritional struggle which in intensity resembled the fighting of World War I. The Allies expected an early breakthrough but became bogged down in the bocage country which was excellent for defense. Allied and German casualties were approximately the same.

▶ **The Allied buildup of 6 June to 31 August 1944** was the most immense supply operation in history. This flood of manpower and materiel eventually enabled the Allies to crack the German defenses. Even though the Mulberry harbors proved a disappointment, Allied supplies passed unhindered over the beaches.

Allied forces

- UK
- USA

Men

Vehicles

Stores (tonnes)

The overriding problem facing the British army after its expulsion from France in 1940 was not when it would return but *how*. Within days of Dunkirk, Churchill issued orders for the planning of an invasion to begin. But the prodigious difficulties that would face any force crossing the English Channel – perhaps the most tempestuous passage of water anywhere in the world in proportion to its size – were a serious deterrent to planning. The fact also had to be faced that, on its own, the British army was not strong enough to undertake the task.

Instead, the Royal Marine commandos were ordered to begin raiding in an attempt to weaken the enemy. By 1941 their raids were sizeable, and included attacks on the Lofoten Islands, Spitsbergen, South Vaagso and Maaloy, and in 1942, St Nazaire. But such pinpricks on the periphery of the Nazi empire were no substitute for a full-scale onslaught on "Fortress Europe".

The origins of "Overlord"

No matter how forcefully Lord Beaverbrook and others might press for an invasion, however, the wish alone offered no solution to overcoming the massive problems such an operation faced. This was brutally confirmed by the failure of the Dieppe raid in August 1942, when a force of 6,000, mostly Canadians, left behind 3,670 casualties.

The entry of the USA into the war changed drastically the material balance. But an amphibious operation, if launched prematurely against an enemy as skilful as the Germans, would end only in disaster. If an invasion of France was repulsed, a Dieppe on a grander scale, the consequences for the Allies would have been incalculable. Nonetheless, in 1942 President Roosevelt, in his casual way, gave Stalin a promise that the Allies would open a second front in Europe that year. Roosevelt's friend and adviser, Harry L. Hopkins, was dispatched to London on a mission to begin preparations, accompanied by an unknown major-general, Dwight D. Eisenhower. As the bulk of the force for this enterprise would be British, the chief of the imperial general staff, Alan Brooke, had no difficulty in brushing aside the somewhat hazy arguments of the Americans, and Roosevelt was persuaded that the main Allied effort should be directed to the North African landings in November 1942. Here American troops could be "blooded" without risking heavy casualties.

Nevertheless, the US army's doctrine was dedicated to the principle of massive concentration; the overwhelming use of firepower and material resources to defeat the enemy at the earliest opportunity in the decisive theater of war. George Marshall, the US chief of staff, was suspicious that further Mediterranean adventures

THE SECOND FRONT IN EUROPE

would sap Allied strength to little profit. No serious planning for a cross-Channel invasion began, however, until after the Casablanca conference (12–23 January, 1943). Here a joint Allied staff was agreed upon and a chief of staff to the supreme Allied commander, COSSAC, was appointed – Lieutenant-General Sir Frederick Morgan – but no supreme commander. At the Washington conference in May 1943 it was finally agreed that Operation "Overlord" should be given the highest priority. Morgan had inherited Eisenhower's preliminary planning which emphasized a landing on the tip of the Cotentin Peninsula, near Cherbourg. The only alternative was the Pas de Calais, which enjoyed the shortest sea route. But this had the disadvantage of an inadequate springboard for launching the assault, as it would have to depend exclusively on Dover and Newhaven. Normandy was much more central, all the southern English ports could be used and the direction of attack would be less obvious to the Germans. Morgan planned for an assault on a frontage of three divisions, with a buildup

to 18. It was reported that the Germans had 60 divisions deployed in the West.

At last, in November 1943 at the Cairo Conference, the command structure was approved. As the operation was scheduled for May 1944 this was not a moment too soon. Eisenhower was chosen as the supreme commander and Air Chief Marshal Tedder as his deputy. Montgomery was appointed to command the ground forces (21st Army Group). For the invasion there would be two armies, US 1st Army (under Lieutenant-General Omar Bradley) and Br 2nd Army (under Lieutenant-General Sir Miles Dempsey). Montgomery's first act was to scrap Morgan's plan, asserting that a three-divisional frontage was much too weak. Montgomery's criticisms were undoubtedly correct.

Montgomery's concept envisaged a five-divisional attack on a front demarcated by the Rivers Vire and Orne. Three further airborne divisions covered the flanks, two on the right flank to ensure the early capture of Cherbourg. The total host comprised 50,000 men, with a

▼ Wasted strength: the German Atlantic Wall. So convinced were the Germans – and this included Rommel – that the Allies would land in the Pas de Calais region, they concentrated their defenses in this region.

The Allied Invasion of France 1944

British landings
→ Seaborne
▼ Airborne

US landings
→ Seaborne
▼ Airborne

■ Beachhead 6 June 1944
▨ Bridgehead
➤ British attacks
➤ US attacks
▨ Trapped German troops

Front lines 1944
— 12 June
— 1 July
— 24 July
- - - 8 Aug
- - - 16 Aug
- - - 25 Aug

English Channel

OPERATION OVERLORD

Alderney
Cherbourg
Cotentin
Jersey
la Haye du Puits
Carentan
Coutances
St Lô
NORMANDY
Bayeux
Caen
Odon
Orne
Le Havre
Dieppe
Falaise
Risle
Seine
Mantes
Oise
Paris
St Malo
Avranches
Flers
Argentan
Mortain
Verneuil
Dreux
Versailles
BRITTANY
Fougeres
Alençon
FRANCE
Chartres
Étampes
Rennes
Vilaine
Mayenne
Sarthe
Loir
Le Mans
Châteaudun
to Orleans 16 km

UNITED KINGDOM
NETH
GERMANY
BELGIUM
LUX
Paris
Orleans
Nantes
FRANCE
SWITZ
Lyons
Grenoble
ITALY
Marseilles
Toulo
SPAIN

June 1944
➤ Allied deployments
➤ Allied landings
Aug 1944
→ French landings
▨ Liberated area

Scale 1 : 2 000 000
0   50 km
0   35 mi

June 6–12
Operation Overlord. The Allies return to France with airborne landings and amphibious landings on five beaches in Normandy (D Day). Beachheads are established. By June 12 they have been joined and Bayeux taken.

June 13–30
US forces seal the Cotentin Peninsula and advance on Cherbourg. The port holds out until June 27.

June 26
(to July 1) Operation Epsom. British forces attempt to obtain bridgeheads on the Odon and Orne. They succeed on the Odon (June 28–29) but meet fierce resistance. Strong German attacks are eventually beaten back.

July 3–18
The Battle of the Hedgerows. US forces move south from the Cotentin peninsula, but make slow progress in the bocage.

La Haye du Puits falls on July 7, but St Lô is besieged for 7 days (July 11–18).

July 8–20
A British assault on Caen succeeds (July 9). Operation Goodwood succeeds in gaining a crossing on the Orne (July 20).

July 25
(to Aug 8) Operation Cobra. US forces attack west of St Lô and break the German line (July 27) and capture

Avranches (July 31) and Le Mans (Aug. 8).

August 6–21
Germans counterattack at Mortain, but are beaten back (Aug. 6–10). The Allies quickly trap German troops south of Falaise. British forces advance from the north and capture Falaise (Aug. 16). US troops drive north and take Alençon (Aug. 12) and advance on Argentan. On Aug. 20 the Falaise "pocket" is sealed.

August 14–25
To the south of the pocket the advance eastward continues. US forces capture Chartres, Dreux and Orléans (Aug. 16–18) and cross the Seine at Mantes (Aug. 20). As the Allies approach Paris there is an uprising in the city (Aug. 19). A Franco-American force liberates the city on Aug. 25. Meanwhile US and French forces have landed in the south.

further 2 million to follow in 39 divisions, 138 major warships, 1,000 minesweepers and auxiliary vessels, and 4,000 landing craft or ships. It was to be the greatest seaborne armada in history, the most hazardous operation of its kind.

The Allied conquest of northern France
The most careful planning may sometimes be overturned by the whims of fate. The weather on 4–5 June was atrocious. Eisenhower shouldered the awesome responsibility of ordering the invasion on 6 June with the mundane instruction: "Let's go". His gamble succeeded. All five divisions got ashore safely, though the casualties on Omaha beach were severe. The major problem by the end of June was whether the Allied build-up could outmatch the German. Here the weather

turned against the Allies and one of the "Mulberry" harbors (artificial jetties) was destroyed – though this was perhaps less serious than the dislocation of shipping.

The German CinC West, Field Marshal von Runstedt, planned to hold his reserves back until the Allies had committed themselves. Rommel, commander of Army Group B, was conscious of the strength of Allied air power, and urged that the beachhead be destroyed before it grew too strong. A compromise was reached. The infantry was posted near the coast and the armor was held back. In addition, both field marshals had been fooled as to the real direction of the Allied assault. Both expected it to come in the Pas de Calais area. This was an intelligence triumph of immense significance. A brilliant deception plan combined

▲ Montgomery's plan was to draw the German armor on to the British flank, so enabling the Americans to break out on the left. In operations Epsom and Goodwood he fought two great battles of attrition. He did not break out himself, though he often gave the impression that he could have. But these battles made the American advance to Avranches possible.

with the "turning" of German agents convinced the German high command. Thanks to Ultra the Allies could read German signals intelligence and knew that the plan was working. Over half the German strength remained in the north waiting for a phantom army.

Montgomery's "master plan" envisaged that the British army on the left should draw the German armor on to it, permitting the American forces on the right to break out. He had also hoped to take the road center at Caen on the first day. He failed, but its seizure was vital to the security of the expanding bridgehead. Caen, like Tobruk, assumed symbolic importance. Montgomery organized two massive offensives, "Epsom" and "Goodwood" to seize Caen and draw Rommel's armour to the left. He employed massive artillery bombardments and strategic bombers to provide a "colossal crack" at the enemy's defenses. Such a weight of firepower only increased the devastation and rubble blocked the roads, impairing the advance. Mobility was sacrificed for hitting power, but this was unimportant so long as the German armor continued to move eastward on to the British Front.

In this aim Montgomery was successful. Seven of the nine Panzer divisions faced the British 2nd Army by the third week of July. But as usual he claimed too much. He said that the plan had gone "without a hitch", which was clearly untrue. He also claimed that he had never intended to break out on the left flank. This may have been true as far as the letter of the plan was concerned, but not its spirit. Fundamentally, Montgomery was contemptuous of American military ability and believed that he could break out toward the Seine *and* draw the German armor simultaneously on to

his front. In this he was wrong, and his failure to break out permitted his enemies, Morgan and Tedder, to gain the ear of the supreme commander, and urge that he be sacked.

Meanwhile, the American forces moved slowly toward St Lô, another road junction. The fighting here was laborious. The terrain — the *bocage* – was ideal defensive country: high hedgerows, winding lanes and numerous hamlets. St Lô eventually fell on 18 July. On 26 July the US 1st and 3rd Armies broke out of the Normandy beachhead in Operation "Cobra". Hitler now took a dramatic hand in the campaign. He had earlier replaced von Rundstedt with von Kluge and ordered a counterstroke toward Avranches. By advancing in the opposite direction to the Americans, the Germans guaranteed their envelopment. The Allies monitored the anxious signal traffic between Hitler and von Kluge eagerly. The Germans were entering a trap of their own making. Then on 20 July occurred the "July Plot" against Hitler. Von Kluge disappeared from view and then committed suicide. But the real significance of these events was that the German command system was paralysed.

The Germans hastened to escape in terrible confusion through the Falaise Gap. By the end of August the salient was finally eliminated. The Battle of Normandy was a tremendous victory. The Germans had suffered half a million casualties, including 210,000 prisoners, and lost 2,000 tanks and self-propelled guns. The Allied pursuit began. Patton advanced into Lorraine and Montgomery took Brussels. When on 1 September Eisenhower took over command of the Allied ground forces from a reluctant Montgomery, it seemed that the war would be over in 1944.

▲ American soldiers come ashore on Utah beach. The American experience during the Overlord landings was mixed. At Utah the GIs walked ashore, meeting only light resistance. At Omaha beach they met strong resistance, and gained a toehold very slowly and with heavy casualties. The sea was covered with bodies – like gruesome seaweed.

▼ Vehicles of US 1st Corps are landed at Utah beach. The great array of amphibious landing vehicles added considerably to the flexibility of amphibious operations. Amphibious vehicles permitted the landing of troops and mobile fire power much more quickly than during World War I.

Dwight D. Eisenhower 1890–1969

Eisenhower was the first of a new generation of "political generals", whose strength was politics rather than operational command. Before taking command in the Mediterranean after Operation "Torch" in November 1942, he had not seen a shot fired in anger. He overcame this inexperience with a skill for making difficult personalities work together. He was particularly adept at developing a "team" which dropped national prejudices. Not a great strategist, Eisenhower was the model coalition leader, tactful and cheerful.

Bernard Montgomery 1887–1976

"Monty" had dedicated his life to the profession of arms. He neither smoked nor drank and had no other interests outside the British Army. He was the most proficient operational commander produced by the British army in World War II. Although prudent and enjoying vast material superiority over the enemy, he could put together an ambitious plan on a great scale and see it through to a successful conclusion.

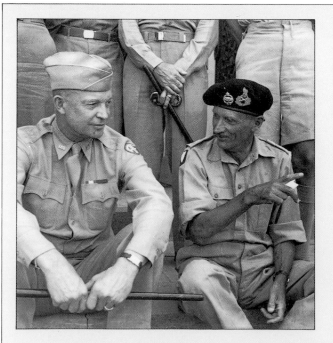

▲ US 82nd Airborne Division dropping over Nijmegen. The concept of operations for the Battle of Arnhem, Operation Market Garden, belied Montgomery's reputation as a cautious commander. It was a bold stroke to secure the bridges over the Rhine and thus secure lines of communication to outflank the Rühr from the north. Most bridges were captured, but the vital bridge at Arnhem was "a bridge too far". The British troops who landed there were isolated and virtually annihilated.

From Belgium to Germany: debates and disaster

Though great in magnitude, however, the Battle of Normandy was another incomplete triumph. The Germans had escaped, and it can be argued that they should not have done. The advance into Brittany was an unnecessary diversion from the main front. Too many Allied commanders showed undue caution in exploiting their success. There is justice in both of these criticisms. But the Allies were, to some degree, prisoners of geography. Because the Americans had to cross the Atlantic and use western British ports, the maneuver wing perforce had to be on Montgomery's right, and not his left. To guarantee the annihilation of Army Group B, the maneuver wing should have been on the left flank so that it could engage the Germans west of the Seine and cut their lines of communication. But to sustain *their* lines of communication across the Atlantic, the Americans needed the Brittany ports.

The extent of Allied success ushered in the most acrimonious debate yet over the course of Allied strategy. Montgomery, perhaps the only Allied commander who was the conceptual equal of his German counterparts at the operational level, urged that a narrow but concentrated thrust be mounted in the north to seize the Ruhr and advance on Berlin. However justified this concept was at the operational level, Eisenhower, highly attuned to political factors, realized that such an operation, carried out by predominantly Commonwealth forces commanded by a British general, was unacceptable to American public opinion. In any case, Eisenhower was temperamentally disposed to military operations in which "the whole team" kept "kicking the ball forward" all along the line. This "broad front", in so far as it can be described as a concept, was his preferred style. It minimized political difficulties.

Montgomery nevertheless gained Eisenhower's permission to mount Operation "Market Garden" to seize the bridges over the Maas and Waal. These would serve as a springboard for an offensive toward the Ruhr that autumn. The American airborne landings at Eindhoven and Nijmegen secured their objectives. The landings of the 1st British Airborne Division at Arnhem did not. The troops were landed too far from the bridges and their fighting power was diffused over too great an area. Of the 10,000 men who landed only 2,163 survivors broke out.

This setback dealt Montgomery's case for a narrow front a severe blow. Indeed, his attention had been so focused on the Rhine that he had overlooked the paramount importance of the port of Antwerp, which he needed to supply his columns. An intricate and time-consuming operation was required to break the German blockade of the port. But Montgomery's greatest enemy was himself. He took no pains to conceal his disdain for the supreme commander. He behaved in such a truculent manner that Eisenhower, urged on by Tedder, moved to have him relieved. Montgomery's chief of staff, de Guingand, realized the danger and after a dramatic flight to Montgomery's tactical HQ persuaded him to write a diplomatic note agreeing to abide by Eisenhower's instructions. The supreme commander

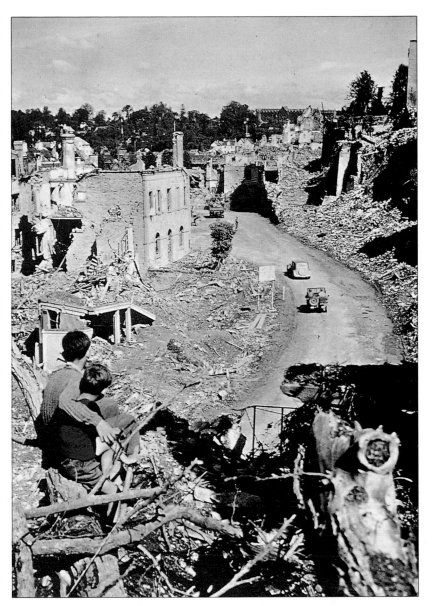

▲ The fruits of liberation, St Lô in July 1944. The only antidote the Allies could find to fanatical German resistance during the Battle of Normandy was overwhelming firepower and systematic destruction. Consequently, Allied offensives were accompanied by massive artillery bombardments which destroyed towns, villages and roads on a greater scale than in 1914–18. During Operation Cobra, the breakout, strategic bombers were used to supplement artillery fire.

was placated and Montgomery survived – this time by the skin of his teeth.

The issue over which Montgomery and Eisenhower clashed was the need, as Montgomery saw it, for a ground forces commander interposed between the supreme commander and his army group commanders. Montgomery only had one candidate in mind for the job: himself. If introduced, this measure would have denied Eisenhower any effective direct control over his armies. Montgomery wanted to see more "grip" over the course of operations. At the operational level, Montgomery was probably right. The Allied forces were overstretched and barely coordinated. The Germans were now fighting on their own soil and contesting every centimeter.

It did not occur to the Allies that this was a prelude to a major counteroffensive. A new commander, Field Marshal Walter Model, had rebuilt Army Group B. It now comprised two Panzer and one infantry army. It was poised for an onslaught toward Antwerp via Namur. This was to be a reprise of the victorious thrust through the Ardennes in 1940. But then the Germans had enjoyed air superiority.

Omar N. Bradley 1893–1982

Bradley had risen to prominence on taking over US II Corps in Tunisia. Unlike the flamboyant Patton, Bradley was a reserved and diffident man. A skilled tactician, Bradley was initially Patton's subordinate, and his rise to command 12th Army Group left their relations, at best, as ambivalent. Bradley performed soundly during the Battle of Normandy. During the Ardennes counter-offensive he appeared to lose his grip, but he survived and in 1945, during the advance to the Elbe, commanded the largest force ever raised by the United States.

George S. Patton 1885–1945

Patton was a ruthless cavalry general, at his best in the pursuit. His skill was less evident in the bloody battles in Lorraine in 1944. Although from a wealthy family and himself well-read and cultured, Patton developed the almost obsessive element in his personality. He became the embodiment of the "fire-eater": vulgar, insensitive and foul-mouthed. Hardly the natural diplomat, his snide asides at the British and his temper – notably the notorious "slapping" of a shell-shocked patient in Sicily in 1943 – almost destroyed his career.

I found Miley, Commander of the 17th Airborne, in Bastogne. While there we had considerable shelling, including airbursts. The flashes of our own guns and those of the enemy in the gathering darkness against the white snowfields were very beautiful, but not too reassuring. In my diary I made this statement on the afternoon of January 4, and it is significant, as it is the only time I ever made such a statement: "We can still lose this war."

GEORGE S. PATTON

The Germans' last offensive

As Montgomery wrote, the Allied armies "sprawled all over the place". There was no reserve. Even Ultra intelligence gave no hint of the attack. When the Germans struck on 16 December the surprise was complete. But the German offensive soon ran into difficulties, as progress in the center was less than hoped for. The Americans held Bastogne, an important road center – a thorn in the German rear. Montgomery had to be given command of all forces north of the breakthrough. This amounted virtually to the ground forces command he had advocated. Montgomery provided a steady hand and slowly but surely took control of the battle and provided himself with a reserve from 21st Army Group.

Eisenhower now planned a counteroffensive in which both Bradley and Montgomery were to advance simultaneously. This Montgomery considered a waste of strength. He could not understand that this move was required for political rather than military reasons. The USA was by now the dominant partner in the Alliance. American generals were calling the tune.

Patton relieved Bastogne. The Germans withdrew, and on 16 January 1945 American forces linked up at Houffalize, effectively pinching out the German "Bulge". The significance of the battle was that it shattered Hitler's last strategic reserve. By throwing this against the western Allies rather than the Russians, Hitler guaranteed that a great chunk of Germany, including Berlin, would fall to the Red Army.

Across the Rhine – to victory

West of the Rhine, the Germans now faced seven armies. In a great pincer movement reminiscent of the Normandy campaign, Montgomery advanced to the Rhine (Operation "Veritable"), drawing what remained of German strength northward to permit Bradley to smash his way to the Rhine (Operation "Grenade"). This strategy exceeded expectations when Bradley seized an intact bridge at Remagen. But the material inferiority of the German army did not diminish its fighting power, and the fighting during "Veritable" was some of the bitterest of the war.

On 22 March Patton crossed the Rhine and Montgomery the following day. On regrouping Eisenhower decided that once the Ruhr was encircled, US 9th Army, previously under Montgomery, would revert to Bradley. The US 12th Army Group would now comprise 48 divisions, the largest single command in American history, and the source of patriotic pride. The political impossibility of a British officer commanding this force was now apparent.

▶ It is a much quoted axiom that in war an attacker must have a 3:1 superiority. The Allied crossing of the Rhine illustrates the massive superiority the Allies now enjoyed – amounting on some fronts to 10:1. It was not so much numbers but equipment which overwhelmed the last legions of the Third Reich

The Battle of the Bulge 1944-45

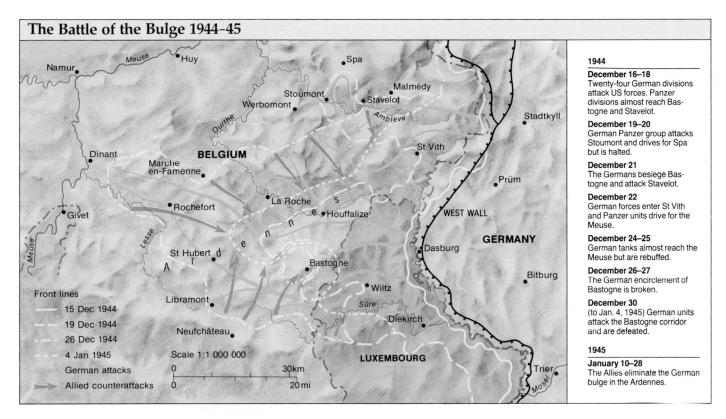

Front lines
— 15 Dec 1944
— 19 Dec 1944
— 26 Dec 1944
— 4 Jan 1945
→ German attacks
➤ Allied counterattacks

Scale 1:1 000 000

0 ——— 30km
0 ——— 20 mi

1944

December 16–18
Twenty-four German divisions attack US forces. Panzer divisions almost reach Bastogne and Stavelot.

December 19–20
German Panzer group attacks Stoumont and drives for Spa but is halted.

December 21
The Germans besiege Bastogne and attack Stavelot.

December 22
German forces enter St Vith and Panzer units drive for the Meuse.

December 24–25
German tanks almost reach the Meuse but are rebuffed.

December 26–27
The German encirclement of Bastogne is broken.

December 30
(to Jan. 4, 1945) German units attack the Bastogne corridor and are defeated.

1945

January 10–28
The Allies eliminate the German bulge in the Ardennes.

After the great victories west of the Rhine, the movement of Allied armies was barely contested. In a great double envelopment the US 9th and 1st Armies completed the encirclement of the Ruhr. On 18 April this offered up 400,000 prisoners – the greatest single capitulation of the war. On 21 April Model committed suicide. Hitler now lived in a world of daydreams.

As the end neared, Eisenhower's generalship became increasingly cautious. The main objective of the US 12th Army Group, he ordered, was to be the Elbe. The 21st Army Group was to protect Bradley's flank and move on Lübeck. Churchill protested and claimed that Eisenhower's objective should be Berlin. Roosevelt supported Eisenhower in overruling Churchill's protests. They claimed that Berlin was no longer of strategic importance. This was untrue. Here lurked Hitler, still exerting his will over the German people.

What was more in doubt was not the importance of Berlin but the practicality of its capture. By 31 March the nearest Allied troops were still 440 km (275 mi) away, while the Russians were only 65 km (40 mi) from the city. Any drive to

Berlin also had to take into account the possibility that American and Russian troops might accidentally clash. As ever, Eisenhower erred on the side of caution. As his armies closed to the Elbe, Eisenhower knew that the Allies had already agreed at Yalta on the division of Germany into zones. Any further advance eastward would have had to be withdrawn after the war had ended.

The war in Europe moved to a close. On 1 May 1945 Hitler's death was announced. Admiral Dönitz succeeded him as *Führer*. On 4 May Montgomery received the unconditional surrender of all German forces in Holland, Northwest Germany and Denmark. In dealing with Eisenhower, Dönitz attempted to extend the negotiations so that the greatest number of German soldiers and refugees "will find salvation in the West". Jodl, his plenipotentiary, tried to play for time. Eisenhower threatened to seal the Western Front, and Jodl had no choice but to sign the instrument of unconditional surrender on 8 May.

▲ Hitler's last throw. The immediate object was the Meuse crossings at Namur. The plan was over-ambitious, and could not be sustained even with surprise and poor visibility which grounded the Allied air forces.

◄ American troops greeted with joy by the citizens of Aachen. Elsewhere their encounters with the former citizens of the Third Reich were less enthusiastic.

▼ Montgomery in solemn mood signing the 21st Army Group instrument of surrender. Nothing was done to spare the sensibilites of the emissaries. On being introduced to the field marshal, each member of the German delegation received the withering reply, "Never heard of you."

Datafile

In summer 1945 Japan had under arms more than twice the number of men with which it had started the Pacific conflict, and it was clear that most of them would fight like the garrisons of the Pacific islands and sacrifice their lives for relatively light (in proportional terms) American casualties. These casualties, of course, were viewed very differently by the Americans, who feared that an invasion of the Japanese home islands would cost hundreds of thousands of lives. But Japan's power to resist was being undermined, by a submarine blockade and by a remorseless aerial offensive which the Japanese airforce could no longer oppose effectively.

Japanese forces July 1945

3%
2%
15%
35%
19%
25%

July 1945
Total 4,625,000

☐ Japan
▨ China
☐ Manchuria and Korea
▨ SE Pacific
▨ C Pacific
☐ SW Pacific

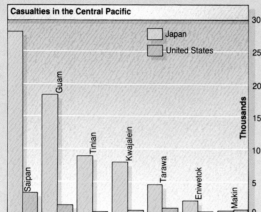

Casualties in the Central Pacific

☐ Japan
☐ United States

Saipan, Guam, Tinian, Kwajalein, Tarawa, Eniwetok, Makin

Thousands (0–30)

▲ Despite the fact that Allied invasion forces were assembling in the Philippines and Okinawa, in July 1945 more than 2 million of Japan's 4.6 million soldiers were still deployed on the Asian mainland. The relatively large forces still holding out in the Central and Southwest Pacific and in Southeast Asia were cut off and could be of no assistance in the event of an invasion of the home islands, so the Japanese government attempted to mobilize civilians to face the Allies.

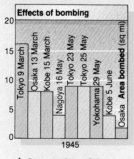

Bombing raids on Japan

B29s per raid (0–600)

Tokyo 9 March, Osaka 13 March, Kobe 15 March, Nagoya 16 May, Tokyo 23 May, Tokyo 25 May, Yokohama 29 May, Kobe 5 June, Osaka 7 June

1945

▲ The casualty statistics for the Central Pacific "island hopping" campaign graphically illustrate the Japanese method of sacrificing every man of a garrison in order to maximize the loss to an invader. The knowledge that their enemy would fight to the end had a demoralizing effect on even elite US units.

Frontline air strength

Aircraft (thousands) (0–25)

United States
Japan

1943   1944   1945 July

Effects of bombing

Area bombed (sq mi) (0–20)

Tokyo 9 March, Osaka 13 March, Kobe 15 March, Nagoya 16 May, Tokyo 23 May, Tokyo 25 May, Yokohama 29 May, Kobe 5 June, Osaka

1945

▼ Initial US high-level bombing raids from June 1944 did little damage to Japanese cities. On 9 March 1945 the first low-level incendiary raid was carried out and within three months nearly 40 percent of Japan's five major cities, Tokyo-Yokohama, Kawasaki, Osaka, Kobe and Nagoya, had been destroyed.

Aircraft production

Thousands (0–100)

United States
Japan

1937   1939   1941   1943   1945

▲ A comparison of the nine heaviest raids showing the number of bombers employed and the area destroyed. The most devastating raid was the first, though the largest came on 23 May 1945 when 562 B-29s hit Tokyo. By this time much of the city had been burnt out so the raid was relatively less effective.

Major Japanese cities

38%
62%

Total 275 sq mi

☐ Area remaining
▨ Area bombed

▲ A graphic presentation of aerial supremacy. By 1945 America deployed five times as many war planes as Japan did. It was not just the B-29s which wreaked havoc. By the summer of 1945 fighters from Iwo Jima also and fighter bombers from American and British carriers roamed at will in the skies over Japan.

Between March and June 1943 America prepared for the next round. The Japanese, determined to hold an 8,000km (5,000mi) perimeter running from Attu via the Marshalls and Gilberts down to the Central Solomons and Eastern New Guinea, concentrated Yamamoto's Combined Fleet at Truk, a central position from which any penetration could be countered. For their part the Americans planned a two-pronged breakthrough. MacArthur's forces, supported by Halsey, were to advance on Rabaul (Operation Cartwheel) in June while Nimitz's forces would drive into the Gilberts in the fall. From March onward Japanese airstrikes sought to disrupt Allied preparations but incurred crippling losses while Allied squadrons penetrated ever deeper into Japanese territory. On 18 April 1943 one such foray sent Admiral Yamamoto, who was flying from Rabaul to Bougainville, to a fiery death.

From island hopping to leapfrogging

Halsey's forces – 1 New Zealand and 6 American divisions, 1,800 aircraft, and the 3rd Fleet which included 2 carriers and 6 battleships –

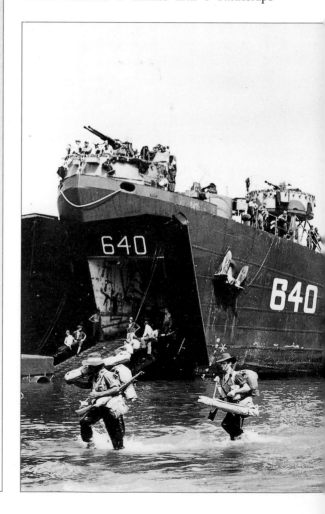

THE DEFEAT OF JAPAN

struck Japanese-held New Georgia on 2 July. Despite a superiority of 4:1, it took five weeks to capture the enemy base at Munda, only 16km (10 mi) from the beachhead. At sea the Japanese displayed equal tenacity, though their loss of 17 ships for 6 American showed that the balance of skill had shifted.

The increasing effectiveness of their navy notwithstanding, the Americans knew that if the reduction of all Japan's outposts proved as costly, the war could drag on into the 1950s. The joint chiefs of staff (JCS) now decided on a fundamental change in strategy, from "island hopping" (taking each base in succession) to "leapfrogging" (bypassing large Japanese concentrations and using naval and air forces to seal them up). It fell to Halsey's forces to put this into effect. On 14 August his assault forces sailed past heavily defended Kolombangara, the next island in the Solomon chain, and the following morning landed on Vella Lavelle to the northwest, surprising the small garrison. A brilliant success, this operation set the pattern. Bougainville, the next target, was defended by 60,000 Japanese. On 27 October

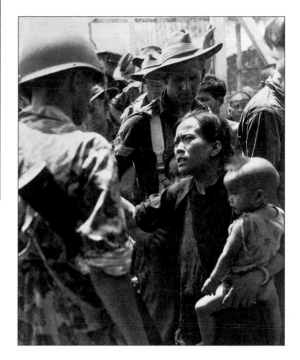

▶▼ Australia played a key role in the Pacific War. Right, "Diggers" and "Yanks" care for bewildered Indonesians after the bitter fighting for Tarakan in Borneo, 1 May 1945. Below, Australia's 9th Division lands on the Huon Peninsula, 22 September 1943 when they cleared the way for an American landing in New Britain.

Allied landings on two small islands to the east and southeast, convinced the Japanese that the attack would come from this direction. It did not. On 1 November the Americans landed at Empress Augusta Bay on the remote west of Bougainville. The following night they defeated a desperate naval counterattack and three months later smashed a belated land assault.

Meanwhile MacArthur's forces – 11 Australian and 4 American divisions, 1,000 aircraft and the 7th Fleet – had been carrying out their own part of "Cartwheel". In a complex operation, beginning on 4 September, three Australian divisions took the Japanese bases of Lae and Salamaua on New Guinea's north coast, and a month later captured the Huon Penisula which controlled the approach to southern New Britain. The JCS had already decided that heavily defended Rabaul was also to be isolated, a task which was effected by the US marines' seizure of southern New Britain in December, followed in succeeding weeks by the capture of islands which dominated the northwestern and eastern approaches to the base. By March 1944 the 140,000 Japanese in Rabaul and on the neighboring New Ireland and Bougainville were for all intents and purposes out of the war.

With Rabaul isolated MacArthur pressed ahead with the most ambitious bypass operation yet – Operation Reckless, a leap to Hollandia 800km (500mi) west of the most forward Allied base. The landing on 22 April completely surprised the Japanese. During the next three months the Americans continued to leapfrog westward until on 30 July they occupied Sansapor on the north-

Chester W. Nimitz 1885–1966

Appointed to command the US Pacific fleet shortly after Pearl Harbor, Nimitz achieved a near incredible defensive victory at Midway in June 1942. During the following 17 months, while his surface fleets were expanded, Nimitz launched a submarine offensive which within two years had crippled Japan's merchant marine. In November 1943 Nimitz's task forces went on the offensive, leapfrogging across the Central Pacific, and defeating the Combined Fleet in the Battle of the Philippine Sea and the Battle of Leyte Gulf.

William F. Halsey 1882–1959

The epitome of the aggressive "seadog", the American press christened the Admiral "Bull" Halsey after he had commanded America's first counterstrokes against Japan. Due to ill health he missed Midway but later in 1942 he was ordered to the South Pacific in which theater he cooperated closely with MacArthur and the forces of Southwest Pacific Command. Halsey was brave but impetuous. His decisions during Leyte Gulf indicated that he was not a strategist of the first rank.

Curtis Emerson Lemay 1906–

Known by his men as "Iron Ass", Lemay first saw combat as commander of the 3rd Bombardment Division based in England in June 1943. The following summer he went to China, where, with Claire Chennault, he launched a brilliantly successful low-level B-29 raid against Japanese-occupied Hankou on 18 December 1944. A month later Lemay, now commander of the Mariana-based 21st Bomber Command, introduced new low-level methods of attack which bore fruit in spectacular incendiary raids from March onward.

western tip of New Guinea's Vogelkop Peninsula, only 1,300km (800mi) southeast of Mindanao in the Philippines.

By now Japan was also reeling from the assaults of Nimitz's forces – Admiral Spruance's 5th Fleet, consisting of 7 battleships, 11 carriers with 1,000 aircraft, and 44 cruisers and destroyers and the 5th Amphibious Force and V Amphibious Corps, which together could transport 150,000 men. In mid-November 1943 this mighty force struck into the Gilberts and on the 20th the Americans stormed ashore on Makin and Tarawa. They captured Makin quickly but took four days and 3,000 casualties to eliminate Tarawa's 4,700 strongly entrenched defenders.

The consequences of Tarawa

Like New Georgia, Tarawa caused a reevaluation of strategy. When Nimitz's fleets surged into the Marshalls in January 1944 they bypassed heavily defended atolls on the rim of the group and while fast carrier task forces wreaked havoc as far apart as Eniwetok and Truk, the Americans attacked and captured Kwajalein in the center of the group, suffering relatively light casualties. Exploiting this success, between March and May a fast carrier force rampaged through the Carolines, encouraging the Japanese to think that they were the Americans' next target. But on 15 June Spruance's fleet arrived off Saipan, the main island of the Marianas, only 2,000km (1,300mi) from Japan and within bombing range of Tokyo.

The 9 carriers, 5 battleships and 41 cruisers and destroyers of Japan's Combined Fleet had been husbanded for just such an occasion. Admiral Ozawa, the operational commander, ordered it to Saipan, hoping that its 473 carrier aircraft, combined with 100 aircraft from in the Marianas, would tip the balance in Japan's favor. Disaster struck

▶ The climax of Operation Cartwheel saw a series of devastating raids on Rabaul Harbor. This picture, taken by the bomb-aimer of a B-24 "Liberator" on 30 December 1943, shows bombs bursting across the anchorage, as warships desperately seek to escape the confines of the harbor.

▶▶ Beginning in June 1943, America launched twin offensives to break through Japan's defensive perimeter. In the Southwest Pacific, Operations Cartwheel and Reckless (see inset) isolated large Japanese armies in the Solomons and northern New Guinea and brought MacArthur's forces to within striking distance of the Philippines. Meanwhile Nimitz's fleets in the Central Pacific smashed through the Gilberts, and leapfrogged their way through the Marshalls and the Marianas, bypassing the heavily defended Carolines to link up with MacArthur's forces for the Philippine invasion.

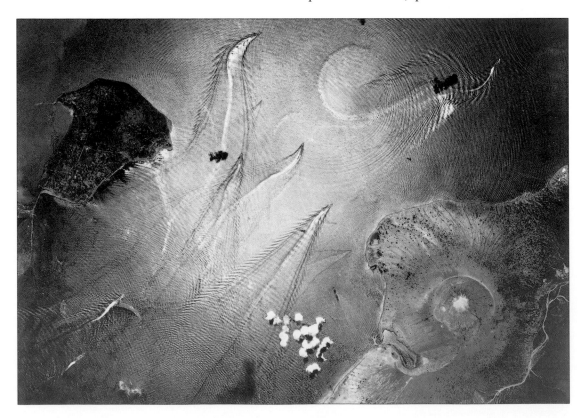

The Defeat of Japan 1943-45

Scale 1: 45 230 000

| 0 | 800 km |
| 0 | 500 mi |

PACIFIC OCEAN AREAS
Nimitz
HQ Pearl Harbor

SOUTHWEST
PACIFIC AREA
MacArthur
HQ Brisbane

Legend:
- ● Allied base
- ── Command boundaries
- ➤ Attacks
- ⇀ Air strikes
- ☐ Occupied by Japanese forces, 15 Aug 1945

Equatorial scale 1: 54 000 000

1943

March 12
(to April 6) Allied conference decides on a two-pronged offensive: in the Southwest Pacific Area (SWPA) New Britain is to be isolated; in the Central Pacific Area the Gilberts are to be recovered.

SWPA OPERATION CARTWHEEL
July 1
(to Nov. 25) Phase 1: in the Solomons US forces recapture important islands (New Georgia, July 1–Aug. 25; Bougainville, Nov. 1–April 1944).

September 4
(to March 23, 1944) Phase 2:

US and Australian forces land on northeast New Guinea. Lae falls on Sept. 16.

December 15
(to March 20, 1944) Phase 3: US troops land at Arawe (Dec. 15), and in southern New Britain. The seizure of Emirau (March 20) isolates the 100,000 troops on Rabaul.

NORTHERN NEW GUINEA
1944

March 12
(to July 30) MacArthur's offensive continues along New Guinea. American forces overrun Holland and Aitape (April 22–August 5) and eventually Sansapor (July 30).

CENTRAL PACIFIC OFFENSIVE
1943

November 13–24
US forces assault the Gilbert Islands. Makin falls quickly, Tarawa only after bitter fighting.

1944

January 29
(to July 25) The US offensive then moves on to the Marshall Islands, Carolines and Marianas. Kwajalein atoll falls after heavy fighting (Feb. 1–7), then Eniwetok (Feb. 17–21). Japanese land forces on the Carolines are bypassed. Instead US forces capture Saipan (June 15–July 13).

THE PHILIPPINES
July 26
After initial air strikes against Mindanao US forces head for Luzon. Landings begin. The Battle of Leyte Gulf (Oct. 17–25) destroys the Japanese fleet. The Americans capture Leyte (Oct. 20–Dec. 31) and then Mindoro (Jan. 1–3, 1945). The US fleet fights its way into Lingayen Gulf (Jan. 6–8). Manila is taken on March 4.

AIR OFFENSIVE
1944

June 15
Initial bombing raids on Tokyo from Chengdu in China and the Marianas (from Nov. 24) have little effect.

1945

March 9
(to Aug. 14) Daytime raids produce firestorms in Japanese cities.

THE ADVANCE ON JAPAN
February 19
(to June 22) Marines recapture Iwo Jima (Feb. 19–March 24). Okinawa is next, but its capture takes almost three months (April 1–June 22).

August 6 – 15
Atomic bombs dropped on Hiroshima (Aug. 6) and Nagasaki (Aug. 9) and the Soviet declaration of war (Aug. 8) cause the Japanese to surrender. Hirohito announces the capitulation on Aug. 15.

▲ American troops use flamethrowers to incinerate Japanese in bunkers in southern Okinawa, 18 April 1945. On that day XXIV Corps Commander Major John Hodge said: "It is going to be really tough. There are sixty-five thousand fighting Japs holed up in the south end of the island and I see no way to get them out except blast them out yard by yard." He was right.

The ten-day battle was a bitter one, from its inception to the destruction of the last organised resistance. The enemy had taken full advantage of the terrain which adapted itself extraordinarily well to a deliberate defense in depth. The rugged coral outcroppings and the many small precipitous hills had obviously been organized for a defense over a long period of time. Cave and tunnel systems of a most elaborate nature had been cut into each terrain feature of importance, and heavy weapons were sited for defense against attack from any direction.

MAJOR-GENERAL L.C SHEPHERD
OKINAWA, 13 JUNE 1945

almost immediately: American submarines and aircraft sank three carriers and shot down 411 Japanese machines. It was the end of Japan's carrier aviation. By mid-July the Americans had secured Saipan and in August took Guam and Tinian, giving them firm control of the Marianas.

On 24 July 1944 MacArthur, Nimitz, and Roosevelt met in Hawaii to determine strategy. Nimitz wanted a navy-dominated thrust from Saipan to Formosa and China, bypassing the Philippines, while MacArthur urged the reconquest of Mindanao and then a drive north to Luzon. Roosevelt supported MacArthur. The liberation of the Philippines was a moral obligation; besides, it seemed unwise to leave a 350,000 strong Japanese garrison active to the American rear. He now ordered MacArthur's and Nimitz's thrusts to converge on Mindanao.

By 15 September MacArthur's forces had secured Morotai, halfway between New Guinea and Mindanao, while Nimitz's marines fought for Pelelieu, 800km (500mi) to the northwest. Feeble resistance to airstrikes against Mindanao bases now convinced the JCS that the southern Philippines could be safely bypassed and MacArthur's forces were ordered to link up with Nimitz and land at Leyte in the central Philippines.

On 17 October, as 700 Allied vessels carrying 200,000 troops, approached Leyte, Japan launched a daring counterattack. The entire Combined Fleet (64 warships) converged on Leyte from three directions. From the north came Japan's four surviving carriers, their object to lure Halsey's 3rd Fleet away from the beachhead. Meanwhile a central and a southern force, in total seven battleships, threaded their way through a maze of islands to catch the unprotected transports in Leyte Gulf. On 23 October Halsey's submarines and aircraft detected and attacked the central force, sinking a battleship and forcing it to put about. Believing he had seen off this threat and having received word of the approach of the carriers, Halsey sped northward and on 25 October intercepted and sank all four off Cape Engano, the northeastern tip of the Philippines. Meanwhile

the Americans had located Japan's southern task force approaching Leyte through the Surigao Strait. All the battleships covering the landing force sped south to the entrance of the strait and on the night of 24–25 October ambushed the southern force, sinking two more battleships. During the night, however, the central force had reversed course, and at dawn debouched unopposed from the San Bernadino Strait onto the now lightly protected transports. A desperate running fight ensued. Japanese battleships sped after the Americans but at the very point of victory put about once more, in the mistaken belief that airstrikes from small escort carriers had in fact come from Halsey's 3rd Fleet. This failure of nerve turned the Battle of Leyte Gulf into an unmitigated disaster for the Japanese. They had sacrificed their carriers to no avail and had also lost 500 aircraft, three battleships, and 14 other warships. It was the end of the Imperial Navy.

Ashore resistance was fierce. The Japanese commander, General Yamashita, boosted Leyte's garrison to 70,000 but by year's end it had been overwhelmed. Yamashita determined upon a desperate expedient to prevent the capture of Luzon. During the Battle of Leyte Gulf newly formed suicide squadrons known as kamikazes (the word meant "divine wind") had crippled several American ships. Used en masse in the first week of Janauary 1945 the kamikazes badly damaged 20 ships of the invasion fleet as it approached the west coast of Luzon, but they could not prevent a landing. By 9 January 4 divisions were ashore striking south and east. In conformity with a preconceived plan the Japanese avoided pitched battles in which the Americans could bring their fire power to bear and withdrew to the Manila Bay area and the mountains of northeastern Luzon. The Americans reached the craft, and inflicted nearly 10,000 casualties. This, the most sustained aerial assault ever mounted against a fleet, cost the Japanese a staggering total of 8,000 aircraft. In the midst of the aerial attacks the Imperial Navy despatched the monster battleship *Yamato* on its own kamikaze mission against the Allied fleet, but swarms of American aircraft sank her well to the north of Okinawa. Ashore the fighting was the bloodiest of the Pacific War. The 300,000 troops landed in the first days of April took 11 weeks and 39,000 casualties to kill 137,000 enemy troops and 100,000 Japanese civilians – a grim foretaste of the likely cost of an invasion of the home islands.

Plans for a landing on Kyushu scheduled for 1 November (Operation Olympic) were well advanced, and while invasion forces assembled and trained pressure was kept up by an intensification of both the submarine blockade and strategic bombing raids. Since the beginning of their campaign in 1942, America's submarines had sunk more than 1,100 merchant ships amounting to 4,800,000 tons, around 56 percent of the total lost by Japan. The effect on Japanese industry had been apparent as early as 1943 and by early 1945 the import of food was also being severely disrupted, leading to widespread malnutrition and in some areas actual starvation. America's strategic bombing campaign was also becoming effective.

Japan's situation was hopeless, but on 27 July the government of Admiral Kantaro Suzuki (Tojo had resigned the previous July after the fall of Saipon) rejected the Allied demand of unconditional surrender made at Potsdam. Nothing remained but to fight it out – Japan might lose but Allied casualties would be horrific. It planned to meet the invasion fleet with 8,000 carefully husbanded aircraft (many of them kamikazes) and hundreds of explosive-packed suicide boats and "human torpedoes". Ashore two million regular soldiers and a vast "home guard" would dispose of even more invaders.

The Americans were aware of Japan's preparations. On 16 July the secret "Manhattan Project" had borne fruit with the explosion of an atomic bomb at Alamogordo in New Mexico. President Truman (Roosevelt had died on 12 April) immediately authorized its use. At 8.00 am on 6 August a single B-29 dropped an atomic bomb on Hiroshima, destroying the city and killing 80,000 instantaneously. Japan's cabinet met on 8 August but still a majority wished to fight on. On the morning of 9 August Japan reeled under two new shocks – a second atomic bomb devastated Nagasaki and Japan's ambassador in Moscow informed Tokyo of a Soviet declaration of war, which was followed within the hour by a massive Soviet invasion of Manchuria. Now at war with two superpowers, its cities being systematically destroyed by incendiary raids and a new and terrifying bomb, its industrial production at only one third of prewar levels and many of its population starving, Japan's cabinet on 10 August accepted the Potsdam Declaration, asking only that the emperor remain sovereign. It was a request to which the Americans readily acceded and on 15 August Hirohito broadcast Japan's capitulation.

▲ The official surrender of Japan, Tokyo Bay, 2 September 1945. On the quarterdeck of USS *Missouri*, Admiral Nimitz's flagship, Japan's delegation, led by top hatted foreign minister Manoru Shigemitsu, approaches the Allied commanders. Worried that the ceremony might be marred by an unseemly conflict between arch rivals MacArthur and Nimitz, US secretary for the navy, J.V. Forrestal, arranged a compromise. Both men would witness Japan's surrender – MacArthur as supreme commander and Nimitz as representative of the United States.

◄ 11.00 am, 9 August 1945. A photograph taken from the "Great Artiste", one of the observation B-29s. Ten kilometers (6mi) below in the inferno that was Nagasaki 35,000 are already dead and another 60,000 seriously injured.

capital on 3 February but it took them a month of bitter fighting, during which the city was destroyed and more than 100,000 Filipinos were killed, to eliminate the garrison. By the end of March Luzon had been secured except for a pocket in the northeast where Yamashita and 50,000 survivors continued to hold out until Japan's capitulation.

The approach to Japan
The battle for Manila was still raging when Nimitz's fleet sailed into the Bonins, an island group only 1,100km (700mi) southeast of Japan, to secure advanced bases for an invasion of the home islands. On 17 February two marine divisions stormed ashore on 20sq km (8sq mi) Iwo Jima, and took five weeks and 26,000 casualties to exterminate the 25,000 strong Japanese garrison. In the last week of March the largest armada ever assembled in the Pacific, 1,450 ships including the carriers and battleships of the newly formed British Pacific Fleet, sailed for Okinawa in the Ryukyu Islands only 560km (350mi) south of Kyushu. Tokyo was determined to hold it at all costs – a 130,000-man garrison and hundreds of kamikaze and conventional squadrons defended the island. During the next eight weeks Japanese airstrikes – kamikaze and conventional – sank 36 and damaged 368 Allied ships, destroyed 800 air-

THE
FIGHTING
SERVICES

Datafile

The land war was a massive struggle of attrition, its outcome determined by the ability to field, arm and supply huge armies, and to replace the losses they suffered in the slow process of wearing down the enemy. On the battlefield, firepower and transportation capability were the essential ingredients necessary to transform manpower into military advantage. Away from the frontline, industrial output and an intensive supply system were the driving forces which kept the armies fighting. Only the most highly mobilized industrial state could hope to stand the strain of a prolonged military campaign.

El Alamein tank forces

Allies Total 1,530 — 61% / 39%

Axis Total 1,090 — 85% / 15%

Tanks remaining
Tanks lost

Equipment at Stalingrad

Soviet
Axis

Thousands — Armored vehicles, Guns and mortars, Aircraft

◀ At El Alamein (October 1942), Rommel's depleted tank force was destroyed by a larger force, equipped for the first time with vehicles of similar fighting power. The hard fighting in a mine- and artillery-infested battleground took a heavy toll of both sides' armored forces, but when the battle was over the Allies still possessed substantial reserves and the capability to make good losses; the Germans had neither.

▲ The Soviet forces at Stalingrad (1941–42) enjoyed a substantial quantitative advantage in machinery, which ultimately proved too great for Germany's diminishing qualitative superiority to overcome. Strategic blunders aside, Germany was defeated at Stalingrad because it was unable to match the USSR's growing military strength or to bring new tanks, guns and transport equipment into the frontline at the same rate. German forces were outnumbered, outgunned and outsupplied.

▼ Germany did not win the Battle of France (May–June 1940) as a result of numerical superiority. Even the figures for motorized and armored formations are misleading because the Allies had large numbers of vehicles in nonspecialist units. German victory was the product of a very quick and well-organized strike.

Firepower of German infantry division, 1944

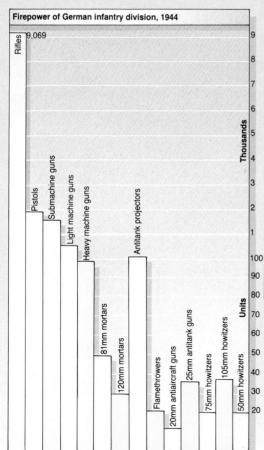

Rifles 9,069; Pistols; Submachine guns; Light machine guns; Heavy machine guns; Antitank projectors; 81mm mortars; 120mm mortars; Flamethrowers; 20mm antiaircraft guns; 25mm antitank guns; 75mm howitzers; 105mm howitzers; 50mm howitzers

Thousands / Units

Battle of France

German
French and British

Infantry divisions; Motorized divisions; Armored divisions

◀ Properly equipped infantry formations could deploy an impressive weight of firepower, sufficient to give them immense killing power. The large casualties of modern military engagements are ultimately the product of the greatly increased density of fire which soldiers are able to unleash on each other.

The armies of World War II retained the same basic organizational structure as that employed in World War I, itself the product of steady evolution in the 19th century. The structure of the British army can be used as an example: similar organization was found in most armies.

The smallest component was the section, composed of eight men; four sections were combined to form a platoon under the command of a subaltern. The next organizational component was the company of 120 men succeeded by the battalion of 700–800. The battalion was a permanent formation which retained the traditional regional or ethnic identity of the parent regiment, be it Highland Scottish, West Country English, Sikh or Bengali. Battalions were combined into brigades of 3,000–4,000 men, and brigades into divisions of 12,000–14,000 men. Divisions were given generic identifications, most commonly armored or infantry, although this only identified the predominant arm and all in fact included subsidiary formations of all arms. Finally divisions were combined to form corps of 30,000–60,000 men, and corps to form an army, containing 60,000–100,000 men. In most theaters, British military might was incorporated in a single army command, such as General Bernard Montgomery's 8th Army in the Western Desert in 1942, but in larger theaters, such as the Eastern Front, several armies would fight under higher organization. The German army in Russia operated as three army groups: North, Center and South.

Asian armies followed European organization closely. Indeed, most had been reorganized in the late 19th or early 20th century on European models and with the help of European advisors.

While World War II military forces were often broken up into a series of separate commands to fight in different theaters, they were at heart huge collections of men and equipment. On the eve of its defence of the Kursk salient in mid-1943, the Soviet Red Army mustered 6,442,000 officers and men, 103,085 guns and mortars, 9,918 tanks and self-propelled guns, and 8,357 aircraft. Forces of such size required a large number of high echelon formations (divisions and above) to control them. The German order of battle in May 1940 comprised some 135 divisions, including 10 armored and 9 mechanized/motorized formations. On 1 July 1944, with German ground forces stretched to the limit on the Western, Eastern and Italian Fronts, the order of battle included 139 infantry divisions, 11 air-force field divisions, 29 static infantry divisions, 11 Jäger divisions, 7 mountain divisions, 10 Panzer grenadier divisions and 24 Panzer divisions, all supplemented by 16 Waffen SS divisions.

Army formations required a massive amount of equipment, some idea of which can be gained

ARMIES AND LAND WARFARE

from a partial list of German materiel captured by the Red Army on the Don Front during the successful Stalingrad campaign: 5,762 guns, 1,312 mortars, 156,987 rifles, 10,722 automatic weapons, 10,679 motorcycles, 240 tractors, 3,569 bicycles, 933 telephone sets and 397km (248mi) of signals cable. Modern warfare made particularly heavy demands on vehicles; in 1942 alone, Germany built 4,278 tanks, the UK 8,611, the USSR 24,668 and the USA 24,997. Motorized transport was always in short supply, simply because the supply and support of fighting formations required the presence of tens of thousands of vehicles which never actually saw combat. So severe was the demand that the German army, the army most clearly associated with the development of mechanized warfare, remained heavily dependent on the horse until the very end of hostilities.

Communications and morale

Advances in communications made the World War II commander's job slightly easier than that of his World War I counterpart. Thousands of radio and telephone sets linked all components of a field force, from forward outposts all the way to general headquarters; but the sheer size and complexity of the modern battlefield, and the volume of communications engendered by the confusion of battle always made some loss of control inevitable. Under adverse conditions, brigades, divisions and even entire army corps could still collapse in complete chaos and resist all the efforts of command and technology to restore order. On the Eastern Front in particular whole formations could disappear in days, if not hours, and everywhere the confusion of defeat could produce tens of thousands of prisoners and huge hauls of perfectly functional equipment.

At the individual level, land warfare remained a matter of morale and small group cohesion. The most important unit to the common soldier was not his battalion or division, but his section or other group of close comrades. These five or ten men were the comrades with whom he shared danger, the messmates with whom he sought food and shelter, and the friends to whom he

▼ US soldiers at rest. Despite mechanization, most World War II soldiers moved and fought on foot, and, like all foot soldiers in history, were exposed to constant, wearying physical effort.

gave support and from whom he received the same in return. While World War II as a whole was probably distinguished by a higher level of identification with national cause than many wars before it, it nonetheless remained the case that small-group loyalties kept most men in the firing line. With the exception of nations, like Italy, whose general commitment to the war was never high, instances of mass surrender or abandonment of duty occurred only in militarily hopeless situations or after prolonged severe fighting. One of the most noteworthy features of the land war of 1939–45 was the ferocity and effectiveness with which the armies of the two major Axis powers (Germany and Japan) continued to fight after any rational hope of victory had long since disappeared. This durability, the product as much of sheer professionalism as of national culture or political indoctrination, ensured that there were few easy victories, even in 1944–45, and that casualties among all participants remained high to the very end.

Characteristics of land warfare

World War II on land is usually presented as an entirely different kind of conflict from World War I. It is seen as a war of movement rather than a war of static positions; as a war of tanks, aircraft and mechanized columns rather than a war of trenches, barbed wire and machine guns. These images are not entirely misleading. Technology did transform the face of war in dramatic fashion between 1939 and 1945, most obviously in the capability it gave to the general to move men and guns quickly across large distances. World War II saw the course of whole campaigns change in a matter of days as a result of rapid outflanking moves or armored breakthroughs. This notwithstanding, there was much that did not change. The vast majority of soldiers were infantrymen, who covered most of the ground they crossed on foot. Most German soldiers marched into Russia in 1941, just as Napoleon's *Grande armée* had done in 1812, and those who survived marched back

out again. In most theaters rapid movement was the exception rather than the rule and much time was taken up with static or near-static warfare, the two sides holding well dug-in positions against each other.

In terms of strategy, the combination of the availability of large mechanized forces and a widespread desire to avoid the bloody stalemate of World War I (in which most senior officers would have served their military apprenticeships) placed a lot of emphasis on variations of the indirect approach – outflanking maneuvers designed to avoid head-on confrontations with strong enemy positions – and on the quick breakthrough by armored forces followed by rapid exploitation of the ensuing chaos (the idea at the heart of the German concept of Blitzkrieg or "lightning war"). Against the unprepared French and British armies of 1939–40, or in the vast interior of Russia and open sands of the Western Desert in North Africa, such approaches were sometimes viable. When operating along a coastline, the greatly improved Allied amphibious capacity of the second half of the war also allowed outflanking maneuvers to be undertaken by sea (as was tried at Anzio in Italy in 1944). In most campaigns though, the nature of the terrain or the strength of the enemies' defenses allowed little scope for such freewheeling operations. Ground had to be taken kilometer by kilometer in slow, close and often confused combined infantry, armor, and artillery operations. When a breakthrough did come, it was often only after the enemy had been ground down by weeks if not months of hard fighting and at a heavy cost in casualties. Despite air power and the tank, the German defenders of Monte Cassino were operating with many of the same advantages as the German defenders along the Somme in 1916 and, despite the technological revolution in warfare, they proved just as difficult to dislodge. Overall the machine gun, artillery piece and well-constructed entrenchment were as important as the tank and motorized troop carrier.

▲ Rouen in flames, May 1940. As German armies moved swiftly through northeast France, they seized one center of communications and supply after another. Air attack would disrupt efforts to restore broken lines of command and regroup retreating ground forces. The motorized leading elements of the Wehrmacht would follow swiftly to complete the process of disintegration.

◀ Rommel's 7th Panzer Division drives for the Channel in May 1940. Although his tanks were lightly protected and undergunned, and much of his infantry support was trailing far behind him, Rommel maintained the momentum of Blitzkrieg by pressing relentlessly on, giving the Allies no time to rally their forces for a counterattack.

◄ The winged weapon of terror and disruption. The German air force or Luftwaffe played a vital role in Blitzkrieg. Close air support helped the armored spearhead to break through defended positions, while constant air attacks on rear areas disrupted efforts to reorganize resistance, destroyed communications and produced panic among the flood of refugees seeking to escape the advancing military forces. The JU87 Stuka, specially equipped with sirens to make its dive-bombing attacks even more terrifying, became the symbol of all that was irresistible in the German attack.

Land warfare in Europe: Blitzkrieg

Blitzkrieg, or "lightning war", was a strategy for using new mechanized military technology. It had been developed in Germany between the wars and dominated the early years of World War II in Europe. The German victories of 1939–41 were notable for their speed and totality. They were based neither on overwhelming numbers nor on a heavy qualitative superiority in equipment. In the first instance German attacking spearheads were often dangerously over-extended and vulnerable to counterattack. In the second instance German Panzer divisions were largely equipped with light tanks which were no match in armor or armament for their French or British opponents, while later experience was to prove that the much-feared JU87 Stuka dive-bomber was a mediocre machine which could not operate in the face of determined fighter opposition. The key components of the German victories, and of the doctrine of Blitzkrieg that lay behind them, were actually speed, surprise, sheer unconventionality, and the comprehensive man-

ner in which the various parts of the military machine were integrated and employed. Blitzkrieg was less a matter of men and materiel than of how they were used.

In the Norwegian campaign of April 1940 the Germans gained the advantage by taking the risk of sailing their invasion fleets straight into Norwegian harbors, seizing as many key points as they could regardless of shortages of forces, and by deploying supporting aircraft to forward bases as soon as these became available. In France and the Low Countries a month later, the Germans attacked unexpectedly out of the supposedly impenetrable Ardennes Forest, outflanking the well-prepared French defenses of the Maginot Line and isolating French and British forces further to the north in Flanders and Belgium. After making their initial breakthrough the Germans did not stop to consolidate their position, but rather continued to push their mechanized forces forward toward the coast. While their flanks were unprotected, their supplies running low, their equipment wearing out, and their supporting

▲ German success depended to a considerable extent on the engineering and logistical skills of the army's support formations. The ability to construct pontoon bridges, such as the one pictured here, allowed the advancing motorized forces to press forward despite the destruction of bridges and the presence of a multitude of rivers which might otherwise have given the defenders a vital breathing space in which to regroup and reorganize.

Supply on the Eastern Front

Supply has always been crucial to military success, but in World War II it assumed greater significance than ever. On the Eastern Front, the logistical problem of keeping armies moving and fighting was further complicated by the huge distances between factories and the front lines. By the beginning of 1943, the Red Army, then over 6 million strong, was using about one-fifth of its field manpower for supply and support duties. The Main Military Roads Administration, for example, employed 125,000 men to service 86,000km (54,000mi) of military highways and overhaul 185,000 lorries. The materiel demands of the war were huge as well: by the middle of 1943 the USA had shipped in 900,000 tonnes of steel and 1.5 million tonnes of food to help sustain the Russian war effort.

The Stalingrad campaign brought the problems of supply into stark contrast. When the German 6th Army was ordered to hold out after being surrounded in the city, it radioed that it would need 750 tonnes of supplies a day just to meet the minimum needs of standing on the defensive (380 tonnes of food, 250 tonnes of ammunition and 120 tonnes of fuel). The German air force could have provided only half the necessary capacity under ideal conditions. Faced with bad weather, disorganized airfield facilities and strong Russian air resistance, it never came close to meeting even that target. By mid-January the beleaguered 6th Army was living off the huge herd of horses which provided it with the largest part of its transport and had already eaten 39,000 of the unfortunate beasts. When resistance was finally crushed at the end of the month, the remnants of the 6th Army were almost completely without food, ammunition or fuel.

troops were often far behind them, the Panzer divisions so disrupted enemy forces that no effective response could be planned or executed. Having knocked the enemy off balance the Germans simply kept pressing until he collapsed in complete confusion.

The vital tactical device behind these lightning assaults was close cooperation, not just between the assorted units of the German army, but also between the army itself and the air force. The Panzer divisions did not consist entirely of tanks: rather they combined tanks with motorized infantry, artillery, and other supporting services to form semiautonomous strike forces capable of dealing with almost any situation that might confront them. Thus, for example, they were able to blunt an attempted British armored attack on their flank, not just with tanks, but with artillery, antitank guns, and even antiaircraft guns (the 88mm AA gun provided a particularly effective tank destroyer). As the Panzer divisions incorporated their own infantry formations, they would not have to launch unsupported tank attacks against defended positions. They were not, however, expected to deal with pockets of resistance and isolated enemy detachments left behind by their advance – these were the responsibility of the infantry divisions which followed along more slowly, in the wake of the armored spearhead. Finally, Blitzkrieg depended not just on aerial superiority but also on direct air intervention in the land engagement. The German air force generally succeeded in gaining the advantage in the sky by launching preemptive strikes to destroy enemy air power on the ground. It then carried out a comprehensive program of tactical air support – a role for which it had been specifically designed and trained. Enemy communications and command structures were disabled by attacks on bridges, railways, roads and population centers well ahead of the advancing German armor while that armor itself could call on close air support to help it push through any obstacle that blocked its path. Overall, Blitzkrieg was as destructive to enemy morale as it was to the physical fabric of his fighting forces, and, as was the case with France in 1940, it was the loss of the will to fight rather than the absolute destruction of the means that produced surrender.

War of attrition: the example of Stalingrad

The Stalingrad campaign was almost certainly the key turning point in the war on the Eastern Front. It began with the Germans driving deep into southern Russia, reaching as far east as the Volga and as far south as the foothills of the Caucasus. It ended with the Germans reeling back beyond their start line leaving an entire army cut off and doomed to surrender far to the east in the ruins of Stalingrad. The campaign itself can be broken into three distinct phases: the initial German offensive, the battle for the city of Stalingrad itself, and the Russian counteroffensive with its attendant siege of the trapped German 6th Army.

The Russians enjoyed a decided advantage in manpower throughout the campaign, but the German army still enjoyed qualitative superiority

◀ A German soldier dug in at Stalingrad. "General Winter" was the great ally of the Soviet resistance. Weather played a crucial role in the German defeat: snow and freezing temperatures played havoc with the inadequately equipped German forces. German morale and fighting effectiveness declined steeply as men froze and weapons failed to function.

▲ Fighting in the Red October Tractor Factory, Stalingrad. The German army in Stalingrad was swallowed up in confused street fighting among the ruins of a devastated industrial city. Unit cohesion disappeared in a maze of broken buildings and rubble-filled streets. Von Paulus's forces were gradually worn down in a series of confused and vicious local actions which destroyed central command, made resupply impossible and broke elite fighting units into isolated groups of exhausted and desperate street fighters.

at the start of the Stalingrad drive. This advantage was lost through the overextension of German forces in pursuit of distant geographical objectives and a growing strategic obsession with the capture of Stalingrad itself. Eventually, an entire army of 22 divisions was sucked into the ruined city, leaving its long and vulnerable flanks protected mainly by second-rate Hungarian, Romanian and Italian forces. As the German advance ground slowly forward, the Russians had time to build up massive forces to the north and south of the city. On 19 November 1942 the Russians attacked, cutting off Stalingrad completely in two days. The Germans failed either to break out from the trap or to push a relieving force through. After Luftwaffe attempts to supply from

the air had failed, the 6th Army was overrun and forced to surrender between 30 January and 2 February 1943. Of a force originally numbering more than a quarter of a million, only 80,000 men were left alive to march into captivity.

The fighting around Stalingrad followed a pattern common to much of the Russian war. Each side counterattacked in turn as the other overextended itself; the Russians used mass infantry assaults to overwhelm enemy positions by sheer weight of numbers; and armored columns repeatedly broke through, causing massive confusion and precipitate retreat.

The fighting inside the city itself was entirely different in nature. Stalingrad was a modern, heavily industrialized center which stretched for

▶ Free French armored cars in the Western Desert. Desert warfare was a mixture of set-piece engagements in which armor, infantry and artillery were used to attack heavily defended positions, and mobile pursuit or outflanking operations in which light armored forces such as the column pictured here played a vital role. The requirement for fast-moving light forces made armored cars and small reconnaissance tanks a far more important component of the desert armies than of military formations in other theaters of war.

▼ Italian infantry move forward in a sandstorm. The Western Desert presented unique problems to the men expected to fight across its arid terrain. Blowing sand reduced visibility, clogged equipment and produced severe personal discomfort. Temperatures varied widely, ranging from baking heat by day to bitter cold at night, and supply was a constant problem in a land which offered little by way of natural resources and rendered transportation extremely difficult. As was the case in so many other theaters, the infantryman's lot was grindingly hard and unpleasant.

18km (11mi) along the high west bank of the River Volga. As two German armies – 6th and 4th Panzer – fought their way in from the west, and as the Russians reinforced the defenders from the east to a strength of five armies, the whole battle degenerated into confused street fighting. Units lost all cohesion as they were fed into the ruined buildings and rubble-choked streets of the inner city. Combat revolved around small group struggles for individual houses and factory buildings, and the morale of both sides was stretched to breaking point by the daily hazards of snipers, boobytraps and ambushes.

As the weather deteriorated, snow, wind and cold were added to the soldiers' problems. After they were cut off and thrown on the defensive, the Germans gradually ran out of food, ammunition and fuel. Russian reinforcements were ordered across the Volga and instructed not to come back, while the Germans missed whatever chance they might have had of an early breakthrough by waiting for definite orders from Hitler. The beleaguered 6th Army was slowly pushed back within an ever-shrinking perimeter. By late January 1943 the enclave was only 16km (10mi) across and the last airfield had been captured. Shortly afterward the Germans were cut into two pockets and overrun.

Desert warfare

Warfare in North Africa's Western Desert was unique for several reasons. The terrain was barren, dry and hostile, and provided little by way of either supplies or natural obstacles to movement. Supply was the critical factor and the strength of the rival armies was generally determined by their distance from their main bases (Tripoli for the Axis and Alexandria for the Allies). Rapid advances tended to outstrip supply capability, leaving the attacker vulnerable to a counterthrust from an enemy who had retired closer to his own supplies. As a result the campaign seesawed back and forth several times across the entire length of the North African desert.

The terrain exercised a decisive impact on the fighting. In the absence of major natural obstacles or easily defensible positions, both sides relied heavily on barbed wire and mines to provide defensive boxes in which they could group their infantry and artillery. Around these the armored forces of both sides enjoyed great freedom of movement, and there was always scope for outflanking moves or surprise attacks on lightly defended areas of the front. For most of the campaign the Germans got more out of their tanks than the Allies did from theirs. Until mid-1942, when American-built Grant and Sherman tanks began to arrive in numbers, British armor was generally slow and undergunned. In Rommel they were confronted by an enemy commander with an instinctive flair for tank warfare. Finally, the Germans possessed the most effective anti-tank gun in their dual-purpose 88mm weapon. They had no hesitation in deploying these weapons at the very front of positions where they were often able to destroy British tanks before the latter could get close enough to do any damage.

Overall the campaign has been justly compared to sea warfare with both sides operating from fixed bases in an almost featureless and generally hostile environment. The campaign also involved polyglot forces on both sides. While the German Afrika Korps attracted most of the attention on the Axis side, it was in fact supported by a large Italian contingent. This force was inferior in equipment and had suffered severely in the opening stages of the campaign, but under Rommel's direction it could not be completely written off by its opponents. On the Allied side almost all of the British Commonwealth and Empire was represented, the 8th Army comprising Australian, New Zealand, South African and Indian formations as well as native British ones. It also included a Free French detachment and by 1942 was looking to the USA for some of its equipment, most importantly Grant and Sherman medium tanks to allow it to take on Rommel's Panzer MkIIIs and MkIVs on equal terms. In the final stages of the campaign, after Rommel's defeat at El Alamein and the Allied landings in French North Africa, American troops also became involved, picking up hard-earned combat skills at the hands of their outnumbered but much more experienced opponents.

All armies coped well with the peculiar demands of the desert climate, and despite the profound swings in temperature and the eye- and engine-clogging clouds of sand, the standard of military performance was generally very high.

Rommel has been criticized for attempting too ambitious a campaign with the forces at his disposal, but, whatever the strategic ramifications, there can be no doubting the fact that his units achieved as high and as consistent a level of battlefield performance as any German military formation during the entire war. His victories were triumphs of improvisation based on the excellent training and spirit of his men. In defeat, the Afrika Korps maintained its morale and fighting capability to the very end, delaying the final Allied triumph for several valuable months. For British and Imperial forces, the campaign was significant because it allowed them the opportunity to recover their morale and develop their fighting skills in preparation for the reconquest of mainland Europe. After the disasters of 1940–41, North Africa was the only theater in which the land forces of the western Allies were in regular combat with the German army. While they were frequently outmaneuvered and outfought by their highly professional opponents, they emerged from the campaign with a far better knowledge of the requirements of modern mechanized warfare than they had been able to draw upon in Norway, France or Greece. Furthermore, the heroic defense of Tobruk, the stout performance of men and machines in the seesaw campaigns of 1941–42, and the final triumph of El Alamein gave the units of the 8th Army a faith in their ability to defeat the enemy which had been sadly lacking by the end of the first campaigns in northern Europe. Overall, there can hardly have been another theater of military operations which saw the opposing sides perform so well and so consistently over such a prolonged period of time.

▼ The critical engagements of the desert war were set-piece battles fought around entrenched defensive positions. Mines (below), dug-in artillery and infantry emplacements equipped with periscopes (bottom), barbed wire, etc were employed to stop armored assaults. Only when such barriers had been destroyed or outflanked did the war assume its more famous mobile character.

◀ A raiding party of the British Long Range Desert Group. The open flanks of the desert armies and the long, vulnerable lines of communication behind them allowed great scope for light mobile operations. Fighting in the tradition of Lawrence of Arabia, small formations like the LRDG caused disruption well out of proportion to their size, but the issue was always ultimately settled in a set-piece battle between the main armies.

▲ The RAF drops supplies to Slim's 14th Army on the River Irrawaddy in Burma. The fighting forces' need for constant supply was all the more critical in the jungle where the terrain made traditional modes of transport impossibly difficult, and the appalling climate rendered mass disease the inevitable consequence of lack of good food and medical supplies. British success in the Burma campaign of 1944–45 was firmly based on air superiority and the massive air supply effort which command of the skies and possession of a large transport fleet allowed. While the British were able in this way to feed the fit and evacuate the sick, their Japanese opponents were ravaged by sickness and malnutrition.

▶ The sheer volatility of the jungle climate produced problems of its own. In the monsoon season, whole areas were inundated and normal patrolling became a matter of amphibious operation, with all manner of craft being employed to move men to areas of suspected enemy activity. In many cases, the volume of water pouring down from the skies was such as to make military movements on any but the smallest scale a complete impossibility.

Jungle warfare: the case of Burma

In their Burma campaign of 1944–45, Allied forces succeeded by utilizing advantages and tactics similar to those employed by the Japanese in the preceding two years. They were also aided by a preemptive Japanese attack (March 1944), the initial success of which overextended General Mutaguchi's 15th Army and exposed it to a devastating counterthrust. Initially Allied attacks met stiff resistance, but when the defensive Japanese barrier finally cracked, the advance gathered momentum. The Japanese lost first Mandalay (20 March 1945) and then Rangoon (3 May 1945), falling back toward the Thai border in complete disarray, and leaving the Burmese army to defect to the Allies.

Japan's successful conquest of Burma in 1942 (see p. 46) had been based on superior air power and better jungle-fighting techniques. British positions were consistently infiltrated and outflanked, and position after position had to be abandoned to prevent encirclement. By 1944 air superiority had passed to the Allies. This enabled them to support deep penetration raids which were aimed at disrupting enemy supplies and communications.

On the British sector of the front, along the Indian frontier, these raids were mounted by General Orde Wingate's Chindits. On the Chinese-American sector further inland, the raiders were a US formation known as Merrill's Marauders. The efforts of these semiguerrilla forces were supported by conventional offensives. General Joseph Stilwell's Chinese-American forces in the north eventually managed to reopen the land link to China along the Burma road, while Slim's British 14th Army advanced on Akyab through the coastal mountains and on the Chindwin river in central Burma.

The second of these offensives was disrupted by a massive Japanese counterattack which broke through the mountains into India. The Japanese invaded the Manipur plain, encircling the strategic towns of Imphal and Kohima. In the case of both the coastal and Imphal campaigns, Slim did not allow his troops to retreat when outflanked and threatened with encirclement. Rather he ordered his garrisons to hold firm and depended on his superior air resources to supply and support them. He then ordered his own relieving forces into the jungle to outflank and encircle the Japanese besiegers. The critical battle took place at Imphal where the siege lasted 88 days (29 March–22 June 1944). When it was finally broken, the Japanese 15th Army had been all but destroyed, severely reducing the defender's ability to resist a renewed offensive in 1945.

For both sides Burma was a remote theater of war, girdled by mountains and cluttered with difficult jungle terrain. The key to success for both sides was their ability to supply and support frontline forces fighting kilometers away from prewar lines of communication. The Japanese managed to complete the Burma railway, running from Moulmein on the coast of Burma to their supply bases in Thailand – its construction the Japanese sacrificed more than 50,000 lives, the bulk of them Asian laborers and Allied prisoners of war – and to conquer terrain. The Allies built a whole series of airfields and a new mountain road from northeast India across the Naga Hills into Burma. Altogether, it required several hundred thousand laborers and support troops to keep the Allied fighting effort in Burma going. In terms of terrain difficulties and the quality of enemy opposition, it was one of the most exacting campaigns of the war. At the tactical level, Slim's 14th Army might have won the war in Burma because it successfully adopted the flexible techniques of jungle fighting, but at the strategic level the outcome was undoubtedly decided by the organization of a massive supply and support service making very heavy use of transport aircraft. Slim's generalship of the 14th Army was particularly distinguished, and his conduct of the Imphal-Kohima battle alone would be sufficient to place him in the front rank of World War II commanders.

Jungle Warfare

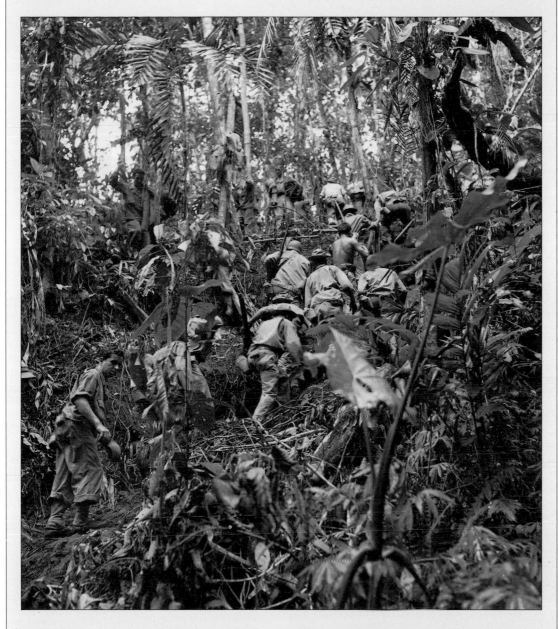

▲ Near-impenetrable terrain on Guadalcanal, 1943.

Then one day we had our first shower. This was the end. The rains. The steep sides of the ridge became a bog and a treacherous foothood. The water seeped into our foxholes and ran in great gushes down the slope, carrying the mud with it. The track from the airstrip was an adventure, but for those who carried the stretchers down to the strip it was a nightmare. The strip itself was soggy. The shower soon passed off, but it left a feeling that we could not get rid of. Rains, misery and sickness, vistas of mud stretching into the endless future, tearing at our boots, covering our bodies, filling our bivouacs and folding over us as we slept.

RICHARD RHODES JAMES
BURMA, 1944

▲ Well-trained and tightly disciplined, the Japanese soldier was all the more fearsome for his willingness to surrender his own life to destroy the enemy. This soldier was crouching in a foxhole in Burma with an explosive device between his legs which he hoped to detonate when an enemy tank passed over his position. Such suicidal bravery ensured that Allied victory could only be completed by the systematic destruction of the entire defending force — a slow, dangerous and bloody business, however inevitable the final result.

War in the jungle was dominated by terrain and climate to a greater extent than war in any other landscape. Much of the jungle terrain fought over by the Japanese and Allied forces between 1942 and 1945 was a cluttered nightmare of dense undergrowth, stagnant water and overgrown tracks. The climate, alternately arid and extremely wet, often almost unbearably hot, made things much worse, not only through the sheer physical discomfort it brought, but also because it bred disease at an army-destroying rate. Success in jungle warfare was thus largely a matter of limiting the impact of natural hindrances on operations and the maintenance of effective fighting capacity.

In the Burma battles both the Japanese in the early years of the campaign and the British and Allied forces in the battles of 1944–45 succeeded by ignoring the conventions of normal strategy and tactics. Armies which stuck to the established road network or attempted to hold fixed positions in open terrain usually found themselves outflanked through the surrounding jungle. Operating in the jungle itself placed a heavy emphasis on independent action by small units, and as a result only troops with high morale and good training could be expected to survive. It was essentially an infantryman's war; tanks operated in small numbers tightly constricted by terrain, while only light artillery could be moved around with sufficient ease to be of any use.

Jungle casualty lists resembled those of the wars of the preindustrial age with far heavier losses through sickness and disease than through enemy action. This was partly a result of climate and partly a result of difficulties in maintaining adequate supplies of food and medicine. The army that could fight best in the jungle was the one which could keep its sick list down by maintaining the flow of food and medical supplies.

Datafile

The sea war involved tens of thousands of fighting and merchant vessels – more than any other campaign before or since. The introduction of the aircraft carrier, and the impact of airpower generally, added a new dimension to seaborne conflict. Once again, industrial might played a crucial role. Nations incapable of replacing losses to torpedoes, bombs, mines and shells were swept completely from the seas.

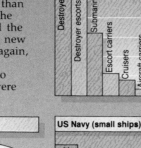

US Navy (large ships)

U-boats

Boats
Total 1,150

- Lost
- Scuttled
- Surrendered

Personnel
Total 40,000

- Killed
- Taken prisoner
- Remaining

▲ The German U-boat service paid a heavy price for the damage inflicted on Allied shipping. In the second half of the war, improved air and surface antisubmarine techniques took such a heavy toll of the German submarine force that by the last year of the war it was powerless to interfere with the enemy's supply effort.

▼ In the first half of the war, Allied merchant shipping losses were horrendous, but from 1943 new building programs, particularly that launched in the USA, were more than compensating for losses, and the faltering German U-boat campaign could not prevent a progressive growth in Allied seaborne carrying capacity.

US Navy (small ships)

▼ The Western Allies enjoyed a substantial numerical superiority over Axis naval forces at the beginning of the war, but the early removal of the French navy from the scene, the diversion of British forces to meet threats away from home waters, and the growth of the German U-boat force dramatically changed the situation. Between 1940 and 1942, Allied naval forces in European waters were stretched very thin, and even isolated Axis surface units could pose a dangerous threat.

UK merchant shipping

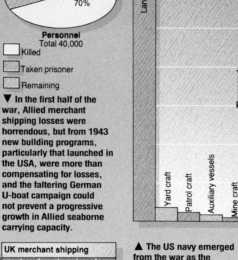

4,034

Losses

Gains

1939   1942   1945

▲ The US navy emerged from the war as the greatest fighting armada ever seen. A huge shipbuilding program, based on the country's dynamic heavy industrial sector, produced not only an impressive fleet of modern carriers, battleships, cruisers, destroyers and submarines, but also tens of thousands of small craft to carry the amphibious landing forces which reconquered the islands of the Pacific and opened the second front in Europe leading to the defeat of Germany.

Comparative naval strengths – September 1939

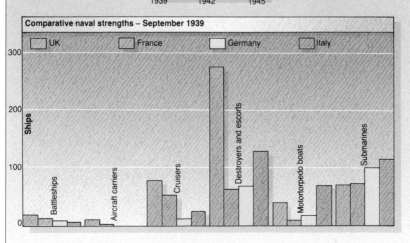

The navies of World War II were fighting services caught in a period of transition. The navies of the late 19th and early 20th centuries had been built up around the battleship, as a result of the introduction of steampower, armor-plating and the long-range rifled gun firing high explosive ordnance. Naval thinking revolved around the employment of battleships in fleet-to-fleet gun duels, with the result that the entire navy would be built around the battleline.

By World War II the introduction of submarines and aircraft had been changing this pattern for several decades, but in none of the combatant forces was the transition to a more balanced fighting fleet complete. Submarine forces were still expanding and in many cases had yet to evolve a coherent strategic doctrine for use in war. Antisubmarine technology was still in its infancy and very few purpose-designed antisubmarine vessels were actually in service. Battleships were still being designed and built, and indeed the last such example of the type was not to enter service until World War II was over. Finally, carrier aviation was in an advanced state of development only in Japan and the USA, and even there naval high commands had not completely rid themselves of a belief in the battleship as the ultimate arbiter of seaborne warfare.

The organization of naval forces

Naval organization was far more flexible than that of land and aerial forces. Vessels were grouped in permanent squadrons and flotillas, but this was mainly for administrative convenience rather than operations. Fighting fleets were usually put together as situations required and the availability of units allowed. Thus a modern light cruiser might find itself operating alone searching for a commerce raider, or helping to screen a battle-group of capital ships, or leading a mixed task force of cruisers and destroyers on a raid against enemy coastal forces, or on escort duty with a convoy fighting its way through the aircraft-dominated Mediterranean. The multiplicity of roles and the frequent unavailability of purpose-built types often exposed warships to challenges they had not been designed to meet.

The war itself saw a tremendous change in the nature of the naval balance. In 1937 the Imperial Japanese Navy (IJN) was the world's third largest force, operating the entire range of aircraft carriers, battleships, cruisers, destroyers and submarines. By 1945 the IJN had been all but annihilated and its place as number three had been taken by the Royal Canadian Navy. This force had entered the war with nothing but a handful of destroyers, but had expanded as one of the major participants in the Battle of the Atlantic. Designed almost entirely as an antisubmarine

NAVIES AND SEA WARFARE

force, it controlled hundreds of frigates and corvettes but nothing resembling a modern capital ship. The navy that experienced the most dramatic expansion, however, was that of the USA. With the full resources of a massive shipbuilding industry behind it, it left the war with between two and three times the number of modern capital ships and cruisers that it had begun with, to say nothing of an armada of amphibious warfare vessels capable of launching major operations simultaneously in the South Pacific and Northern Europe.

The roles of technology and morale

Technology played a crucial role in naval warfare, and the outcome of battle was often determined by the quality of radar or communications equipment, the intensity and accuracy of antiaircraft fire, and the ability to use established systems to limit the impact of fire, explosion and other battle damage. Training and coordination were crucial if the complicated machinery of the modern warship was to be used to full effect in combat.

While morale is always important in war, it did not exercise a decisive influence over the sea campaigns of World War II – simply because most navies almost always fought to the best of their technical abilities. Both the German U-boat force and the Imperial Japanese Navy suffered appalling losses in the second half of the war, due to industrial and technological advances on the part of their enemies, but both forces continued to fight hard to the bitter end. Neither British forces dive-bombed by the Axis out of the waters of Crete and the Aegean in mid-1941, nor US forces, swept from the island waters of the South Pacific six months later, suffered any decline in fighting spirit. Only the Italian navy demonstrated a poor appetite for fighting the enemy. A partial explanation for this may be its low level of politicization: it was disinclined to fight because it saw the war more as a fascist adventure than a matter of national survival. The French navy was denied the chance to distinguish itself. Equipped with some of the most modern warships in the world, it was first attacked in harbor by its ex-ally, Britain, and then scuttled in harbor to avoid capture by its rather dubious friend, Germany.

Trade, supply and the sea war

Beyond the drama of fleet engagements and amphibious operations, naval warfare in the modern age has always centered around the control of sea lanes for the purposes of supply and trade. The blockade of enemy coasts, the marshalling of huge escorted convoys of merchantmen and the employment of the free-ranging surface commerce raider had all been essential features of naval campaigns for centuries before the aircraft

▼ Funeral at sea: American casualties of the naval war in the Pacific are prepared for a watery grave.

and the submarine appeared on the scene. World War I had introduced the submarine as the most potent threat to a warring nation's seaborne trade. World War II saw the underwater threat intensify, with German submarines in the Atlantic and US submarines in the Pacific sending millions of tonnes of enemy merchant shipping to the bottom. The coming of age of the aircraft added a whole new dimension to the situation. Merchantmen had to be protected against a threat from above as well as one from below, and the achievement of air supremacy over the sea could allow the destruction of trade and supply on a scale of which not even the submarine was capable. In World War II the navies of the world refought the age-old battle for control of the sea lanes with new weapons as well as old on a scale unimaginable in any earlier conflict.

The UK and Japan were the major combatants

most dependent on seaborne supply for survival and suffered most at the hands of these new weapons. The victory of the first and the defeat of the second were inextricably linked to their performance in the war between merchant shipping, submarines and aircraft. Beyond the convoy battles on the major sea lanes, however, many other naval engagements were also fought over trade and supply. Perhaps the best example of this phenomenon was the German surface commerce raiding campaign, which involved operations in every major ocean.

Beyond its participation in the invasion of Scandinavia, the only major role of Germany's small surface fleet was to pose a threat to British commerce. Either by operating against independently routed vessels in distant waters (a role left largely to converted merchantmen with concealed armaments) or by descending suddenly in force on a single north Atlantic convoy, German surface raiders could cause heavy damage and even more serious disruption. Perhaps most importantly, they could tie down large numbers

Convoy Organization

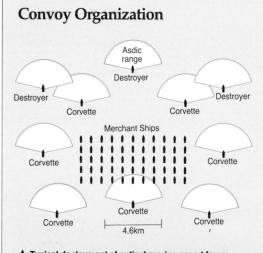

▲ Typical deployment of antisubmarine escort forces.

The basic principle of the convoy is to concentrate merchant ships in large groups so that they can be protected by warships. A typical convoy of 45 ships in 9 five-ship columns would cover an area of 13sq km (5 sq mi), and with the underwater detection device Asdic normally only capable of picking up submerged submarines at distances shorter than a kilometer and able to sweep in an arc of 80 degrees ahead of the vessel, only a strong escort could expect to prevent a determined mass U-boat attack from getting through to the merchant vessels.

Until the mid-way point of the war, overworked escorts could rarely take enough time away from screening duties, shepherding straying vessels back into formation and rescuing survivors to depth-charge a submarine to destruction. Only after sufficient vessels became available to provide large screens and independent groups to cooperate with aircraft in a hunter-killer role, did U-boat losses begin to climb and merchant ship sinkings decline. Before that the convoy only served to keep losses within manageable proportions. When U-boats concentrated in numbers a massacre could ensue.

of British warships needed in other theaters.

German surface raiders caused intermittent trade crises in areas as far from their homeland as the South Atlantic, the Indian Ocean and the coastal waters of Australia until the middle of 1942. Germany's fleet in Norwegian waters posed a serious threat to the Arctic Convoys from the USA and UK to the USSR between 1942 and 1944, playing a central if indirect role in the destruction of the ill-fated convoy PQ17 and tying down the best of Britain's handful of modern capital ships until the two main German vessels, the battleship *Tirpitz* and the battlecruiser *Scharnhorst* were destroyed. The most famous action of the campaign, however, was fought in the North Atlantic in 1941 when Germany's first modern battleship, the *Bismarck*, was hunted down and destroyed. This campaign revealed the strengths and weaknesses of the German position. At a time of the war when it was severely stretched in other theaters, the Royal Navy was forced to deploy a huge force of capital ships, cruisers and destroyers to prevent a single enemy capital ship (with only one heavy cruiser as a consort) destroying entire convoys. On the other hand, by committing this formidable vessel on what was always likely to become a one-way mission, the Germans were throwing away a valuable asset, which could have been better deployed.

Attrition at sea: the Battle of the Atlantic
The Battle of the Atlantic was essentially a struggle of attrition, in which the German U-boat force attempted to sink Allied merchant vessels at a faster rate than they could be built, while not themselves accepting losses too high to allow the growth of submarine strength. It was also a struggle of technology, in which complicated machinery was continually under development either to conceal or detect the movements of the submarine; in which new weapons were added to both surface and underwater arsenals; and in which the rival intelligence services struggled to break each other's codes while keeping their own

▲ A U-boat commander uses his periscope to survey the surface. The secret of the submarine's effectiveness was its ability to approach its target undetected. But the necessity of constructing a vessel small enough to avoid easy detection yet capable of carrying a mass of special technology, a full complement of torpedoes, and two different engines produced a cramped and uncomfortable environment for the crew. Submariners spent long hours trapped in a metal tube which a single depth-charge would transform into their coffin.

impenetrable. Ultimately the U-boat force was defeated because it failed in both struggles.

While U-boats in other theaters had the luxury of operating against single unescorted merchant vessels, their counterparts in the North Atlantic had to contend with escorted convoys from the beginning of the war. Because of this fact, U-boats were concentrated in ad-hoc wolf packs under the general coordination of their head-quarters in France whether a convoy was detected or not. While the U-boats themselves could not cooperate closely without risking detection of their radio signals, the general intention was to overwhelm the escort by force of numbers and sink as many merchant vessels as possible while they remained a concentrated target.

Both the geographical focus and the tech-nological balance of the U-boat war changed several times during the war. In the early months German submarine activity was concentrated in the western approaches to the United Kingdom, but increasing patrol activity gradually drove them out into the Atlantic, where, in late 1940 and early 1941, they enjoyed a period of great success. Improved antisubmarine techniques brought this period to an end in spring 1941, but when the USA entered the war at the end of the year, the U-boats were able to find easy pickings along the

▲ Overhead view of part of the secondary armament of the US battleship *Arkansas*, taken while the vessel was on convoy duty in the Atlantic. Such vessels had a limited role in protecting convoys against German surface raiders, but it was the far smaller destroyers and corvettes, usually operating in far worse weather conditions than those portrayed here, which represented the last line of defence against the far more dangerous German U-boat force.

◀ An Atlantic convoy at sea. The escort in the foreground is a British destroyer of World War I vintage modified for antisubmarine duties. Convoys of 40–60 merchant ships occupied sea space of several square kilometers, presenting U-boats with a huge target and escorts with a dangerously overextended perimeter to defend.

▲ USS *Bunker Hill* on fire after being hit by two kamikazes off Okinawa in April 1945. Kamikaze attacks often did spectacular damage to the plane-crowded, wooden flight decks of US carriers, but the effect was rarely decisive. The huge Japanese losses incurred in such suicidal assaults failed to destroy the American capability to dominate the Pacific battlefield with naval airpower.

American coast for several months, until routine wartime measures like blackouts and convoys were introduced.

The convoy battles reached their peak in the winter of 1942–43 far out in the mid-Atlantic away from the ever-increasing patrol areas of land-based aircraft. After a final burst of success in the early spring, U-boat losses rose sharply, and merchant ship sinkings fell by a corresponding margin. Under almost constant threat on the surface from long-range aircraft, not only in the Atlantic but also on their outward and inward passages through the Bay of Biscay, and hunted down by free-roving groups of anti-submarine vessels (often accompanied by a small escort aircraft carrier), the U-boats had difficulty even reaching attack positions near convoys. New devices like the schnorkel and new submarines of advanced design came too late to change this situation, and although U-boats remained at sea until the end of

the war, their low success rate made them a nuisance rather than a menace.

The Battle of the Atlantic was fought at great cost on both sides. Many torpedoed merchantmen sank so quickly as to allow no chance of crew survival, and many of those who survived the actual sinking were never rescued, either because they were not found or because escort vessels were too busy trying to deal with enemy submarines. The U-boat force itself suffered the unprecedented casualty rate of 90 percent, and in most cases the entire crew would perish with the vessel. The outcome of the battle, however, was determined by ship-building capacity and technological development. After the introduction of extensive Anglo-American merchant-ship building programs, the U-boats could no longer sink vessels at a rate sufficient to reduce the pool of available tonnage. With aircraft able to patrol almost the entire ocean, with newly built escorts

► Royal Navy deckhands
push a strike aircraft into
position on the flight deck
of HMS *Indomitable* in the
Pacific in 1945. By this time a
British carrier force had joined
the already huge American
fleet. The aircraft carrier was
a floating airfield as well as
a warship, and the need to
maintain fully equipped
hangars with all the necessary
repair, maintenance and
refueling machinery produced
crews of over a thousand per
vessel – a floating community
of specialists in the
complicated art of naval
air warfare.

appearing in sufficient numbers not only to protect convoys but to form extra support groups as
well, and with the technology of detection and
destruction developing heavily in favor of the
anti-submarine forces, the U-boats of the last two
years of the war were more often the hunted than
the hunters.

The impact of carriers

The naval war in the Pacific was dominated by
the use of aircraft operating from carriers. Fought
around the North Pacific island of Midway on 4–5
June 1942, the Battle of Midway marked the turning point in the naval war between the USA and
Japan. In it, Japan lost two-thirds of its main
carrier strike force, and a similar proportion of
highly-trained flight crew. Neither the ships nor
the men could ever be replaced, and, stripped at
one blow of its most valuable asset, the IJN was
doomed to eventual defeat by superior American
air power.

The Japanese defeat was due largely to poor
planning, confusion of objectives, and over
confidence, although sheer bad luck also played a
role. Admiral Yamamoto dispersed his forces too
widely, sending a small but valuable detachment
(including two light carriers) on a futile diversionary attack on the Aleutian Islands, and splitting his main body into separate invasion, battle,
and carrier groups, thus denying the carriers
themselves adequate escort. While the successful
occupation of Midway Island would have been a
valuable gain, this mission could only be successfully completed if the opposing US carrier force
was first destroyed. In fact, the latter objective was
of far greater strategic importance. Despite this,
Japanese attention remained focused on the island until it was too late, with the result that the
Americans were able to get in the first and, as it
turned out, decisive blow.

The battle began with Japanese air strikes on
Midway itself. Aircraft were being readied for a
second strike, when aerial reconnaissance reported the presence of the American carriers to
the northeast. By this time an American strike
force was already on its way and, when this arrived overhead on the morning of 4 June, Japanese

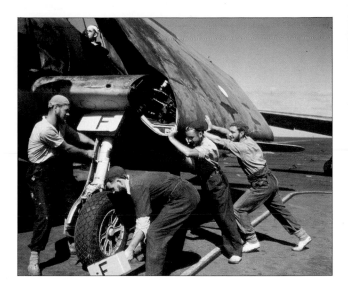

deck crews were still frantically at work rearming
aircraft for antiship operations. By sheer coincidence low-flying American torpedo bombers
found the enemy first, and, although these were
all but wiped out by Japanese fighters, they did
pull the latter down to sea level, leaving the way
entirely clear for the higher-flying dive-bombers
which followed. At about 10.30 am these began
their attacks, and within five minutes the outcome of the battle had been decided. The carriers
Akagi, *Soryu*, and *Kaga* received two, three, and
four bomb hits respectively. These, by themselves, might not have been fatal but, with flight
decks and hangars crowded with fuel lines, uns-
towed ordnance, and flight-ready aircraft, a series
of secoary explosions and uncontrollable fires
soon reduced all three vessels to wrecks.

The one undamaged carrier, *Hiryu*, managed to
launch two airstrikes against the enemy, but,
again by coincidence, these both found the same
target, the carrier *Yorktown*, leaving the other two
US carriers, *Hornet* and *Enterprise*, (which were
sailing in a separate detachment) free to find and
disable the *Hiryu* at 5.00 pm. All four Japanese
carriers proved unsalvageable, and those which
remained afloat were eventually scuttled to prevent capture. The sole US carrier casualty, the
Yorktown, was badly damaged, but remained
afloat until 6 June, when it was sunk by a
Japanese submarine in an attack which also accounted for one of its escorting destroyers. By this
time Japanese surface forces, bereft of air cover,
had begun to withdraw. In the confusion of the
retreat two Japanese cruisers, *Mogami* and
Mikuma, collided, and were then subjected to
heavy air attack. While the former eventually
limped home, the latter was sunk by a hail of
bombs, drawing the IJN's disastrous battle to a
close.

Although the IJN was not so superior in carrier
airpower as the overall size of its fleet at Midway
would indicate, the Japanese should have been
able to win the battle, or at least to have avoided
complete disaster, had the operation been more
clearly conceived and better planned. Their failure
to do so left them with insuffiient naval airpower
to fight the remainder of the war with any chance
of success.

▼ Mealtime at sea on a
US aircraft carrier. A large
warship was an entirely
self-contained fighting unit.
An important requirement for
efficient operation was the
ability to feed the crew from
on-board resources – a
major exercise in supply,
preparation and organization
in a vessel which might be
expected to operate for weeks
without resupply.

Datafile

The air war swallowed up aircraft and aircrew by the thousands. The greatly increased firepower of the aircraft themselves, the massive growth of ground- and sea-based antiaircraft weaponry and on occasion the use of aircraft as suicide missiles all contributed to increase the high wastage rates normally associated with aerial operations. All of the combatants had to launch massive industrial efforts to keep abreast of the constant need for expansion and replacement. They were also faced with the problem of training enough personnel. Toward the end, the Axis powers could no longer sustain their replacement programs and were all but driven from the skies.

Battle of Britain

24%
4%
8%
35%
29%

Total 3,400 aircraft

Luftwaffe
- Bombers
- Fighters
- Dive-bombers
- Reconnaissance

- RAF Fighter Command

Kamikaze missions

Okinawa
Philippines area
Formosa area

Returned
Expended

Hundreds

◀ In the last year of the war, the Japanese expended hundreds of planes and pilots in desperate one-way missions aimed at reversing the course of the war by using aircrafts as flying bombs. Most kamikazes did not survive the flak and defending fighters sent up to meet them. Those which did reach their targets could not do enough damage even to delay the Allied advance, and the cost in irreplaceable aircraft and aircrew was such as to destroy Japanese airpower.

▲ The RAF entered the Battle of Britain heavily outnumbered, but a large part of the attacking German force was made up of lightly armed bombing aircraft ill-suited for their task. The opposing fighter forces were closely matched in equipment, training and numbers, and the British aviation industry was actually able to outbuild its opposite number. With the advantage of fighting over its own territory, the RAF was not in quite as severe a position as has often been thought.

Kamikaze damage

11%
89%

Total 222 ships

- Warships damaged
- Warships sunk

Battle of Britain

- Aircraft lost
- Aircrew killed

Luftwaffe
RAF

◀ Enjoying all the benefits of fighting over its own territory, RAF Fighter Command suffered appreciably lighter losses than the Luftwaffe. While the balance of losses was not as favorable as portrayed by wartime propagandists, it was sufficient to force the cancellation of the German offensive.

▲ While the kamikazes did not inflict damage on a large number of vessels, much of the effort was expended on destroyers and other small vessels on screening duties. No major Allied capital ships were actually lost to kamikaze attacks, and those which did suffer damage were quickly replaced or repaired.

▶ The air battle of the Philippines Sea was almost completely one-sided. Ill-trained Japanese pilots in obsolescent aircraft proved no match for US carrier fighters and Japan's naval air capacity was destroyed for good in a few hours of hectic action without a single US naval vessel receiving either bomb or torpedo damage.

Battle of Philippines

6%
94%

Total 429 aircraft lost

- Japan
- USA

Aircraft exercised a profound influence on the course of hostilities, but at the start of the conflict Europe's air forces probably mustered fewer frontline machines than their predecessors had at the end of World War I in 1918. The French air force, for example, had over 2,000 aircraft in November 1918, but in early 1940 could place only 1,147 machines in the front line, and of these only 678 could be described as modern designs. Only the German air force (Luftwaffe), could really be described as a fully effective striking force. It took 3,530 operational aircraft into the Battle of France in May 1940.

Aircraft construction programs, however, had already become items of urgent priority all over the world before the first shots were fired. As the war developed, the major combatant air forces swelled dramatically in size. By the end of hostilities, the largest of them rivaled armies in the numbers of men employed. The British Royal Air Force (RAF), which had a personnel strength of 175,692 on 3 September 1939, reached a peak of 1,185,833 men on 1 July 1944. The striking might of the aircraft themselves reached levels scarcely dreamed of six years before. In September 1939 RAF Bomber Command could muster 352 aircraft (none of them heavy four-engined types); in the first four months of 1945 it had an average daily strength of 1,420 aircraft (1,305 of them four-engined) and during this period flew 67,483 sorties and dropped over 180,000 tonnes of bombs.

Organization and efficiency

Most air forces employed similar organizational structures: aircraft were grouped into squadrons, wings, groups and finally semiautonomous commands like the US 8th Air Force, responsible for the strategic bombing offensive launched against Germany from bases in the UK. The German air force, which employed a tightly structured command system right through the war, was fairly typical in the way it organized its frontline formations. The smallest tactical unit was the *Staffel* of 12 aircraft (for combat purposes alone the *Staffel* was broken down into three *Schwarmen*, each composed of a pair of two-plane *Rotten*). Three *Staffeln* were combined to form a *Gruppe*, and three or four *Gruppen* in turn comprised a *Geschwader*. Organization up to this level was fixed, but *Geschwadern*, and on occasions detached *Gruppen*, were assigned to *Luftflotten* (air fleets – effectively area air commands) to meet the needs of the operational situation.

The performance of the aircraft was naturally one of the key determinants of combat effectiveness. Pilots unfortunate enough to be sent aloft in inferior equipment, such as those of the Russian air force in 1941 or the Japanese aviators of the last two years of the war in the Pacific, were

AIR FORCES AND AIR WARFARE

bound to suffer crippling losses. Beyond equipment, however, it was the training, experience and élan of a unit which really shaped its fighting efficiency. Flying high-performance aircraft under combat conditions required a degree of individual skill far above that expected of most fighting men. Improved aircraft were of little use without a long and intensive training program and the operational experience necessary to hone individual and group flying skills.

Tactics and resistance

The air war in World War II varied tremendously in nature and intensity. Aircraft were not completely absent from any campaign, and they played an important if not decisive role in most, ranging from Japanese tactical bombing in 1937 to the final bombing attacks on Japan in 1945. Much of the air war was directly related to the land and sea wars below it. The German Blitzkrieg of 1939–41 depended heavily on support from the air and

▼ RAF ground crew gathered in front of a Lancaster bomber in 1944. Keeping a large bombing force operational required a massive force of fitters, riggers, electricians and armorers.

provided the model for later tactical air operations by all the combatants. At sea, aircraft proved a greater danger to warships than other warships, and, even in campaigns as different as those fought in the Mediterranean between 1940 and 1943 and in the Pacific between 1941 and 1945, it was land- or carrier-based air power which exercised the dominant influence.

This was largely the case because the aircraft had developed greatly in range, speed, reliability, and destructive capability since the previous war. The introduction of the metal-framed monoplane with enclosed cockpit and engine/engines of vastly improved power allowed the aircraft far greater scope for interference in land or sea campaigns, enabling it to deliver a large bomb or torpedo payload at great range with considerable accuracy. It also allowed the aircraft to operate as a strategic weapon in its own right, squadrons of bombers being deployed against industrial and population targets hundreds of kilometers from the Front in an effort to cut off the enemy war-effort at its roots.

The tactics of the air war varied with its nature. In the classic fighter-against-bomber confrontations of the Battle of Britain and the Allied strategic bombing campaign against Germany the introduction of radar, radio-control, and a new generation of fast monoplane fighters such as the Spitfire and the Messerschmitt Bf109 disproved the prewar adage that the bomber would always get through. Even large, concentrated formations of bombers with strong defensive armaments would suffer unacceptably high losses until provided with fighter escorts of their own. In operations of a tactical nature, usually undertaken at lower altitudes, the roles of the fighter and the bomber were often combined in one aircraft, and heavy casualties had to be accepted due to antiaircraft fire from the ground.

Ground-based antiaircraft (AA) weaponry grew in strength as the war progressed. At high altitudes aircraft could be subjected to constant danger from time- or proximity-fused shells fired from large guns like the German 88mm. Lower down they could encounter a wall of automatic and semiautomatic gunfire from heavy machine guns, 20mm Oerlikons, 40mm Bofors, and the like. Major cities and industrial targets were protected by tightly integrated rings of searchlights, guns and control stations, all guided by radar, while both warships at sea and military formations on land carried large complements of AA guns with them wherever they went.

Overall, the air war increased in intensity as the conflict progressed, with Allied forces recovering from early losses to gain gradual ascendancy in a long war of attrition. When the breaking point came, the decline of Axis airpower was swift, and the closing months of the war in both the east and the west were characterized by almost unchallenged Allied air superiority over Axis soil. Axis targets came under attack not only from long-range multiengined bombers, but also from smaller aircraft flying from advanced landing

▲ RAF pilots rush toward their Hurricane fighters in the summer of 1940. Advances in radar and communications technology allowed fighter forces to be deployed rapidly from their bases to make last-minute interceptions of incoming raiders. As a result, it was often possible to break up bomber formations before they reached their targets.

▶ A German bomb-aimer mans the machine gun in the nose of his machine while other aircraft fly in formation beneath him. In 1940 Germany's bomber force was composed entirely of lightly armed two-engined aircraft. Even in tight formation its squadrons could not generate enough defensive firepower to protect them from heavy losses at the hands of attacking RAF fighters.

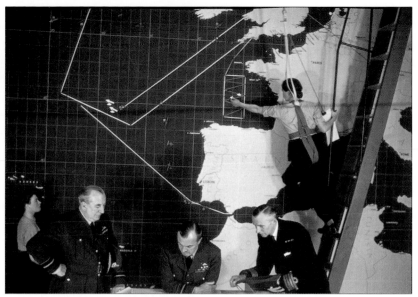

◀ The heart of the air–sea war: British naval and air force officers control operations in the eastern Atlantic. The combination of advanced detection and communications equipment allowed senior officers to monitor and control complicated multiservice operations in far-flung regions from control complexes a long way from the dangers of bombs and gunfire. Ultimate success was the product as much of radio/radar control as of frontline bravery and firepower.

strips just beyond the front or from carrier flight decks just off the coast.

Debate still rages about airpower's claims to be a war-winner in its own right, but there can be no doubt that it made a major contribution. It employed tens of thousands of aircraft to kill hundreds of thousands of people and inflict millions of dollars worth of damage. The dropping of two atomic bombs on Japan in August 1945 gave a sinister warning that in any future war the destruction would be even worse.

Attrition in the air: the Battle of Britain

The Battle of Britain, fought in the skies over southern England in the late summer and autumn of 1940, began as an attempt by the German air force to eliminate Britain's Royal Air Force as a prelude to the planned invasion of the island. As this objective proved elusive, and the invasion itself became a more distant prospect, the German campaign degenerated into an assault on the morale of the British people through the bombing of major population centers. At each stage of the

campaign the Germans failed, not so much because of poor planning or bad intelligence (although these were both factors of some importance), but because the forces at their disposal were not designed for the tasks in hand. They were also severely hampered by recent advances in aviation technology, which had greatly increased the capabilities of the British defenders.

The German air force had been designed first and foremost as a tactical air-support force for military operations on the Continent. It possessed no heavy bombers, and its medium bomber force of JU88s, Heinkel 111s, and Dornier 17s carried small bomb loads and light defensive armaments: they were in no way suited for long-range strategic operations in the face of heavy fighter opposition. The much vaunted JU87 Stuka dive-bomber proved almost useless over Britain and had to be withdrawn after heavy losses in early raids. Finally, the German fighter force could not give its bombers adequate support. The two-engined Messerschmitt Bf110 proved no match for its single-engined opponents, and while the excellent Messerschmitt Bf109 was in every way a match for the British Spitfires and Hurricanes, it lacked the fuel capacity to linger long in the combat zone.

On the other hand the near-simultaneous introduction of radar, integrated radio control of airborne units from the ground, and the fast, low-wing monoplane fighter allowed the British to mount a far more effective defense than would have been possible even a few years before. German air attacks could be detected as their aircraft took up formation over France, and fighter resources could be allocated and moved rapidly to contend with each threat as it developed. As a result, German raids could often be disrupted, if not completely broken up, before they reached their target. The British also enjoyed the added advantage of fighting over their own territory. This allowed pilots, who managed to escape unharmed from disabled aircraft by taking to their parachutes, to return to operations rather than languish in prisoner-of-war camps. It also exposed German aircraft to loss through antiaircraft fire.

Kamikaze Pilots

◄▲ The contest between man and mass machinery: a Japanese pilot (above) ties his nation's flag around his head before departure on a one-way journey to attack the enemy, and the US light carrier *Belleau Wood* (left) burns after being hit by a kamikaze off the Philippines in October 1944. Mass attacks by suicidally brave Japanese pilots exposed US carrier forces to constant danger and heavy damage, but even the mass sacrifice of men and aircraft could not offset the USA's huge material superiority. While damaged carriers were quickly repaired and replaced, the Japanese lost pilots and machines at a rate which their war-effort could not sustain.

German air commanders have been criticized for failing to pursue a coherent targeting policy, but in truth, few of the targets at their disposal were easily neutralized. Radar stations were small and notoriously difficult to put out of commission. Air fields near the coast could be made untenable, but defending fighters could be moved to bases further inland with only a marginal loss of effectiveness. Also, the British aircraft industry was well dispersed, with many of its factories located far to the north in the industrial Midlands. German intelligence persistently underestimated the combat strength and reserves of the RAF, but the more important factor here was simply that the British aircraft industry, more completely mobilized for war, was producing machines faster than its German equivalent.

German losses made their air force the real loser in the war of attrition. It takes nothing away from the RAF's reputation for gallant defense in the Battle of Britain to indicate that the odds against it were not as heavy as has usually been thought.

Air power in the ascendant: the Pacific, 1944–45
In 1944, after a year of steady but unspectacular progress in 1943, the American war-effort against Japan's Pacific empire accelerated. This was most clearly the case in the air war. With the arrival of a new generation of aircraft, a massive expansion of the carrier force, and the continuing growth and success of pilot-training programs, American aviation went from strength to strength. The Japanese case was the reverse. Air services remained heavily dependent on prewar designs of light construction that could not stand up to enemy firepower. Some new aircraft did appear, but were not manufactured in sufficient numbers to make any impact. The carrier force losses of 1942 were never made up, and 1944 saw the extinction of the remainder of the fleet. Worst of all, Japanese pilot-training programs, originally geared to produce small numbers of highly skilled aviators, never adjusted to the demands of the war. The flying skills of aircrews went into such steep decline that the quality of aircraft being flown was scarcely material.

Named "divine wind" after the typhoon that had destroyed a Mongol invasion fleet on its way to Japan in the Middle Ages, Japan's kamikaze pilots were the agents of a last-ditch effort to turn the tide of the Pacific War and save the homeland, yet again, from invasion. The kamikaze, drawing on self-sacrificial ideals, set out from base with the explicit intention of using his aircraft as a guided missile and immolating himself, to cause maximum destruction to the enemy.

The kamikaze campaign began on a small scale on the initiative of a local commander in late October 1944 during the closing stages of the Battle of Leyte Gulf. On their first mission the kamikazes successfully destroyed an American escort carrier, and a number of further successes (and exaggerated reports of others) seemed to provide a desperate Japanese high command with a solution to the US naval threat. In 1945, particularly during the long struggle for Okinawa – the last island barrier between the enemy and the homeland – the kamikaze campaign became the dominant strain in Japanese air policy, with pilots and planes being sacrificed in their hundreds.

The kamikazes inflicted heavy damage and severely shook US morale. They failed, however, to delay or deflect the Americans. Some carriers were temporarily put out of action, but the kamikazes failed to sink any major warships.

There were severe constraints on their effectiveness. The pilots were usually inexperienced volunteers. Their aircraft were not as efficient at destroying ships as the more conventional bomb or torpedo. Much of the damage done affected the superstructure or deck of the target vessel, not its hull or vital machinery. Finally, the inexperienced kamikaze pilots tended to attack the first enemy vessel they saw regardless of size or importance. In many cases this would be a destroyer or similar small craft on picket duty in the outward screen of the invasion force.

American superiority was graphically demonstrated during the Battle of the Philippines Sea in June 1944. While American carrier strike planes were mauling enemy surface units, their fighter aircraft all but annihilated the Japanese attempt to counterattack, in an air battle so one-sided as to earn it the nickname "the Marianas Turkey Shoot". This massacre destroyed Japanese carrier aviation for good. When the navy launched its massive effort to regain the initiative at Leyte Gulf in October 1944, it was so short of planes and pilots for its remaining carriers that they were used merely as a sacrificial decoy force to draw US carrier forces away from the battle area. This battle resulted in further heavy aircraft losses for the Japanese; it also witnessed the first systematic use of aircraft in the kamikaze role – a role in which the aircraft itself became a projectile to be crashed deliberately on its warship target.

In the Iwo Jima and Okinawa campaigns of 1945 the Japanese turned wholeheartedly to the kamikazes in a last-ditch effort to save the final barrier between the home islands and the enemy. Significant damage was inflicted on American naval forces, but it was never sufficient to stem the tide, and Japanese aircraft losses were so high as to leave few resources for more conventional missions, such as the provision of air cover for the giant battleship *Yamato* on its own one-way mission against enemy forces off Okinawa. In the last weeks of the war US and British carrier forces cruised with near-impunity just off the Japanese coast, striking at shore and naval targets in the face of only light and ineffective resistance.

While the naval air war was making its way inexorably toward Japan's shores, Japanese cities were coming under heavy attack from another direction. Using air bases in China and on captured Pacific islands, the Americans launched a strategic bombing offensive against enemy morale and industrial capacity. Strengthened by the arrival of the new B-29 Superfortress, this air assault inflicted massive damage. Under incendiary attack, Japan's lightly built cities proved veritable tinder-boxes. Japanese industry and transport disintegrated far more rapidly than had those of its ally, Germany, under similar attack. Unlike the Germans, the Japanese failed to develop an adequate home air defense system, partially through the sheer unavailability of aircraft and pilots. By the last months of the war aerial resistance to these raids had virtually ceased and the centers of many of Japan's cities had been razed to the ground. The final blow from the air came in early August 1945 when first Hiroshima and then Nagasaki were devastated by single atomic bombs dropped by B-29s. Convinced that further resistance was pointless, the Japanese surrendered, giving American air power the somewhat tainted distinction of being the first to force a modern industrial power's surrender without the necessity of an invasion. The bomber had played a more decisive role in the defeat of Japan than it had in Europe. The crucial difference (notwithstanding the atomic bomb) was that Japan, unlike Germany, did not possess the resilient infrastructure of the modern industrial state, and could not survive a prolonged aerial assault.

This pilot knew his job thoroughly and all those who watched him make his approach felt their mouths go dry. In less than a minute he would have attained his goal; there could be little doubt that he was to crash his machine on the deck of the Enterprise. *All the batteries were firing... but it came on, clearly visible, hardly moving, the line of its wings as straight as a sword.*

FROM USS ENTERPRISE
13 MAY 1945

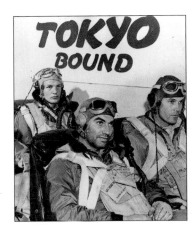

▲ US naval airmen are briefed for a carrier air attack on Japan in early 1945. Although Japanese air units could offer little effective resistance, the strain of even victorious air operations is clearly etched on the faces of these highly trained pilots.

◄ US B-29 bombers on a forward air base in the Mariana Islands. American successes in the naval air war in the Pacific brought the massive might of land-based airpower closer to Japan's shores. Operating from specially built bases, constructed and supplied on captured island groups through a massive logistical exercise, B-29s carried huge loads of high explosive and incendiary bombs directly to Japan's industrial heartland. As one city after another was razed by fire, Japanese air resistance weakened to the point that the bombers' defensive armament was reduced to allow the carriage of even heavier bomb loads.

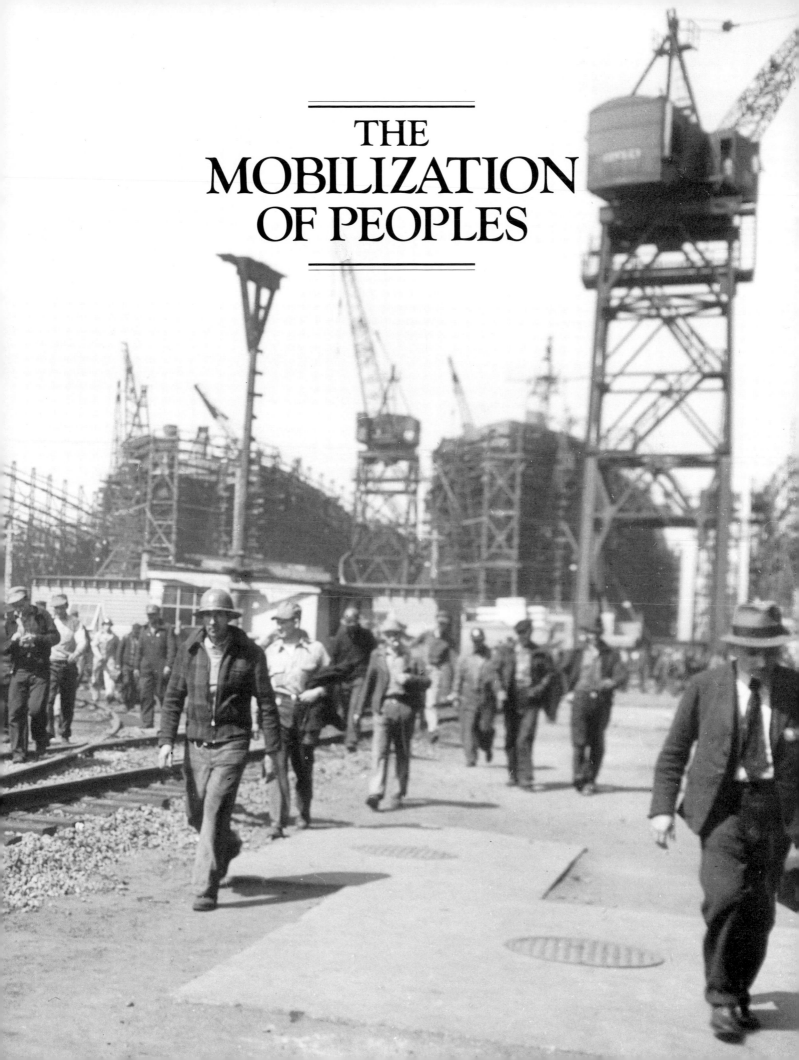

THE
MOBILIZATION
OF PEOPLES

Datafile

The Japanese economy showed remarkable resilience between 1937 and 1945 but the strains of the enormous war effort in China, the Pacific and Southeast Asia took their toll. The vulnerability of an island economy, heavily dependent upon imported energy and raw materials, was demonstrated starkly during the American onslaught between 1943 and 1945. By the summer of 1945 Japan was crippled.

Japanese oil stocks

▲ Oil reserves were built up from the mid-1930s so as to sustain the war effort for a limited period. Because Japan was so dependent on imorted oil, the Us oil embargo of July 1941 was a heavy blow. Stocks were rapidly depleted in the middle and latter stages of the war as Japan lost command of the sea and air.

Main industrial areas

Industrial centers

▲ The principal or home islands of Japan. The central island of Honshu has been most important in industrial development, particularly the area extending from Tokyo to Osaka (right) contains Japan's main coal fields. Much of Japan is so mountainous as to be useless for productive purposes.

Japanese retail prices

◄ The drive to achieve maximum production stimulated serious inflation. The war in China led to a doubling of retail prices between 1937 and 1941, before the start of war against the USA. Thereafter prices doubled again by 1944, a far worse record than the wartime inflation in the USA, UK and Germany.

▶ The American bombing campaign and large-scale evacuation temporarily reversed the long-term trend toward urbanization. The capital, Tokyo, suffered the greatest reduction in population, the former imperial capital, Kyoto, the least. Situated on or near the coast, Japan's major cities were easy to reach for US bombers.

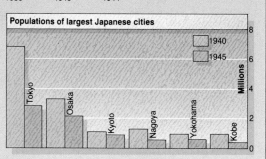

Populations of largest Japanese cities

Chronology

1937	**September** Neighborhood associations revived	**1943**
July Japanese invasion of China		**November** Munitions ministry created
1938	**1941**	**1944**
March All employment brought under government control	**April** Rice-rationing begins	**July** Resignation of Tojo
June Formation of Patriotic Industry Association	**October** Hideki Tojo prime minister	**1945**
	December 7 Japanese attack on Pearl Harbor; USA enters war	**March** USB-29s begin incendiary campaign against cities
1939	**December** Invasion of SE Asia begins	**May 8** VE Day; war in Europe ends
July National Conscription Ordinance to deploy workers	**1942**	**July** 10 pecent cut in all staple rations imposed
September Start of war in Europe	**April** US "Doolittle" bombing raid; losses of shipping begin	**August** Atomic bombs dropped on Hiroshima and Nagasaki; USSR invades Manchuria
1940	**August** US success at Guadalcanal	**August 15** Emperor Hirohito orders surrender: end of war
July Voluntary dissolution of political parties; formation of Imperial Rule Association	**October** Neighborhood associations take over rationing	

After the outbreak of the Sino-Japanese war in 1937, the Japanese government became more authoritarian. But, unlike Germany and Italy, the constitution continued to function and elections took place. Governments comprised a mixture of conservative bureaucrats, and active and retired generals and admirals. Their priority was to consolidate foreign and defense policies. Their aims inside Japan were to stimulate morale and unity, through loyalty to the emperor and commitment to the war effort, and by avoiding reliance upon non-Japanese ideologies and cultures. In theory the emperor's power had been restored in 1868 but in reality the government acted in the emperor's name. During the late 19th century State Shintoism was fostered officially and inculcated through the armed forces and the educational system. The emperor's divinity was given strong emphasis. He personified the essence of the nation and had to be obeyed. Failure to do so could lead to disgrace.

Wartime Japanese leaders were consistent in their aims, seeking above all Japanese leadership in Asia, which was expressed in such concepts as the "New Order in East Asia" and the "Greater East Asia Coprosperity Sphere". Prince Konoye, prime minister from 1937 to 1939 and again in 1940–41, advocated the end of party political struggles and the creation of a new spirit of national cohesion. In 1940 political parties formally dissolved themselves and were replaced by the Imperial Rule Assistance Association formed by Konoye. Superficially this resembled European fascist bodies but in reality it proved hollow and accomplished little. Dissenting party politicians paid lip service to the new trends and bided their time until a more sympathetic climate emerged. General Hideki Tojo, prime minister from 1941 to 1944, was the toughest leader of the wartime era and accumulated greater power through holding several different offices simultaneously. But Tojo had no thought of becoming a dictator and regarded himself as the servant, rather than the master, of the system. Limited criticism of the government could be expressed and this became more overt later in the war. The growing setbacks suffered by Japan from 1943 accentuated unease and led to Tojo's resignation in 1944. His successors realized that Japan could not hope to win but they could not consider unconditional surrender, which was demanded by the Allies.

The majority of Japanese gave loyal support to the war, but in the form of stoic endurance rather than fervent enthusiasm. The middle and later stages brought deprivation and hardship which led to the emergence of some discontent. Yet there was no challenge to the government. The trade unions had enjoyed little freedom before the war and were persecuted. Leftwing parties

JAPAN: CHALLENGE AND RESPONSE

The reorganization of
politics in wartime Japan

Japan's war aims

The success of the war
economy

Reluctance to involve
women in war production

Local organizations used
for sustaining morale

Repercussions of war
for children

had always been weak and were also persecuted. The Japanese police were zealous and brutal in investigating alleged subversion and it was prudent to evade their attention. A watch was kept on rightwing extremists but far more interest was shown in those suspected of socialist inclinations. Ironically the only revolt against the government came from a section of the army which mutinied against the emperor's decision to accept defeat in August 1945.

Expansion and decline in the war economy

From the late 19th century onward Japan's economic development had been remarkable. Industry had developed rapidly, to become predominant within the economy by the 1920s, though it was then hit hard by the depression of the 1930s. The agrarian sector remained large and was regarded as particularly important because rural Japan would preserve essential Japanese values, unlike the modernizing economy which had given rise to the hybrid character of the city. Japan's principal economic weakness was a shortage of vital raw materials.

Japan's invasion of Southeast Asia in 1941–42 gave access to oil, rubber, tin, bauxite, teak, rice

▼▶ Japan prepares for war and moves more closely toward Germany. In a military review, banners waving, Japanese officers express their enthusiasm and dedication in fulfilling the nation's mission (right). This Nazi emblem outside a German club, restaurant and meeting place in central Tokyo illustrates Japan's identification with the Axis powers (below).

▲ Women using machinery in the drive to maximize war production. Pressures for transformation are underlined, as traditional Japan and the kind of roles fulfilled by women were overtaken in the march to Armageddon. Women responded patriotically and wished to contribute more, yet were held back by social conventions linked with male dominance.

and other commodities. Efficient utilization of these resources required integration of dependent territories into the domestic economy, as had occurred with the development of Japanese control in Korea, Manchuria and northern China. In itself this assumed Japan could control sea and air so as to facilitate transport and coordination. In this they failed. From 1943 vast quantities of Japanese merchant shipping were sunk by American submarines. This, plus massive conventional bombing in 1944–45, crippled the economy.

Japan had made a swift recovery from the world economic depression of 1930–34. Production of pig iron almost doubled between 1929 and 1936 while that of steel nearly tripled. Thereafter production was greatly expanded achieving a total of 6.3 million tonnes of pig iron in 1942, nearly 9 million tonnes of ingot steel in 1943, and 6.25 million tonnes of finished steel in 1943. The coal industry boosted production significantly, attaining a total, combined with net imports, of almost 66 million tonnes in 1940. Thereafter production declined to a combined total of nearly 52 million tonnes in 1944 and then to 32 million in 1945. Output in 1941 was one quarter of the UK's total and one ninth of the USA's. Coalfields were inconveniently situated in the northern island of Hokkaido and in the southern island of Kyushu. Production was stimulated in Taiwan (Formosa), Korea, Manchuria and north China–Inner Mon-

golia with creditable achievements. Overall, however, Japan could not compete adequately in heavy industry with the USA. Heroic efforts were made in shipbuilding but Japan experienced disturbing losses in merchant shipping from the summer of 1942. The percentage of vessels built and sunk during the war reached 42 in 1943 and 45 in 1944. In the course of the Pacific war a total of 38 percent of new shipping was sunk.

Japan's extraordinary attempt to secure full economic mobilization can be seen in statistics for the growth of aircraft, army ordnance, navy ordnance, naval ships, merchant ships and motor vehicles. The peak level was achieved in September 1944, but thereafter a catastrophic fall occurred in consequence of the air offensive, sea blockade and concomitant lack of resources. The price of increased production was a decline in employment in agriculture (from 48 percent in 1930 to 42 percent in 1940) and inflation which reached serious levels. The retail price index reached 175 in 1940 compared with 101 in the United States and 104 in Germany. The government tried to depress it with laws to curb excess profits, and price ceilings, but these were ineffective. Cumulative pressures produced by rising national expenditure and insufficient resources produced a black market, most noticeable in food supplies, especially vegetables, seafood and rice. In 1944 black-market prices were about ten times the official ones. With certain commodities the divergence could be much greater: by the end of 1944 rice had reached nearly 50 times its legal price level. Consumer goods fell rapidly as part of national production, from 40 percent in 1941 to 17 percent by March 1945. Most Japanese used the black market for some of their requirements.

Mobilization of the population developed from 1937, but the increase in civilian employment was small: between 1937 and 1942 it rose from 31 to 33 million. But there were notable changes in employment patterns. Women and girls replaced male farmers who had been called up for the army or other work. The total engaged in commerce fell from almost 5 million in 1937 to 2.5 million in 1944. In manufacturing an additional 2.3 million people were employed with nearly 300,000 more in mining. Men between 16 and 40 and women between 16 and 25 were placed on labor registers but only males were conscripted into the armed forces. About 1.5 million men were conscripted for factories. Later in the war the age of registration was lowered and those employed in essential industries were prevented from switching jobs.

Women in wartime Japan

Before 1945 Japanese women occupied a strictly subordinate role in politics. They did not have the vote and attempts to obtain enfranchisement had made little progress. Within industry women were traditionally employed in textile manufacturing, usually for a short term before marriage. During the war female employment expanded, but only within traditional areas. Many labored in fields and markets, in return for low wages.

Social pressures prevented the transfer of women to jobs with higher status and better pay. Nor would men tolerate the promotion of women to more senior positions. Fewer than 1 million women obtained jobs during the war. Shortages of labor were met by transferring men from less essential areas of the economy to important jobs and by importing Koreans and Chinese as laborers. The employment of students and old men was also encouraged.

General Tojo resembled Hitler in disliking an increase in female employment. He told the diet in October 1943 that Japan should not emulate the UK and USA by compelling women to enter into industry. He said, "the weakening of the family system would be the weakening of the nation ... we are able to do our duties here in the diet only because we have wives and mothers at home". His emphasis reflected the magnitude of the war struggle and pressures from the armed forces for population growth.

The birth rate had to be increased, if possible by as much as almost one half. Propaganda urged earlier marriages and government policy dictated a more generous approach by companies to young fathers. As in Mussolini's Italy and Stalin's USSR, prolific mothers were rewarded. However, the birth rate for 1943–44 showed no increase on the 1940–41 figure of about 2.25 million, and thereafter in fact declined significantly. The attempt by the state to achieve a major increase in the birth rate failed.

◀ The government's bid to enlist civilian support extended to children. Here, girls from Tokyo high schools present aircraft-sound detectors to the war ministry.

▼ Pressures on the economy led to intensified savings campaigns. These were important in stimulating savings and in developing the general theme of war mobilization. This poster shows the savings bond drive supported by the ministry of finance and banks.

Japanese Children and War

▲ Evacuation of children from major cities in Japan resembled evacuation in Europe, as bewildered or stoical children departed for temporary homes. The banner in the upper picture ("Evacuated children let's be good friends...") emphasizes the importance of friendship. The militaristic impact in education emerges in the lower picture where boys are undergoing training for military service.

Japanese children were taught to accept arduous work and to show deep respect for the emperor. Individual desires were subordinated to the requirements of the nation. Militarism was pervasive. All children at school in the 1930s grew up against a national background of conflict and exposure to expansionist rhetoric. Great emphasis was placed on the heroic achievements and self-sacrifice of the imperial forces and these had to be emulated. Boys were taught that there could be no higher calling than the military. The idealized figure of the samurai warrior was used to stimulate interest in war.

Japan was opposed by avaricious foes and must defend itself. To accomplish this aim children must accept basic foods rather than relative luxuries and diminished choice in toys. Teachers stressed imperial values and their authority could be reinforced through harsh punishment. Children were influenced by the passion and splendor of militaristic demonstrations amidst the wars in China, the Pacific and Burma. The impact of war communicated itself most forcibly and poignantly with the absence of fathers, elder brothers and other relatives on war service. Many never returned and boys and girls were told that this was inevitable as part of the imperial mission.

While mothers usually bore the brunt of childrearing, circumstances accentuated maternal dominance. Exigencies of war entailed more use of child labor and registration of boys as young as 12 for possible employment. The direct horrors of war were conveyed most savagely through the intensive Allied bombing campaigns in 1944–45. Children were evacuated from large cities and sent to small towns or rural areas. The psychological repercussions of removal from the home environment were profound and caused much distress. Education continued in the cities amidst adverse conditions, sometimes with classes held in underground bomb shelters. Children brought up to believe in the unique progress of Japan leading to the culmination of the imperial mission experienced defeat in August 1945. It was even more bewildering to them than to their parents.

Morale at a local level

To control or influence local opinion, the government attempted to work through local bodies. In September 1940 an edict established community councils and neighborhood associations throughout Japan. They were instructed to achieve moral, social and economic cohesion so as to motivate people correctly. Neighborhood associations were smaller groups, consisting of 10–15 households. In July 1942 a total of 1,323,473 associations existed. In the six principal cities nearly 300,000 associations functioned in April 1942 with around 11 families per association. Associations were instructed to handle local defense, cooperate with councils, prevent crime, support savings movements, and pursue related issues. The most vital single step for councils and associations occurred in October 1942 when the government told them to organize food and clothing rations. Thus the daily lives of all families were affected.

In rural areas leadership came from local elites. In urban areas difficulty was found in securing suitable leaders. Women participated prominently in neighborhood associations and men dominated community councils. Ordinary people were more aware of the work of associations and thought more highly of them than the councils.

A large increase in social legislation also took place, stimulated by the necessity of safeguarding health standards in wartime. In 1938 a welfare ministry was created to supervise medical and social welfare. Measures were introduced to assist mothers and children, orphans and the elderly. Workmen's compensation was improved and hours of work for laborers were defined.

In July 1938 an important health insurance law was introduced. National health insurance associations were created to cater for communities. Families had the choice of joining and premiums were financed by the state and those insured, the latter depending on means. The numbers of insured grew swiftly so that by 1942 almost 16 million people were insured via nearly 4,500 associations. In 1945 these figures had risen to more than 41 million and over 10,000 respectively. Ordinary Japanese benefited appreciably. Public health centers were set up in 1937–38 with the aim of improving general health and sanitary awareness. The impact in rural areas was especially significant. Success was seen in controlling disease including tuberculosis. A health system of basic adequacy existed during the war but younger doctors were usually required for military service.

The positive features of Japan's domestic experience during the war included arduous self-sacrifice, dedication, and acceptance of national objectives. Social cohesion was promoted through enforced cooperation but workers suffered adversely, earning one third less in real terms in 1944 than in 1939 as a consequence of inflation. Absenteeism and poor-quality work in certain spheres showed dissatisfaction with the war. Absenteeism reached 10 percent in war plants in 1943 and was probably higher in 1944. This must be seen in perspective. In total the Japanese people revealed remarkable loyalty to the war-effort, equal to or excelling that seen in the UK or Germany.

▲ The grim reality of war: ambulances convey war injured to hospitals after being landed in ports. The procession of vehicles proceeds through a street market and the citizens betray no surprise at the sight.

▼ Neighborhood associations fostered communal activities and women played an increasingly influential role in them. Some of these children are still helpless infants.

Datafile

The German war machine produced extremely impressive results, supporting the armies in several theaters of war. Slave labor from occupied countries and Germans working long hours helped to compensate for the chronic manpower shortage. Munitions production grew markedly in spite of increasing Allied bombing, with some factories relocated to small towns or rural areas to try to evade the bomber.

Foreign workers

Tank production

▶ With the enlistment of German men, the domestic war-effort depended increasingly on foreign workers. Civilians numbered over 5 million by 1944, POWs almost 2 million. By contrast, the German female labor force remained virtually constant, with fewer than 4 million women industrial workers in 1944, as in 1939.

Women in industry

▲ German tank production increased almost six-fold between 1940 and 1944, in spite of a diminishing labor force. This remarkable achievement owed much to huge investment in industrial plant during the war. It was made possible by the expropriation of plant, machinery and, especially, manpower from occupied countries.

▶ Allied bombing raids became heavier in 1943 as fighters with an increasing operational range were developed. By early 1944 they could defend bombers against German aircraft almost anywhere over the Reich, bringing strategic targets in southern and eastern (as well as northern and western) Germany within range.

Exposure to bombing

Range of allied bombers Nov 1943

Chronology

1939	1942	1944
September 1 Germany invades Poland; start of war in Europe	**January** Wannsee Conference plans extermination of Jews	**June** Allied invasion of Normandy; economy concentrates on quantitative production
September War Economy Regulations introduced	**February** Albert Speer becomes armaments minister	**July 20** Assassination attempt on Hitler fails
1940	**April** Central Planning Committee formed: economy to be mobilized for attrition rather than Blitzkrieg; priority given to qualitative weapons' superiority	**October** *Volkssturm* created
April–June Germany defeats: Norway, Denmark, Low Countries and France		**1945**
1941	**1943**	**February** Allied bombing of Dresden
March "Women for Victory" voluntary campaign launched	**January** Labor conscription for women aged 17–45	**April** Red Army reaches Berlin;
June 22 Invasion of Russia begins	**February** German army at Stalingrad surrenders; Goebbels' "Total War" speech at the Berlin *Sportpalast*	**April 30** Hitler commits suicide
November German troops halted before Moscow		**May** Soviet army enters Berlin; German army surrenders
		May 8 VE Day: war in Europe ends

In Germany, as in all belligerent countries, the home front was vital to the waging of war. Hitler believed this and was determined to maintain domestic support for the war effort. He was obsessed by the need to avoid a recurrence of the "stab in the back", the alleged betrayal of the German army in 1918 by hungry and demoralized civilians, incited by "Jews and socialists". The means were provided by the fruits of Hitler's conquests: occupied Europe was forced to supply foodstuffs, raw materials and labor which cushioned the home front for most of the war.

This strategy was vindicated: throughout the war there was virtually no open defeatism, far less popular revolt. But that did not signify enthusiasm for the war. The memory of World War I remained horrifically vivid. Germany's early victories were popular, but there was clear evidence of war-weariness virtually from the start. Even the victorious campaigns in Poland and western Europe in 1939–40 brought casualties and grief. The Russian campaign (launched in 1941), in particular, caused deep anxiety. Especially after the Germans were defeated at Stalingrad early in 1943, there was increasing despair, but also numbing apathy as reality became too terrible to face. Together with increasing Nazi terror, this ensured that Hitler's regime would not be overthrown from within. Germany would have to be defeated by *foreign* foes.

Political stability in Germany was achieved at the expense of foreigners: prisoners of war and civilian workers imported from occupied countries were used as slave labor; within occupied countries a low living standard was imposed. This accorded with Nazi views about the German "master race" which would dominate "inferior peoples", especially those in eastern Europe. Exploitation of occupied countries and of over 7 million foreign workers in Germany allowed the regime to defer or avoid unpopular policies, like conscripting women into war service, or reducing Germans' rations to, or below, subsistence levels. It also disguised contradictions within a system operated by incompetent, self-interested and feuding policy-makers.

Between 1939 and 1945 more than 11 million German men were conscripted into the armed forces. The German civilian population therefore consisted increasingly of older men, children, youths and – the largest single group – women. They felt the impact of war in differing ways, depending on their family circumstances, where they lived, and whether they were employed. By 1945 few had escaped the effects of the war: to that extent, it was a "total war". But even in 1942 victory was still widely expected, with the prospect of indefinite German rule over a continent-wide helot empire. The long road to defeat in

GERMANY: HITLER'S HOME FRONT

1943–45 showed that Germany lacked the resources to hold down its empire at the same time as repelling the forces of the Allies.

The impact of labor shortages

Two major problems afflicted the German war effort: limited materials and shortage of manpower. Resources were already being diverted from domestic consumption to the military before 1939, and further potential for this was limited. While the war necessitated an escalation in armaments production, supplies of food and other essentials had to be maintained to keep German civilians loyal and ready to support the war effort. This was perceived as a short-term problem until plunder from vanquished countries supplied Germany's needs, material and human. By 1939 there was little surplus labor within Germany, since rapid recovery from the Great Depression had absorbed all who wished or needed to work. Labor shortages appeared in critical areas even before the war, while high rates of women's employment in industry, commerce and agriculture indicated that the reserves of willing female labor were already exhausted.

▼ The myth of popular obedience and support for the war-effort was maintained throughout the war. Rallies like this, in the Berlin *Sportpalast* in June 1943, were carefully stage-managed and publicized. Goebbels and Speer used this occasion to stiffen morale among the Party faithful, at a time when the tide of war was turning against Germany.

The shortage of labor on the home front affected businesses large and small. As men were conscripted, factories lost large numbers of workers, including those with special skills. In return, they received substitutes – including foreign workers – who were often unwilling, unfamiliar with the work, and therefore less productive. Almost three million men left industrial work between 1939 and 1944, but the number of women rose only slightly.

In other sectors of employment, including agriculture, trade and commerce, and domestic service, women's numbers actually declined. Even with a doubling of the number of women employed in administration, the total number of employed women in September 1944 was only slightly higher than in May 1939 (14.9 million, compared with 14.6 million). In this "total war" many women, especially from the prosperous middle class, continued their prewar life of relative idleness. The allowance paid to the wife of a serving soldier enabled her to withstand government efforts to attract or shame her into war-related employment. Even after the introduction of labor conscription for women in January

▶ At first, Hitler's regime relied mainly on propaganda to try to bring nonemployed women into work. This slogan, "You help, too!", was typical, urging women to support their men by working in factory or hospital or on a farm. This convinced few while Germany appeared invincible. Conscripting women into war work was debated virtually from the start. But Hitler's reluctance to impose unpopular measures prevailed until the position began to deteriorate, early in 1943.

cruit women into war work less vital, especially in the early part of the war. Nevertheless, the failure to recruit women equitably for war work was one of the most divisive issues in wartime Germany. Scathing attacks were made on leisured women who had all day to shop for scarce goods, while tired working women faced queues and disappointment at the end of a long day.

Many Germans worked in small concerns, for example, family-run shops or farms. The loss of even one adult male worker – a family member or a hired hand – could have a dramatic effect on a business. Where a wife was left in charge, with the burdens of war economy regulations in addition to customary chores, the family shop might close or the farm go into decline. The employment of a servant at home could release a wife to run a business, which helps to account for there being over a million domestic servants during the war. A small farm might receive assistance from young women enrolled in the Labor Service (a compulsory scheme to indoctrinate the young and provide a pool of cheap labor). But the demands of the Labor Service camp, with its duties, parades and classes, curtailed the time available for work. Farmers much preferred to be allocated a foreign worker.

1943, many managed to avoid it, to the disgust of those who had no choice but to work.

It is clear that many middle-class women genuinely dreaded the prospect of factory work. Hitler was determined not to antagonize actual or potential supporters by enforcing an unpopular policy. Resentment at home would – as in 1914–18, he believed – be communicated to soldiers at the front, and sap their morale. The "stab-in-the-back" myth thus had its effect, while the availability of foreign labor made the need to re-

Supplies and distribution

In 1936 the Four Year Plan gave official priority to rearmament and the drive for self-sufficiency in certain raw materials and foodstuffs over the production and import of consumer goods. While this policy was only partially enforced, the replacement of imported goods by indigenous alternatives was strongly encouraged. Nevertheless, German industry continued to depend on foreign imports, notably ironore from Sweden, which provided 40 percent of Germany's needs in

Foreign Workers

Even before 1939 full employment in Germany provided jobs for 300,000 foreigners. Then came Polish prisoners of war and civilian conscripts and, in 1940, French, Belgian and Dutch POWs. After the invasion of the USSR in 1941, hundreds of thousands of *Ostarbeiter* ("eastern workers") were sent to Germany. In the west, there was "voluntary" migration from now depleted industrial centers to Germany's expanding war industries. But increasingly from 1942 coercion was used in western as well as eastern Europe, to provide substitutes for enlisted Germans. From 3 million in 1941, the number of foreign workers in Germany rose to 7 million in 1944, as 20 percent of the labor force. They were fairly evenly divided between agriculture and industry. The French formed the largest group of skilled workers in industry, while unskilled heavy work fell to the *Ostarbeiter*. Poles were often deployed in agriculture, providing vital assistance on small farms which had lost workers to the armed forces. Later, some were even managing farms where no German male labor remained. Foreign labor, male and female, was invaluable to the war effort.

◀ Foreign workers in a German arms factory, 1943.

◀ Hitler's reluctance to conscript female labor left the task of recruiting women for voluntary work to the Nazi women's organization (*NS Frauenschaft*). But even this attracted few, and in 1940 the average effort put in by each volunteer amounted to one hour per week. The regime depended mostly on small-scale, local enterprises, like this sewing circle in Bayreuth in 1941. With German troops stranded in their first Russian winter, in 1941–42, Nazi Party agencies like the NSF and the Nazi welfare organization (NSV) supervised collections of warm clothes and the knitting of socks and comforters. They also provided emergency aid for air-raid victims and welfare work among evacuees from bombed-out cities. But this was all piecemeal, local and uncoordinated effort. Some women preferred work with the Red Cross or the air-raid protection service, partly because they were not run by Party agencies like the NSF or the NSV.

1940 and still around 25 percent during 1941–44. The conquest in 1940–41 of countries producing essential minerals brought Germany ironore from Lorraine (annexed from France); manganese and oil from the Soviet Union; nickel from Greece and Yugoslavia. Friendly countries supplied other goods, including oil from Romania, wolfram from Spain and Portugal, chrome from Turkey. In addition, Germany's own rich coal deposits enabled it to manufacture synthetic oil and rubber, but these were costly processes which deprived domestic consumers of adequate coal supplies. Once German forces were in retreat (from mid-1943) and resources in the shrinking empire inaccessible, these synthetic goods were vital, if increasingly insufficient. But especially under Albert Speer, as minister for armaments and munitions from 1942 to 1945, Germany's capacity to produce heavy industrial goods was formidable.

Throughout the war, civilians faced rationing and shortages. From the end of August 1939 some foodstuffs were rationed, and at frequent intervals rations were reduced and more goods – for example, soap and clothing – brought under rationing control. For "normal consumers", food rations remained limited but adequate until 1944–45, by which time few goods were unrationed and

many commodities completely unavailable. People in special categories, like German workers in heavy industry or pregnant women, received extra rations, while foreign workers received smaller amounts of poorer quality food.

Extra rations might be distributed, on a local basis, in the event of a particularly good crop or to boost morale after a heavy bombing raid. But, otherwise, rations were steadily decreased. Controlling distribution through rationing did not prevent shortages becoming more acute. In winter 1939–40 there was a coal crisis because of transportation problems. Hoarding, bartering and an active black market removed goods from the official economy. Together, rationing, shortages and the black market caused great resentment and a decline in morale.

Other government economic controls, too, were unpopular. Taxation was increased both to raise extra funds and to dampen consumer demand. But the additional "war supplement" tax created problems for small businesses, some of which closed for the duration of the war. Agricultural production was regulated, with regional boards set up to collect and distribute produce such as eggs and milk. This was intended to pace distribution, to avoid periodic shortages, but rural producers greatly resented regulation and

The mood among the working class here is very bad at present! One hears remarks that are very reactionary, provoked by 1) price and wage developments, and 2) the food situation. People from regions endangered by air attacks have been with us for weeks and months now; they can afford the best meals on meatless days and pay cut-throat, profiteering prices for foodstuffs under the counter. It's the working population which has to bear the entire brunt of the economic struggle.

NAZI PARTY OFFICIAL
IN SOUTHERN GERMANY
JULY 1941

▲ Bombing of German cities damaged not only buildings but also services like gas, electricity and water. People then had to queue for a bucket of water. Bomb damage enhanced opportunities for black marketeers, who had exploited shortages from the start. They hoarded goods and then sold or bartered with them when supplies were low and prices high. They also stole, forged or falsified ration cards.

tried hard to sabotage it. Arrests, followed by fines or imprisonment, failed to deter others from breaching the war economy regulations.

Increasingly, civilians stood in queues for staple foodstuffs, exchanging grumbles and blaming the government for failing to eradicate the black market. Security service agents mingled with shoppers and reported their grievances. Monitoring the public mood, by means of a plethora of government and Nazi Party agencies, was regarded as vital for avoiding the risk of a "stab in the back" through disaffection. There was particular anxiety about the susceptibility of the industrial working class to this, and sometimes unpopular measures were rescinded. For example, the wage freeze introduced at the start of the war was quickly abandoned because of protests from employers and Nazi Gauleiters about absenteeism and deteriorating work discipline. To try to raise morale, a state housing program and improved social welfare benefits were promised for when the war was over. But this did not meet specific grievances about the way in

which the better-off could evade consumption restrictions and war work.

Germany under pressure 1942–45

The absence of men at the front disrupted family life, put family businesses at risk, and meant constant worry among the relatives and friends of servicemen. Conscription and military casualties touched most families. Three million German soldiers, sailors and airmen were killed and many more injured.

In the second half of the war, the major threat to civilians came from aerial bombardment. There had been sporadic daylight air raids in 1940 and 1941. But from spring 1942 Allied bombing of German cities became frequent and systematic. Northern ports like Lübeck, Hamburg and Bremen, and western industrial cities like Cologne, Düsseldorf, Essen and Duisburg, bore the brunt at first. But by summer 1943 the bombers were reaching southern cities like Munich and Stuttgart, where they inflicted heavy damage on civilians as well as on known industrial complexes. To continue vital production in safety, factories were dismantled and then reassembled in forest clearings, or even underground.

Life under bombing meant not merely terror but also added discomfort. Sleepless nights in air-raid shelters were followed by a day's work and queueing for food. Worse, it could mean the loss of home and possessions, although the government paid compensation. Bombing of north-western towns led to the evacuation of women and children to the rural south. As Allied bombing intensified, evacuees from central and southern German towns and cities, too, were sent to rural areas which were less at risk. Billeting town-dwellers on the rural population often bred hostility between two kinds of lifestyle and expectations.

In the face of these increasing hardships, the government tried to maintain and raise morale through propaganda. After 1933 Germans became inured to constant, repetitive and mind-numbing propaganda, but the war brought a renewed campaign to try to maintain morale and elicit support for the war effort. Although the outbreak of war had not been welcomed, the early victories were hailed as the just settlement of Germany's grievances. New campaigns, however,

were unwelcome, especially the invasion of the Soviet Union in June 1941. The failure to win quickly in Russia, after victory had seemed both assured and imminent in late 1941, led to disenchantment and apathy, and to diminishing faith in and respect for Hitler from 1942.

But popular revolt was not on the agenda. Civilians faced the obstacles of everyday life with resentful resignation and harassed anxiety. There were instances of disorder and lawlessness, but these mostly involved crowds of consumers competing for commodities like coal or fruit when a delivery was made; or it might mean people plundering freight trains or stealing agricultural produce from the fields where it grew.

Germans fought for Hitler's cause to the end, especially on the Eastern Front where fear of the advancing Red Army was fueled by Nazi propaganda about "Bolshevik atrocities". There was also fear of being subjected to the same appalling treatment that Germans had inflicted on Soviet soldiers and civilians in 1941–44. In the west and south, the arrival of American forces in spring 1945 was welcomed. Yet SS officers tried to enforce resistance to the last by summarily executing "defeatists" who called for an end to struggle, pointless as it had become by March 1945.

At present, the air war dominates people's minds and does most to undermine their faith in a change of fortunes. The enemy's constant attacks have made a deep impression. Everyone is convinced that worse is yet to come. There is growing anxiety that, once the cities are annihilated, the smaller towns, too, will be destroyed. Low-flying raids cause particularly deep concern. There are frequent complaints about the shortage of air-raid shelter space for the civilian population.

SECURITY SERVICE REPORT
MAY 1944

German Resistance

From 1933 opponents of Hitler's regime either fled Germany, worked there in difficult illicit conditions, or were apprehended by the Gestapo. Socialists and communists, particularly, suffered this fate; but liberals, pacifists and feminists, too, were suppressed. Of the few attempts at a viable coup, only the bomb plot of 20 July 1944 had clear potential. It was the climax of a conspiracy by dissident army officers, former diplomats and politicians, and some socialists and clergymen. Its timing, soon after D Day, has drawn accusations that fear of military defeat was their motive. But many had been involved since 1938; their earlier attempts to kill Hitler

had been aborted, often at the last minute. In wartime, opponents faced the additional hazard of being labeled traitors. The burden of resistance to Hitler fell largely on conservatives and soldiers who had earlier collaborated with him, because they had better cover than open opponents. Alarmed by Hitler's war-mongering and sickened by German wartime atrocities, they joined a few former labor leaders and individual Protestant and Catholic clergy in conspiring rather ineffectually against Hitler, more to demonstrate that there was "another Germany" than in the hope of actually succeeding.

◄ On 20 July 1944 a bomb placed close to Hitler in his eastern HQ at Rastenburg by Count Claus von Stauffenberg exploded. The operations room was shattered and injuries sustained, but Hitler emerged almost unscathed. The plotters were quickly apprehended. The refusal of more than a handful of officers to support them (although a great many more knew about the plot) testified to the terror felt by senior soldiers at the prospect of Hitler's vengeance should the plot fail. Their fears were vindicated: around 5,000 people, many merely relatives of the conspirators, were executed in the wake of 20 July. There were no more attempts from within Germany to remove Hitler.

Datafile

UK statistics can deceive the unwary. The "United Kingdom" government was responsible for foreign affairs and defense, but "Northern Ireland" had home rule in domestic matters. Within "Great Britain", Scotland had separate systems of law and education. Foreigners tended to refer to the whole Kingdom as "England" – yet in football Wales, Scotland and Northern Ireland all fielded "national" teams.

UK munitions production

Index (1939=100)

800 700 600 500 400 300 200 100

752

1939 1942 1945

UK external liabilities

Pounds (millions)

700 600 500 400 300 200 100 80

647

1939 1942 1945

▼ **Indictable offences known to the English and Welsh police rose sharply. (The Scottish pattern was similar.) The image of a nation united in self-sacrifice must be heavily qualified: 940,000 working days were lost in strikes in 1940, 3,714,000 in 1944. The latter figure was high by prewar standards.**

▶ **On the graph averaging quarterly production figures, the UK's commitment to munitions production peaks impressively. But the imported supplies and military expenses had to be paid for. During the war the UK suffered an enormous loss of wealth, of which debts as sterling liabilities were only part.**

Offenses in England/Wales

Thousands

500 400 300 200 100 0

1939 1942 1945

▶ **The decanting of child evacuees from likely bombing targets into the countryside was based partly on false assumptions, as the map shows. Sussex (in the southeast) received a lot, but by mid-1940 it was virtually in the front line. Plymouth, later heavily bombed, was a "neutral" area from which evacuation was not supported.**

Reception areas of evacuees in England and Wales

- Town bombed 1940
- Reception areas

Newcastle
Sunderland
Middlesbrough
Hull
Liverpool
Manchester
Sheffield
Birmingham
Coventry
Norwich
Swansea
Ipswich
Cardiff
Bristol
Bath
London
Southampton
Canterbury
Exeter
Portsmouth
Plymouth

Chronology

1939

March
UK abandons Appeasement and offers guarantees to Poland and other countries

June
Women's Land Army formed

August
Emergency Powers (Defence) Act passed

September 1
Germany invades Poland; start of war in Europe; National Service (Armed Forces) Act passed

September
Internment of aliens begins; first wave of evacuation

1940

January
Rationing begins

April
German invasion of Norway

May
Chamberlain resigns; Churchill becomes prime minister; Germany invades France

July
Evacuation from Dunkirk completed; Local Defence Volunteers reformed as Home Guard; free milk for mothers and small children

August
Battle of Britain begins

September
London Blitz begins

October
Hitler postpones invasion of UK

1941

March
Mobilization of labor by Registration and Essential Work Order; US Lend-Lease Act gives aid to Allies

1942

January
First American GIs arrive

December 1
"Beveridge Plan" published

1943

May
Axis forces surrender in Tunisia; end of war in Africa

1944

June
Allied invasion of Normandy; V1 missiles fall in England

1945

May 8
VE Day; end of war in Europe

July
Churchill resigns; Attlee forms Labour government

September 2
VJ Day; end of war in Pacific

The human story of the UK "people's war" has long been told as one of simple triumph. Never before had ordinary people participated so wholeheartedly in a war and with such a glorious result. According to this view, the war can be narrated as follows.

The UK entered the war on 3 September 1939 under a Conservative prime minister, Neville Chamberlain, who had no will to fight. For months people endured the discomfort of conscription, evacuation, the nightly "blackout" of windows and so on, but very little happened. Then disaster struck in the spring of 1940, first in Norway (see p. 27), then on the Western Front (see p. 28). As the People wished, Chamberlain was overthrown by a revolt of members of parliament from his own party and was replaced by a man of indomitable courage and charismatic oratory. Winston Churchill (known as "Winnie") brought leaders from the Labour and Liberal Parties into his new coalition government. After the fall of France (22 June 1940), heroic effort in the Battle of Britain (Britain's "Finest Hour" according to Churchill), supporting the RAF's brave fighter pilots, thwarted the intended German invasion. First London, then city after city, endured bombing raids, but morale did not falter. The UK "stood alone" – but in 1941 found mighty allies, first in the USSR, then in the USA. After massive effort in industry and agriculture, enduring living conditions which were more and more austere, British civilians saw the Allies triumph. The British People had Saved Democracy.

The UK's unmatched mobilization

Certain statistics support this heroic account. Between 1940 and 1944 The UK mobilized its resources with a thoroughness unmatched by any of its allies, or by Germany. In June 1944, at the time of D Day, the USA had drawn 40 percent of its people into the armed forces or civilian "war work". In Britain 33 percent were in "war work" alone, and the combined total was 55 percent. Employment in "war industries" had been raised at the expense of civilian needs. While labor was directed into engineering, chemicals and other work connected with munitions, employment in consumer goods industries slumped, and much of what remained was devoted to supplying the needs of the armed forces, or producing goods for export which helped pay, in small part, the huge cost of the war effort.

Not even Stalin's USSR went so far in conscripting women. By 1943 it was almost impossible for a woman under 40 to avoid "war work" – unless she had heavy family responsibilities or was looking after a war worker billeted on her. By 1944 women formed 48 percent of the civil service. The proportion of women in

THE UK: A DEMOCRACY AT WAR

engineering and vehicle building rose from 9 to 34 percent. Women in agriculture more than doubled, to 204,000 – and "Land Girls" did farm tasks hitherto performed almost entirely by men. An ex-hairdresser won a horse-plowing competition against a field of men. In July 1943 nearly 40,000 Italian prisoners of war were also at work in the fields. British civilians were exhorted to "Dig for Victory" in their scanty spare time. By 1943 there were 1.4 million allotments, an increase of 75 percent on the prewar figure. Hen-keeping and pig-rearing expanded likewise. The islands were besieged. The British had to feed themselves. U-boats prowled in the Atlantic, and in the worst year, 1943, the UK lost 833 merchant vessels. Bread and potatoes increasingly dominated the diet.

Food rationing, introduced early in the war, intensified. At a peak, in August 1942, one adult could hope for roughly half a kilogram (1lb) of butcher's meat a week: children got less. This was supplemented by 115g (4oz) of bacon or ham, 225g (8oz) of sugar, 225g of fats (of which 115

must be margarine, only 55g (2oz) could be butter) – and so on. Eggs were in especially short supply – the average person might get 30 a year – but the State was careful to ensure that expectant and nursing mothers and children received more (maybe three a week), and a half liter (1 pint) of milk per day. Rationing was perceived by the public as both necessary and fair.

In 1942, when a system of "points" rationing had been extended to canned and dried foods, breakfast cereals, chocolate, biscuits and other groceries, and soap was rationed for the first time, Sir Stafford Cripps, returning from his post as ambassador to the USSR, competed for a while with Churchill himself in popularity. He was a vegetarian and teetotaler and stood for more austerity, not less.

Getting home after long hours of work, perhaps having queued on the way first for food, then for scarce public transport, people went out to "Dig for Victory" or serve in Civil Defence, or train with the Home Guard, affectionately known as "Dad's Army". (It was founded in 1940 to fight

The apparent triumph of British society in war

Statistics that support the argument: working women and industrial production

The vogue for planning

Social services in wartime

Two views about wartime Britain

Bevin and trade unionism

▼ This Land Girl was employed on a drainage project in the summer of 1943. The image suggests that women are doing very tough farmwork. Is it a smile or grimace? The side-view, "Socialist Realist" style permits either interpretation.

▲ Women, mannishly dressed for industrial work, are manufacturing barrage balloons. These were still doing useful work in 1942, when this picture was taken, though the heaviest air attacks were long over. In that year the Germans carried out a destructive air raid on Canterbury. The addition of a balloon barrage to the town's defenses ensured that a second attack a week later was relatively ineffective. In 1944 balloons ringing London helped ward off V1 flying bombs.

German invaders had they come.) Elderly people and housewives worked in private homes making aeroplane parts.

Production of aircraft rose from 8,000 in 1939 to 26,000 in 1943 and 1944. Between 1940 and 1942 tank production quadrupled. There was much criticism of graft and inefficiency in "war industry" by workers in it and by outsiders, but this might be attributed as much to a frustrated wish to see Hitler beaten quickly as to the weariness and strains of wartime life. Popular feature films of the day showed people with strong hopes of a better future after victory and a willingness to keep "going to it". Industries and regions which had suffered especially hard in the years of depression between the wars now played their full part. The shipyards of the North were busy again. Scotland got major new industrial works.

The vogue for planning

During the war the prewar regional railway monopolies were run as components of a unified system, prefiguring postwar nationalization. The new ministry of fuel and power (created in 1942) similarly controlled the numerous companies in the coal industry. The idea of "Planning" became immensely fashionable. It was thought that the capacity of the USSR to fight back against the German army (and finally to defeat it) demonstrated the virtues of having a "planned" society.

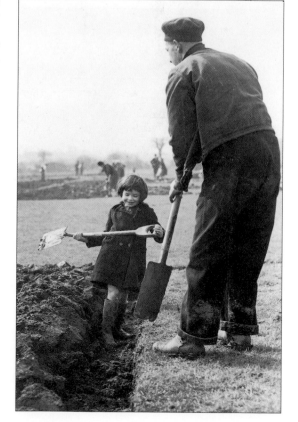

▶ "Digging for victory". Any one, however young, might get open-air pleasure out of growing food. Father and child are spending their Easter Holiday at work together. Potatoes matter far more than sport – a cricket field in North London is being transformed into allotments for people attracted by the "Grow Your Own Food" campaign.

Books, pamphlets and articles poured out from writers of the left and center full of "plans" for a more just, more efficient postwar country. One series of publications, by distinguished experts, included such typical titles as *Make Fruitful the Land*, *Start Planning Britain Now*, *Reconstruction and Peace*, *End Social Inequality*. In this ambience, the success of the Beveridge "Plan" – published in December 1942, is easy to explain. People queued outside branches of His Majesty's Stationery Office to purchase a dry-sounding, boring-looking, and highly technical official report on *Social Security and Allied Services*. This "Plan" eventually sold 650,000 copies. Within two weeks of publication an opinion poll discovered that 19 people out of 20 had heard of it, and that 9 out of 10 thought that it should be adopted.

Ironically, the chief "Planner" of Britain's wartime civilian life was a wholly uncharismatic Scot, a former civil servant, Sir John Anderson. His lord president's committee had central control of home and economic policy from 1941. In the following year, after much public clamor, a ministry of production was created to oversee supply to the armed forces. Despite the unpopularity of controls with businessmen, and the irritation felt by the general public over civil service "Red Tape", it was generally accepted that Total War demanded governmental and official dominance of the lives of all citizens.

Politicians and the people

The central institutions of British public life came out of the war with their prestige enhanced. The House of Commons was physically destroyed in the greatest air raid on London, on 10 May 1941, but parliament continued to meet, a beacon for democrats all over Europe. Buckingham Palace was also bombed, though less severely, but this served to join King and People in a common tribulation. George VI, Queen Elizabeth and their daughters provided a symbol of decent family life in austere and difficult days.

The political parties all had cause for satisfaction. The Conservatives, many of them hostile to Churchill in May 1940 when he ousted Chamberlain, came to delight in possessing the allegiance and leadership of the great man. The Liberals were overjoyed when Beveridge joined their ranks late in the war. But Labour was to be the electoral beneficiary of the Beveridge Plan. The party's leaders served loyally and effectively in the war cabinet, gaining the party a wholly novel reputation for solidity and common sense. At the same time its backbench members of parliament served it well when nearly 100 of them voted against the government in February 1942 over its less than total acceptance of the "Beveridge Plan". The Labour Party was identified with the planned future which so many people wanted, and swept to a landslide victory in 1945 in a general election held before the war with Japan had ended.

The British historian Henry Pelling has commented that "Parliament, the political parties, the Civil Service, local government, the press, the law, the trade unions – all emerged from the war with slightly different surface features but basically

War and Social Services

That many people in the UK lived in dire poverty was dramatized by evacuation. One and a half million school pupils and mothers with small children were suddenly decanted, in September 1939, from cities likely to be bombed into rural and suburban "safe" areas, where verminous slum-bred children shocked genteel householders. Concern for "social welfare" in general was heightened in some quarters.

In early 1941 the Trades Union Congress lobbied the minister of health about inadequate existing provision for health insurance. The government set up a committee of civil servants, chaired by the famous social scientist Sir William Beveridge, to survey all social insurance. The resulting "Plan" took a range of existing schemes and gathered them into one overall scheme to provide for the citizen "from cradle to grave". It was based, Beveridge wrote, on three assumptions: (1) that family allowances would be given for all children; (2) that a National Health Service would be provided; (3) that mass unemployment could be avoided. Before the war ended family allowances were introduced.

▲ During the war milk consumption increased considerably. The decision taken in July 1940 that mothers and small children should get free or cheap milk came to symbolize the beneficial impact of war on social services. This poster's designer, James Fitton, had been well-known before the war as a leftwing cartoonist.

unaltered. There had not been much of that 'inspection effect' which is supposed to be one of the by-products of war; or, if there had, it had found most institutions not unsatisfactory and so served to reinforce the view which so many people in Britain still retained: that somehow or other, things in their own country were arranged much better than elsewhere in the world...".

The UK had escaped invasion, which would have tested all its institutions to the limit. It had endured air raids on a far smaller scale than those which the German economy survived in 1944. Its moral reputation stood, or seemed to Britons to stand, very high in 1945. St George had slain the dragon of Nazism.

▲ The "Dad's Army" image of the Home Guard is typified here by the grizzled veteran closest to the camera. But by 1943 the average age of the 1.7 million part-time soldiers in this service was under 30 – it was used to train boys of 17 and 18 prior to their call-up into the army.

▼ November 1942, King and Queen inspect pies in the canteen of a Manchester aircraft factory. Such shots of royalty mixing with workers emphasized that this was a "People's War". Industrial canteens were amongst Ernest Bevin's favorite causes. In 1943 he pushed through an act fixing catering wages against the votes of over 100 Conservative MPs.

Doubts about wartime Britain

Yet within a quarter of a century of World War II the UK became a troubled, manifestly unsuccessful, country. Not surprisingly, the triumphalist account of the war outlined above came under fire, not only from "New Left" Marxists, but also from the so-called "Radical Right". It can be held that the UK's very success in wartime helped to preserve antiquated institutions and incompetent industrial practices, while confirming its imminent demise as a great power.

There is no contest over the evidence. From 1940 the UK depended on American friendship. "Lend-Lease" from 1941 to 1945 provided vitally important food and armaments but represented client status. On 14 August 1945, the day Japan surrendered, the British treasury advised the cabinet that the UK faced a "Financial Dunkirk". External disinvestment for the sake of the war had reached 4,000 million pounds. Shipping, a source of invisible exports, had been reduced by 30 percent. Visible exports were running at no more than four tenths of their prewar level.

From the right, the British historian, Corelli Barnett, has argued that the establishment of a welfare state, which was incumbent politically on any postwar government, whatever its political coloration, was an economic absurdity in these circumstances. But the apparently successful organization of the war economy had convinced politicians of diverse hues that anything was possible, given Planning.

Barnett argues – with much justice – that the British war economy was in fact bedeviled by longstanding inefficiency ("uncompetitiveness" in postwar terms). Small-minded, small-scale industrialists snarled at trade unionists obsessed with traditional practices. The UK preened itself on its wartime technological feats. Yet it had long lagged behind Germany in applied science and technology. The Germans developed a better jet fighter far more quickly, while British production figures were being boosted artificially by the manufacture of obsolescent planes: the Whitley bomber, almost useless for its task when the war

started, nevertheless continued in production till 1943. An *official* British historian has remarked that of the Whitleys produced – six times as many as originally planned – "many, perhaps most ... scarcely left the Aircraft Storage Units". In productivity, anyway, the US aircraft industry far outstripped the British. The UK's machine tool industry was so inefficient that dependence on America was inevitable. The UK's tanks were so botched in design that, by the summer of 1942, American Grants and Stuarts far outnumbered British Crusaders in the armored divisions of the British 8th Army.

But the view that the British people were deluded by their own propagandists, who were themselves deluded, perhaps points to unusual cohesion and unity within the society. It is said that a high-risk rescue worker, when praised by King George VI for getting a young girl out of a wrecked house after she had been buried for four and a half days, replied, "It's all in the day's work, sir, we all get the same pay." He was wrong; skilled rescue men in fact got more than the basic Civil Defence wage. But such expressions of solidarity abound in writings from the war years, as do memories of them. An aircraft-factory worker recorded: "There was very little absenteeism caused by the raids ... we knew that if we didn't turn up our mates would be worrying. You would see men staggering at their work from lack of sleep, snatching a ten minutes' doze in the canteen over their food, and still, when knocking-off time came, going off with a cheerful, 'See yer in the morning, boys'."

The evidence is contradictory. A coherent society is a tolerant one. The UK interned fascists early in the war, but communists who called for peace until Hitler invaded the USSR were allowed freedom of speech, though their newspaper, the *Daily Worker*, was suppressed. Conscientious objectors to the war were not hounded as they had been in World War I. By-elections continued to be fought, though the coalition partners refrained from opposing each other. From 1942 to 1945 Independents and candidates for the new Common Wealth Party (which was socialist) – eight in all – defeated government nominees and entered parliament. They did not oppose the war; they argued that it should be conducted on a more efficient, usually socialist, basis.

But the hysteria of the summer of 1940, when rumors of "fifth column" activity made neighbors suspicious of each other, and thousands of European refugees from Hitler's Europe were interned as "enemy aliens", does not suggest a self-confidently harmonious UK. It can be argued that resentment between classes intensified in the 1940s. Certainly it was present in the strike wave of 1943–44. There was a rise in working-class wages at a time when people had little to spend them on. But the earnings of farmers rose fastest of all: were these men heroes justly rewarded or profiteers?

Huge crowds cheered Churchill and the King in London on Victory in Europe Day. The last word must rest with them. They believed that they had made history and triumphed.

▲ May 1940, a newly completed housing estate has been converted into a temporary internment camp for "aliens". Some 27,000 people born in enemy countries were rounded up that summer. A few of them were indeed anti-British. The vast majority were not, including many Jewish refugees as well as distinguished German and Italian anti-fascists. Some 11,000 were deported to Canada and Australia; and many of these lost their lives when their ship was torpedoed. Camps on the Isle of Man filled up with the rest. Conditions were fairly comfortable. Gradually most "aliens" were released. Despite their treatment, many joined the services or did other war work.

Ernest Bevin and Trade Unionism

The Conservative rebels who voted against their prime minister in May 1940 wanted a coalition, and so Chamberlain fell because Labour would not agree to join one led by him. The party which commanded the loyalty of the most active trade unionists held a key position in a war which would be won by industrial effort. Even so, it was imaginative of Churchill to bring Ernest Bevin, from outside parliament, into office as minister of labour. Bevin was general secretary of the Transport and General Workers Union. He duly became the most powerful Labour man in the war cabinet.

Self-educated, he had had his first involvement with "Transport" as a drayman. He had not joined a trade union until he was nearly 30, but between the wars had become a leading union figure. Strongly anti-communist, he was also anti-Nazi.

The Essential Work Order of March 1941 and the registration of the entire labor force during that year gave Bevin enormous power over every civilian man and boy, girl and woman. He used it to direct labor to where it was considered most essential. But he also employed it in the promotion of his long-time aims: collective bargaining, recognition for trade unions, and improved conditions.

The Trades Union movement was vastly strengthened by wartime full employment and the propitious work of Bevin. Between 1938 and 1943 the number of unionized workers

▲ Bevin (right) starts a loom to open an exhibition.

increased by over a third, to 8,174,000. Bevin's own TGWU became the first union to top a million members. Paradoxically, Bevin's old enemies the communists, when they switched to support the war effort after Hitler's invasion of the Soviet Union, were able to recruit scores of thousands of new party members. Still more paradoxically, they wielded their new influence against strike action, without much obvious success.

For every five persons killed in the course of World War II, two were Soviet citizens. The toll in blood was horrendous, though the exact tally will probably never be known. Civilian losses reached 7 million due to death, deportation and wartime exertions, to which must be added the wounded, the mutilated and the orphaned. The trail of destruction left a third of Soviet industry in ruins.

Steel smelting

Tonnes (millions)

17.9

8.1

1940   1945

Male workforce

Millions

28.6

18.4

1940   1945

► **Even before the German attack of 1941, Stalin prophesied that the next war would be won in the machine-shops, the factories and the foundries. The USSR won the industrial war outproducing Germany in spite of a vast forced industrial migration eastward and enemy occupation of major industrial regions.**

Tank production

Index (1940 = 100)

296

1940   1945

▲ **German occupation of large areas of the western USSR made huge inroads into the industrial labor force available to the Soviet authorities, losses steadily made good by the vast increase in the number of women and young persons (16–25) employed in factories, and pensioners over 50 recalled to their work-benches.**

► **Between July and November 1941, in the first stage of an unprecedented industrial evacuation, 1,360 major military plants were shifted into the eastern interior, turning the Urals, western and eastern Siberia and Central Asia into a great arsenal. The map shows new or expanded engineering plants east of the Front.**

Major industrial centers 1941–45

◆ Engineering plant

▢ Area occupied by Germany

Leningrad

Moscow
Smolensk
Gorki
Perm
URAL MOUNTAINS
Sverdlovsk
Ulyanovsk
Ufa
Penza
Chkalov
Stalingrad
Rostov

Chronology

1939

August 23
Soviet-German Nonaggression Pact signed

September 1
Germans invade Poland; start of war in western Europe

September
End of Soviet–Japanese border conflict (since July 1938); USSR occupies Eastern Poland

November 30
Soviet-Finnish War begins (till March 1940)

1940

June
Working day increased

1941

June 22
Germany invades USSR

July
Stalin makes first statement since invasion, calling for loyalty to motherland; ration-cards introduced in Leningrad and Moscow

August
Emergency war plan for Soviet economy

September
Siege of Leningrad begins (lifted January 1944)

November
Evacuation of industrial plant completed

1942

March
Soviet economy rallies

April
Nonagricultural labor conscripted for harvest

May
Central partisan staff set up to organize guerrilla warfare

1943

January
State defense committee takes action against abuses in distribution of commodities; Germans surrender at Stalingrad

1944

August
Red Army invades Romania

1945

April
Red Army reaches Vienna and Berlin

May 9
VE Day; end of war in Europe

August
USSR declares war on Japan and invades Manchuria

September 2
VJ Day; end of war in Pacific

It would be difficult to argue with the proposition that even more than the Bolshevik Revolution of 1917, the Soviet–German war, known as "The Great Patriotic War of the Soviet Union 1941–45", shaped the USSR as a world power, cemented its political system and colored its society.

By virtue of the magnitude of the Soviet achievement in defeating Nazi Germany and the scale of Soviet losses this was a war that was militarily and morally different, if not unique. Not only was it the greatest land campaign in history, but also a war of enslavement and extermination on the part of Nazi Germany and one of almost unprecedented barbarism.

During the 1,418 days of the war the Red Army fought along a front varying in length from 3,000 to 6,200 km (1,860mi–3,900mi), launched 9 campaigns and 210 operations by groups of armies; seven of the campaigns and 160 operations were offensive in nature. Each hour of the war cost 587 lives, each day 14,000 died; only 3 percent of the younger generation (17–21) survived. Society suffered the loss of the equivalent of two five-year plans; 30 percent of Soviet industry was left in ruins.

Authority and organization

Certain characteristics of Soviet society stood the state in good stead in time of war. To move to a war footing required surprisingly little administrative adjustment given the complex overlapping levels of Soviet administration and authority. Stalin, after recovering from his stupor during the first days of the German attack in June 1941, imposed his personal authority in a system of "super-centralization", directing military affairs through the *Stavka* (the equivalent of a general headquarters, for which the general staff worked directly) and the state defense committee (the GKO, with Stalin at its head and an entirely civilian membership), the latter body all-powerful and operating either by decree or direct personal intervention.

Thus Stalin had eyes and ears everywhere. The system worked on naked personal authority and personal control, subjecting governmental, military and administrative organs to the communist party and police primacy. Stalin ran the war much as he ruled in what passed for peace, with an all-powerful, rigidly centralized directorate headed by himself as party general secretary, as defense commissar and supreme commander and as chairman of the state defense committee, overriding "legal norms" and with Lavrenty Beria and the NKVD (the People's Commissariat of Internal Affairs) at his back. The system had strengths but was cumbersome; lack of direction from "the center" caused it to seize up.

THE SOVIET GREAT PATRIOTIC WAR

In the western regions a wartime regime was introduced by the hastiest of decrees. The initial military mobilization went smoothly, bringing 5 million men to the colors within little more than a week. But all too soon, as the German army drove deep, the lack of prewar contingency planning for industrial evacuation and strategic dispersion produced a grave crisis. Before the war Stalin had ordered the military authorities to plan for achieving rapid victory through offensive action "with little loss of blood". The Red Army was unprepared for a protracted war. In the German invasion of 1941 it suffered enormous battlefield losses; the invaders overran grain lands, mines and factories and engulfed millions of Soviet citizens, Stalin's labor force. Improvised industrial evacuation under fire accomplished astounding feats on the orders of the GKO, though the real heroes were Soviet railroad workers, who transported 2.5 million troops to the front in August–September 1941 and 1,360 heavy plants to the interior, to the Urals, western Siberia and the Volga region. Once plants were in the interior there came the mammoth task of building new factories, but machines were set down and set to work on the bare earth. Workers lived in grim barracks or in scooped-out dugouts – in a fierce winter.

The USSR survived the rending crisis of the late autumn of 1941. Total collapse was staved off by the fact that the Japanese did not attack Soviet Asia, by communications which did work (unlike those of World War I), by an extraordinary capacity for improvisation and by the ability to operate under conditions of wholesale disorder, by enduring grievous losses, by eliciting effective responses when "the authorities" also did their jobs properly and by the slow but horrifying popular realization what German rule meant: the enslavement and extermination of the "Slav rabble".

Resistance and economic mobilization
The emergency mobilization bore horrendously on the civilian population, called upon to man the militia, dig tank-traps and fortifications, undergo reserve training, patrol as "home guards" and, above all, increase war production. In Leningrad the population stood fast against German besiegers, even though starvation soon began to pierce. It was the start of almost 900 days of siege (8 September 1941–27 January 1944). Moscow endured martial law and siege conditions. Leningrad lived on its civic pride, for there was little else. In mid-November 1941 the GKO accepted revised production plans for 1942: 22–25,000 aircraft and 22,000 tanks, all with a labor force now fallen from 27 million to 19 million. Women and youths were drafted into the work places while in the interior, desperately housed and far from ade-

quately fed, workers in the newly transshipped factories started production as walls went up around them. The Kharkov Tank Factory turned out its first 25 T-34 tanks 10 weeks after it had been reassembled.

Full scale military-industrial and economic mobilization effected what amounted to a second industrial revolution in the USSR. Soviet workers won what Stalin called "the battle of machines", turning out 78,000 tanks, 16,000 self-propelled guns, 98,000 artillery pieces. New production methods speeded up the great flow of tanks. The cost was heavy: 55 percent of Soviet national income now went for war purposes, as opposed to 15 percent in 1940. This was all-out mobilization, demanding everything from the Soviet people.

Under the slogan "All for the front!" the country was ravaged and scavenged, in a hunt for its brain and brawn. Food and shelter, never

▼ The shocking cost of the combat was not borne only by adults. The war bore terribly upon children, through death and the chaos of evacuation.

abundant in the USSR, presented daily problems. A "differentiated" rationing system for bread was introduced at an early stage, with increased rations for miners and the apprentice training schools: by 1943 three million were receiving augmented rations. But the breakdown in transport in Moscow in the winter of 1941–42 meant that only 30 percent of the meat ration and 34 percent of the sugar ration was "honored". At the end of 1941 in Zlatoust (a town to the east of the Urals) factory canteens were so flooded with evacuees that they failed to function. As Soviet war expenditures rose four times, civilian consumption fell by as much as 40 percent, while consumer items – sugar, jams, meat, matches, knitwear – were steadily vanishing. In January 1943 the GKO acted against abuses in the supply of food and goods, enlisting the trade unions to control factory stores and canteens and to combat "speculators". Communal feeding eased the situation, with 25 million being so fed by 1944.

The housing situation, already a chronic problem, now became desperate. In the Volga, Urals and Siberian regions, 8,500 workers survived in dugouts, more than 12,000 workers used derelict barracks. Funds were allocated for housing in the east but the problem remained acute, compounded in 1943–44 by the terrible devastation discovered in the west in the wake of the retreating Germans – millions of dwellings, thousands of hospitals and sanatoria ruined, large-scale depopulation. In addition, a depleted medical service had to deal not only with general public health but with widespread infectious diseases in the liberated areas. Provision had also to be made for the thousands of war orphans as well as the war wounded. Enormous burdens fell from the outset on Soviet women, young and old: women and girls were recruited for industry, the mines and railroads or for front-line service as nurses, snipers and aircrew in a unique bomber squadron. Women formed 26–35 percent of the labor force in mining, 48 percent in the oil industry; in all, a 56 percent increase in the number of women employed throughout industry.

War and agriculture

The Soviet peasantry – work-horse and whipping-boy of Stalin's prewar policies of social reorganization – shouldered an immense burden, supplying 60 percent of the Red Army's wartime manpower, responsible also for feeding the Red Army and the general population in the desperate "battle for bread". During the war the agricultural labor force was more than halved by the beginning of 1943 – (down from 16.9 million men and 18.6 million women to 4 million men and 11 million women) – but the travail began much earlier. Soviet farming, divided into collective farms (*kolkhozy*) and state farms (*sovkhozy*), did not escape the crisis of the early months of the war. It lost most of its mechanized equipment to the Red Army; lorries and tractors were used as gun-tows. Women and juveniles, even the old, had to substitute, literally harnessed to plows. Under the wartime labor regime the compulsory minimum of unpaid work or "labor days" (a labor unit equivalent to one and a half days in peacetime)

was set at 150 in cotton-growing areas, 100–120 in the grain and livestock regions. Severe penalties were enforced by the NKVD and the communist party for violations.

German occupation in the early months deprived the USSR of 47 percent of its grain-bearing lands, 87 percent of its pigs. During the early part of the war, in 1941–42, no tractors were supplied to the farms, whether collective or state, nor were spare parts or fuel readily available. In an attempt to compensate for the lost resources, fresh land was developed in the Urals, in Siberia, Kazakhstan and Soviet Asia but again shortage of labor, constantly drained off for the army and industry, and less fertile land hampered this effort. The low point was reached in 1943 when the harvest produced only 63 percent of its 1940 figure. Yet it cannot be said that the Soviet peasantry failed in the "battle for bread". With astounding resilience, though gripped by extreme hardship and suffering dire poverty, the Red Army was fed and the population at large did not actually starve. Little

money was paid to the collective farmers, only "payment in kind" – minuscule amounts of grain and potatoes, if they materialized at all. As for exploiting the "private plots" (peasant's allotments), these too were subject to compulsory state deliveries with a *fivefold* swingeing tax increase on any income derived from them or from livestock. The peasant could hardly be described as a war profiteer on these terms.

German barbarism and Soviet resistance

Not only protracted hardship and constant sacrifices but also terrible savageries came to dominate this war. Behind the German wire an inhuman fate awaited Soviet prisoners of war. They were deliberately left to die, used in death-camp experiments or simply murdered, though from their massed ranks the Germans plucked Soviet non-Russian ethnic minorities for forced service under German arms. From the ranks of Soviet prisoners General Vlasov, a Soviet army commander captured in 1942, attempted to form an anti-Stalinist movement and a "Russian Liberation Army", only to run foul of Nazi political and racial fanaticism. In search of slave labor the Germans deported some 5 million Soviet citizens to operate their factories or run their farms. Stalin, out of revenge for real or suspected "collaboration", brutally deported ethnic-German Soviet citizens, the Crimean Tartars and ethnic minorities from the north Caucasus to Siberia and Central Asia.

The partisan movement in occupied Soviet territory, which grew from an organization dominated by party members and the NKVD into a geniune mass movement, generated more atrocity and unbridled savagery as the Germans intensified their war of reprisal and retribution, employing ferocious anti-partisan units in the

◀◀ The war launched the USSR on a second industrial revolution, with a huge arsenal building up in the deep rear, in Siberia, far from roving German bombers. In this tank factory, workers were reminded of the front: "The Red Army needs *Your* tanks, it needs *Your* aircraft – Stalin", "The Red Army needs modern combat aircraft like it needs bread…".

◀ Peasants are exhorted to year-round work to produce food. "The Battle for Bread" was vital to the survival of the USSR. Its most difficult year was 1943, when the harvest yield fell to 20.6 million tons, but this crisis was overcome. This war differed from World War I in that the population and the armed forces were fed, not luxuriously but enough to keep body and soul together.

Winter had already come when Sverdlovsk received Comrade Stalin's order to erect two buildings for the plant evacuated from the south. … It was then that the people of the Urals came to this spot with shovels, bars and pickaxes: students, typists, accountants, shop assistants, housewives, artists, teachers. The earth was like stone, frozen hard by our fierce Siberian frost. Axes and pickaxes could not break the stony soil. In the light of arc-lamps people hacked at the earth all night. … Their feet and hands were swollen with frostbite, but they did not leave work. … On the twelfth day, into the new buildings with their glass roofs the machinery began to arrive. … And two days later, the war factory began production.

"PRAVDA"
18 SEPTEMBER 1942

◀ Women, children and old men dig antitank ditches outside Moscow. Soviet women, young and old, bore the full brunt of the war. In a land of brutal shortages and hardship, women were called upon to work as air-raid wardens, to dig the huge antitank ditches, and to labor in the munitions factories.

▲ Peasants donate money for the defense fund.

▶ "Russia's sons are on the march! Young and old together. Strike down the insolent invader, take your revenge! Let the tyrant tremble…his hour has struck. In each fighting man there stares out a hero." In an evocative poster the emphasis is on Russia: Red Army troops, "ancient Russia" in the background. Stalin himself called the sons of Russia to war in a speech of November 1941, invoking the great names of Russia's past. This was a confession that the people might not fight for communism but they would struggle for "Mother Russia". The victory of patriotism was celebrated with this great parade in Red Square, Moscow, on 9 May 1945.

May 9 was an unforgettable day in Moscow. The sponaneous joy of the two or three million people who thronged the Red Square that evening – and the Moscow River embankments, and Gorki Street, all the way up to the Belorussian Station – was of a quality and a depth I had never yet seen in Moscow before. They danced and sang in the streets; every soldier and officer was hugged and kissed … Nothing like this had ever happened in Moscow before.

ALEXANDER WERTH

Bandenkrieg (guerilla war). Soviet authorities steadily expanded their control, the partisan movement acquired its own central staff supervised by Stalin who shrewdly insisted on sending partisans printing paper and duplicating machines, as much a weapon as machine guns for re-establishing a Soviet presence. With 88 million people under enemy occupation the reintroduction of Soviet authority, however, indirect, assumed great importance, discouraging collaboration and encouraging resistance.

Once the USSR was in control of the former occupied areas, "re-Sovietization" followed. Programs frequently included harsh measures – mass propaganda, the closing of churches, the reimposition of collectivized agriculture, the struggle against "nationalist" (ie separatist) movements, notably in the Ukraine and in the Baltic states. Among the younger generation, deprived by the Germans of elementary education, Russian literacy had to be established.

The victory and the cost

Eventually the victory was won. The Soviet system, for all its imperfections, had withstood a test to destruction. Total breakdown, confidently predicted by Hitler, had been averted. Total mobilization, going into high gear in 1942–43, ensured victory. The communist party, initially discredited and displaced, recovered ground as it aligned itself, as Stalin did himself, with a "patriotic culture", though in 1944 the ideological screws were again tightened. The *Komsomol*, the Young Communists League, made an enormous effort, marching to the battlefields and into the factories and suffering a slaughter of the innocents. The younger generation suffered hideously.

Within a population so often "brazenly coerced or rudely abandoned", popular attitudes varied widely, but morale and motivation held up. To some the war actually seemed to be a boon; to others the generation of a "front-line morality", demanding but satisfying, brought relief from the cynicism and parasitism of prewar days. The realization of the dread nature of German occupation policies exercised a powerful, all-pervasive influence: a captured Soviet official put it bluntly: "… in the long term the people will choose from two tyrants the one who speaks their own language. Therefore, we will win the war". The resurgence of Soviet power did not fail to have an impact, though recognition of the cost induced a certain war-weariness in 1943–44, offset in turn by the "promise of better things to come", "a party in our street" (a promise not fulfilled). Communal resilience and personal fortitude, coupled with the encouragement of patriotism, encouraged and deepened popular responses.

The alliances with the USA and UK, whatever the strains, and even the late opening of the Second Front in Western Europe, bolstered feelings that Russia was not alone. To their amazement but deep satisfaction and self-esteem, Soviet people discovered that leadership, discipline and patriotism brought results, engendering devotion to duty and steadfastness in danger.

Church, State and People

On the day of the German invasion of the USSR, Sunday 22 June 1941, Stalin maintained a sinister public silence. It was eventually broken in early July, not by Stalin but by Metropolitan Sergius of the Moscow Orthodox Patriarchate. He denounced "the Fascist brigands", vowed that the Church would not forsake "its people" and blessed the "forthcoming heroic exploit" of these same people. This was the first of many unofficial but strikingly effective Church announcements, urging in the name of Russia and the cause of Christianity all-out resistance to Hitler and his pagan hordes.

Far-reaching consequences for Church, State, party and populace flowed from wartime tribulations. If party purists sneered that it was only the "weak-minded" and the "ideologically unstable" who turned to the Church and to religion for individual or collective solace, comfort or hope, this confirmed that ideology alone could not sustain flagging spirits or inspire complete confidence in the Soviet cause.

Stalin himself recognized this, reduced the ideological rasp and embraced Russia's heroic past which he acknowledged as encompassing the Orthodox Church as a staunch defender of Russia. In return the Church not only encouraged morale but made collections of money from the "weak-minded".

On 4 September 1943 Stalin met with the three patriarchs of the Russian Orthodox Church and later concluded a compact or concordat. Though very far from ushering in religious freedom, it at least emplaced the Orthodox Church as a recognized, legitimized institution within the Soviet system.

Ecclesiastical government (the holy synod) was re-established, a limited number of seminaries were opened to meet the dire shortage of priests, the number of bishops was increased and churches long closed reopened. Thanks to the war the Orthodox Church won for itself a legal position which it has never entirely lost: it was a gain of historic proportions.

РОССИИ ДВИНУЛИСЬ СЫНЫ

СТРАШИСЬ, О РАТЬ ИНОПЛЕМЕННЫХ!
РОССИИ ДВИНУЛИСЬ СЫНЫ;
ВОССТАЛ И СТАР И МЛАД; ЛЕТЯТ НА ДЕРЗНОВЕННЫХ,
СЕРДЦА ИХ МЩЕНЬЕМ ВОЗЖЕНЫ.
ВОСТРЕПЕЩИ, ТИРАН! УЖ БЛИЗОК ЧАС ПАДЕНЬЯ.
ТЫ В КАЖДОМ РАТНИКЕ УЗРИШЬ БОГАТЫРЯ"...

Datafile

Although far from the fighting, the American home front experienced great and transforming changes: substantial internal migration resulted in permanent shifts in the population, the rapid increase and improvement in health care led to a healthier and longer-living citizenry, and the growth in industrial production fueled by the war consolidated the USA's position as the world's leading industrial power. Less amenable to counting were changes in attitudes: the birth of the teenager, the change in the expectations of many women, and the tendency for the electorate to ask not what they could do for their country, but what their country could do for them.

Male life expectancy

▲ The development of health care and the increase in well-paid jobs both contributed to the rapid increase in life expectation of black and white males – although the black male had considerably further to go.

◄ One reason for the improvement in the lot of the black population was migration from sharecropping and scrub farming in the South to better jobs in the cities of the South and North. The white farm population also joined the rush.

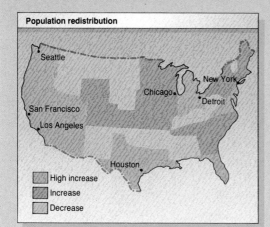

Population redistribution

- High increase
- Increase
- Decrease

US industrial production

◄ The chart well demonstrates the role played by the war in pulling the USA out of the Depression. In 1932 the US government's Index of Industrial Production stood at 52; by 1940 it was 125 and in 1943 239. Production then began to fall as the USA began if anything to overproduce: by 1946 it was back to 170.

Chronology

1940

July
US embargo on war trade with Japan

September
Germany invades Poland; start of war in Europe; conscription begins

1941

March
US Lend-Lease Act

December 7
Japanese bomb Pearl Harbor

December 8
US declares war on Japan

December 9
Germany and Italy declare war on USA

1942

January
Establishment of War Production Board

February
Roosevelt sets up War Relocation Authority (WRA) to intern Japanese-Americans; prohibition of nonmilitary automobile production

April
War Manpower Commission (WMC) formed

June
Roosevelt sets up Office of War Information (OWI) to facilitate propaganda

August
Women's Advisory Committee to WMC formed

September
Gasoline rationing introduced

November
Secretary of agriculture calls for 18 million "Victory Gardens"

1943

May
Office of War Mobilization established

June
Smith-Connally Act

1944

June
Allied invasion of Normandy; Servicemen's Readjustment Act ("GI Bill of Rights")

1945

April 12
Death of Roosevelt; Truman becomes President

May 8
VE Day; war in Europe ends

August
Atomic bombs dropped on Hiroshima and Nagasaki

September 2
VJ Day; war in Pacific ends

The American home front was turbulent and disorganized, but productive. Mobilization, of both the economy and the labor force, developed over a long period and intentions were never completely implemented. It produced social tensions, between races, between capital and labor, between army camps (and munitions-making boom towns) and local populations, and between the generations. Civil liberties were an early casualty. But order eventually emerged out of chaos, and by good luck, an abundance of resources and planning, the USA developed into the Arsenal of Democracy, producing a substantial proportion of the arms, munitions and ships used by the Allies. The USA proved to be a good example of the truism that war is an engine of economic, social and political change. During World War II the average standard of living vastly improved, and the relationship of the citizen with the government was transformed. Seen in a long perspective, World War II produced social developments that were more notable than the economic achievement.

Business and mobilization

Because the USA contained a very vocal isolationist and antiwar element, and had remained neutral during the early days of Japanese and German expansion, there had been little preparation for war. At first, mobilization of the economy was difficult to effect. American business had suffered profoundly during the Depression (1929–36), and once the economy began to pick up in the first years of the war (1941–43), it was loath to forgo production for the profitable domestic market in order to concentrate on war-related contracts. The automobile industry, for example, anticipated selling 4 million cars in 1941: consequently it fought against converting factories for the production of military aircraft instead. While the country was neutral, the political costs were too high for President Roosevelt to attempt to force business to act against its will. Once war was declared (8 December 1941), new rules came into play. But throughout the war big business successfully insisted that war-related contracts be drawn up with provisions which ensured very healthy profits.

The economy was never fully mobilized. During 1940–41 reluctance to convert was a key reason; thereafter the reluctance of major industries (such as steel, electric power, automobile manufacture and railroads) to expand capacity constituted a drag. Businessmen had acute fears that if they did so expand, postwar markets would be flooded, and yet another depression would ensue. Consequently, after wartime expansion, production was hardly greater than output during 1921–25. Unemployment did not dwindle until mid–1943.

THE AMERICAN WAY OF WAR

The slack in the economy can be illustrated by looking at the mobilization of the female population. From 1940 British women were subject to the draft, and 70 percent were engaged in full-time work. In the USA the figure was 29 percent: in short, 71 percent of the female population over 18 stayed at home. This was partly due to male insistence that they were fighting for the right of women to remain in their traditional sphere; as one soldier protested, if, for example, women joined the armed services, American men "would throw away our own self-respect – our right to pledge in earnestness to 'Love, Honor and Protect' the girls we want to marry when we get back." This sentimental servitude, however, could not have been imposed if the economy and the armed forces had seriously needed their services. As it was, at the peak of war production in

▼ **Employees in Chattanooga form a "V" for victory, to celebrate their work on defense orders.**

November 1943 the country was turning out 6 ships a day and 6 billion US dollars' worth of war-related goods a month; a year later many such factories were being closed, as output exceeded requirements.

Wartime social problems

Mobilizing the economy to such an extent caused great upheavals and social tensions. New factories were built and old ones enlarged, with the result that many areas of the country were transformed. The mushrooming of munitions plants produced boom towns to which thousands flocked for work. Migrants suffered a lack of adequate housing, health provision and schools, while inhabitants saw their home towns change from prudish small places into rambunctious and immoral boom cities.

One result was the widespread phenomenon of teenage prostitution. Many were in fact as young as 12 years old; they were called Victory Girls, Patriotutes, Cuddle Bunnies or Roundheels. When arrested by the police, they frequently claimed to be performing a patriotic service by maintaining military morale. However, it was a service sometimes performed for free: federal housing projects spawned what were called "wolf packs" – clubs for teenagers where girls paid their dues by copulating with every male member. One historian has noted that "one determined young initiate joined a club with ninety members."

These developments were amongst the saddest but least surprising results of mobilization, since by mid-1942 there were hundreds of thousands of "eight-hour orphans" wandering the streets of the cities and boom towns, their latchkeys frequently hanging around their necks. The fact that it was "teenage" prostitution which was decried is notable. Before the war there were two age categories for the population, adults and children; during the war an adolescent subculture developed. By 1945 teenagers as such attracted a considerable amount of parental, sociological and advertising interest; several magazines devoted to their interests had sprung up, such as *Seventeen*.

Mobilization also encouraged a substantial internal migration. Sixteen million men and women left home to join the armed services, and another 16 million moved around the country, either wives and sweethearts following the servicemen, or workers moving to other jobs. A million blacks moved from rural areas in the South, some to southern urban areas, but a substantial proportion to urban areas in the North and West. The West, and particularly the Pacific Coast, was the main gainer in the great wartime population shifts. Shipbuilding and munitions-building centers drew workers in particular to California, which rejoiced in a 37-percent gain in population during the war. Rural blacks were not alone in leaving the land for the bright lights: the farm population as a whole fell by 20 percent.

Indeed, the stampede of workers from the land to the towns might well have caused a serious food crisis, but for the Victory Gardens. At first they sprang up spontaneously, but the farm security administration then launched "An Acre for a Soldier" in rural areas. The idea was that the cash proceeds from the crop grown on that acre would be devoted to such things as soldiers' canteens. City dwellers pitched in as well and by April 1942 more than 6 million people were digging "for vitamins and victory". At first the federal department of agriculture was pretty scathing about the movement, but as the number of military conscripts increased and others moved to well-paid jobs in the munitions factories, ordinary agriculture faced a serious crisis in manpower as early as 1942. In fall 1942 the secretary of agriculture called for 18 million Victory Gardens. The gardens were now seen as a resource that might help to offset the threatened loss of millions of tonnes of food.

The economic results of the migration from the land to urban areas, then, were beneficial: production was increased and overpopulation of the land was eased. But the consequence was social problems, particularly as a result of the shift in the black population. Racial tensions erupted in areas of the country where they had previously been unknown. Conflict followed, sometimes violence.

Over one million blacks joined the armed forces, but segregation into separate fighting units, and the relegation of blacks to the most menial duties, ensured deep-burning resentment. Similarly, there was an increase of 800,000 blacks working in manufacturing, but there too their positions were overwhelmingly low-paid and menial. What this did was to underline for all to see the gap between American protestations of equality and democracy, and the reality for those of a different color or race. (Japanese-American citizens suffered even more acutely, those on the West Coast being rounded up and herded into concentration camps.) The reaction of blacks to their treatment during the war may have been the basis for the civil rights protests of the 1950s and 1960s.

Living standards and the state

In short, minority groups suffered, but so did those in the majority, if they were perceived by those in power to be working against the war effort. One such group was labor, both organized and unorganized. Attempts by businesses to ensure that they did not suffer losses, but indeed profited, during the war were seen as perfectly natural; attempts by workers to ensure that their wages kept up with prices and that they retained the freedom to move jobs were seen as attacking the war effort. One result of the New Deal recovery program during the 1930s had been to bring labor into the center of the political process. It had been acknowledged that the political wishes of the workers were as important as those of business interests. During the war this position came under attack, from business and from a Congress dominated by the Republican Party. They combined in an attempt to turn back the clock. In 1943 the Smith-Connally Act was passed,

▼ The USA as the Arsenal of Democracy. President Roosevelt called for the USA to assume this role on 29 December 1940. His purpose was to encourage the public to buy Victory Bonds. The V-for-Victory campaign, launched by the BBC to encourage people in the occupied countries, swept the USA in 1941.

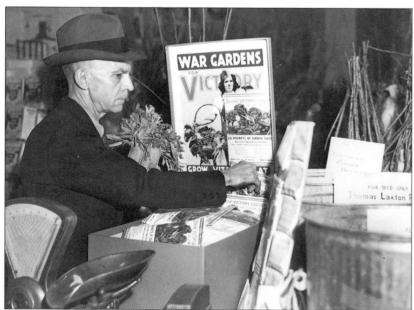
▼ This man is buying seeds for his Victory Garden. Such gardens were an important source of food by late 1942, given the flight from the farms.

which forbade unions from contributing to candidates for office in national elections. The unions' response was to set up the Political Action Committee to canvas and get out the vote for favored candidates.

Indeed, labor managed largely to sustain its recently won political position because of its crucial role in the war effort. Workers' patriotism was frequently much more obvious than that of business: for example, inmates of San Quentin prison in California staged a near-riot to support their demand that they be allowed to produce war materiel. Skilled labor was relatively scarce, and employers found it necessary greatly to improve working conditions in order to keep their work forces. Certainly the economic position of labor was far better in 1945 than it had been in the late 1930s.

Overall, in spite of the many problems which erupted during the war, by 1945 the USA was in

◄ The proportion of women over 18 who worked outside the home — only 29 percent — was much lower in the USA than in any other belligerent country save Germany. Of those who worked in industry, the proportion who were black increased enormously. At the same time, the numbers of black women who worked as farm laborers and domestic servants dropped sharply.

▼ This Dodge plant near Detroit produced army truck bodies, but the lack of a fast-moving production line and the relaxed attitude of the workers produced a scene different from that of today. At least some of these workers had either been unemployed or working in lower-paid jobs before the war.

Japanese Internment

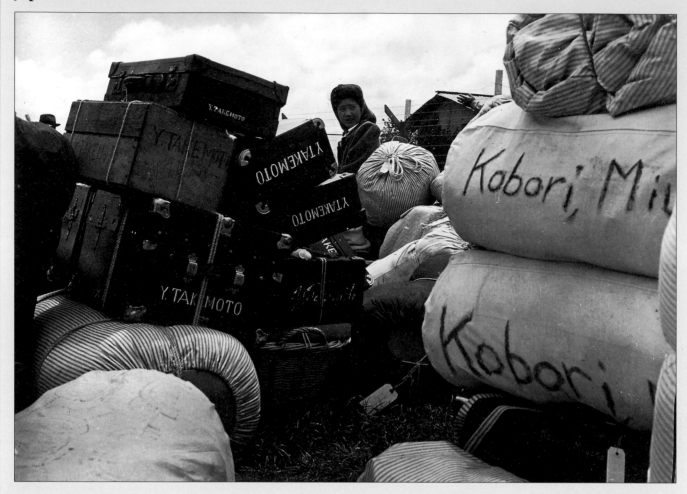

One consequence of the bombing of Pearl Harbor (7 December 1941) was the American government's decision that all those of Japanese ancestry living on the West Coast, whether immigrants or native-born American citizens, constituted a threat to national security and should be removed from their homes and incarcerated in camps. The US army argued that no military necessity required such a step, and the FBI had in any case already rounded up those Japanese aliens whom it deemed dangerous. But the idea of a security threat was pushed by Henry Stimson, the secretary of war, and by his assistant secretary, John J. McCloy, with the support of various politicians and pressure groups. President Roosevelt supported the civilians' assessment of danger and in February 1942 signed the order authorizing the establishment of a War Relocation Authority (WRA) to move the Japanese-Americans away from the Pacific Coast.

On the ground that speed was of the essence, no hearings were granted to the "evacuees", and within weeks 110,000 residents of Japanese ancestry, 65 percent of whom had been born in the USA, were resettled in ten WRA camps. The WRA insisted that there was no coercion, but the reality was camps surrounded by barbed wire and watchtowers, forced loyalty oaths, attempted dispersal of the internees all over the USA to "Americanize" them and in general, their treatment virtually as enemy aliens.

There is a good deal of evidence that the wartime fear of subversion was driven by racism, since there was no general round-up of German-Americans or Italian-Americans purely on the basis of their nationality. A statement by the governor of California, Culbert L. Olson, in February 1942, is enlightening: "You know, when I look out at a group of Americans of German or Italian descent, I can tell whether they're loyal or not. I can tell how they think and even perhaps what they are thinking. But it is impossible for me to do this with the inscrutable orientals, and particularly the Japanese."

The task of the WRA was aided by the cooperation of the leadership of the Japanese American Citizens League and of the national leadership of the American Civil Liberties Union. It was left to the Northern California branch of the ACLU, by arguing the cases of some of the internees, to make clear publicly the illegality of the WRA's procedures.

On 17 December 1944 the war department announced the revocation of the order excluding Japanese Americans from the West Coast, and on the following day the Supreme Court ruled that the WRA had no legal authority to detain a "concededly loyal" US citizen and no legal authority to impose conditions for his release.

▲ A young evacuee of Japanese ancestry identifies her baggage at the assembly center in Salinas, California, prior to being sent to a War Relocation Authority Center. She may well have ended up in one of the ten concentration camps set up to incarcerate 110,000 persons of Japanese ancestry, the majority of whom were American citizens. It took the American government a generation to admit that a great injustice had been done to a group of citizens against whom no charge of attempted subversion or sabotage was ever made.

economic and social terms a much fairer place than before the war. It is clear that civilians in the aggregate did not suffer serious inroads into their material standard of living: on the contrary, total personal consumption rose in real terms during the war. Expenditure per head on food, for example, rose from 560 US dollars in 1941 to 700 in 1945. Overall, real disposable personal income rose 25 percent during the same period. What is equally important is that the economic benefits were spread across the board. The economy expanded substantially, and from 1941 every group benefited. By 1945 the average annual income was almost 3,000 dollars, more than double what it had been in 1939.

One of the most important developments during the war was the very great increase in medical provision. Medical care had been wholly inadequate before the war: although the population had increased by nine million between 1929 and 1939, the number of doctors and dentists had remained static. Added to this were hunger and pollution, and limited public-health facilities. Consequently, the physical condition of a substantial proportion of the recruits for the army and navy was appalling: the overall rejection rate was 50 percent, rising to 70 percent in some areas. One benefit of the 1939–41 defense boom was the building of thousands of new health clinics and community hospitals. But in many cases, no sooner were they built than they lost their doctors, drafted into the armed services. By 1943 there was one doctor for every 100 servicemen and one doctor for every 3,500 civilians. This was ironic, because the civilian death rate of over 10 per thousand in 1941 was higher than that of the armed services, at only 5 per thousand in 1942–45.

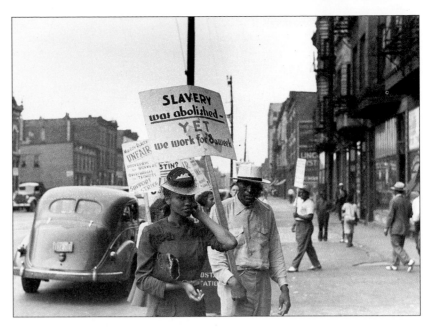

▲ Employers and white trade unions combined to freeze blacks out of defense industries, or to restrict them to low-paid jobs. Black leaders threatened a march of 50,000 to 100,000 blacks on Washington in July 1941 to demonstrate that American democracy was a mockery. Eleanor Roosevelt, the president's wife, convinced them to call it off, but other strikes, such as this one in south Chicago, continued.

Improving health care was given a much higher priority than it had received in peacetime. By 1944 the numbers of doctors and dentists graduating were double the highest numbers in any prewar year, while the number of hospital beds per thousand people increased by 50 percent. Before the war the American Medical Association had objected (solely from greed) to such improvements as health insurance and group practices. Now they were swept away by court order, and by the end of the war the amount of money spent on accident and health insurance was 100 percent greater than in 1939. The results were astonishing: life expectancy rose by three years in the period 1939–45, and for blacks by five years, while the death rate for infants dropped by more than a third.

These wartime gains were consolidated by the Servicemen's Readjustment Act of June 1944, popularly known as the "GI Bill of Rights". This provided a wide range of benefits for the 16 million veterans and their families, who by 1950 constituted about one-third of the population. Veterans were entitled to government help to attend high school or college, to buy a house or take up farming. Millions availed themselves of the provision, particularly to get an education. The results of this aid – welfare wholly without stigma – was to enhance "a powerful wartime trend to the creation of a genuine middle-class democracy".

The GI Bill of Rights was symbolic of another permanent change in American life: the transformation of the relationship between the state and the citizen. Before the war, contact between the average citizen and the government hardly occurred. But contact was regularized during the war, with the draft, social security and the office of price administration. Furthermore, the growth in wage and salary levels and the lowering of the tax floor ensured that many came into contact with the internal revenue service for the first time. The availability of veterans' benefits extended this trend. In short, the war saw the growth of "big government", a permanent development of American life.

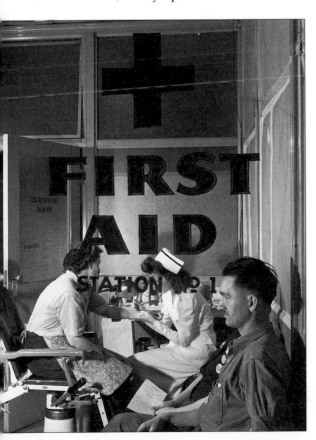

◄ The health crisis was probably most acute in the war industries: its workers had frequently been rejected by the draft for health reasons, the machinery was often dangerous, and conditions could be squalid. Notable exceptions were those run by Henry J. Kaiser. He provided a modern clinic or hospital for each factory or shipyard, and pioneered a health insurance plan for all of his workers and their families. In other war plants, the presence of women workers benefited all, in that sanitary and safety conditions frequently improved dramatically: hot meals might be provided, and operations requiring heavy manual labor were often mechanized. This aircraft factory had first-aid stations dotted throughout the plant.

THE
FRONTLINE
CIVILIANS

Datafile

Bombing campaigns against civilian populations began in World War I. Raids made then caused little damage but had considerable psychological impact. The experience led to two contradictory strategic positions: first, a belief in the power of bombing to devastate enemy civilian populations, destroy morale, and bring about defeat; second, a fear of bombing, which stimulated preparations against bombing raids. In World War II the initial Japanese and German successful use of tactical bombing in China and western Europe seemed to confirm the efficacy of bombing. But the larger and sustained bombing campaigns of the Allies failed to destroy morale.

Casualties of atomic bombs
- Percentage killed
- Percentage injured
- Percentage uninjured

(Hiroshima, Nagasaki; distances 0 to 1km, 1 to 2.5km, 2.5 to 5km)

▶ The impact of bombing was determined more by the existence or absence of protection than by the number of bombs dropped. The short US bombing campaign against Japan caused far more casualties than the Allies' sustained bombing of Germany. The Japanese urban population was concentrated in lightly built cities, where it was exposed to enemy planes for want of defenses.

- UK 1939-45
- Germany 1939-45
- Japan 1944-45

Bombing campaigns

10% 4% 85%
Tonnage dropped on countries
Total 1,591,000 tonnes

7% 35% 58%
Civilians killed by bombing
Total 860,500

▲ The atomic bomb, first used in 1945, raised the power of bombing from disruption to obliteration. Chemical bombs produced local explosions. An atomic "explosion" created a huge yield of energy. It almost totally destroyed the square kilometer around the blast and sent out waves of intense heat and radiation up to 5km (3.1mi). Two bombs were dropped before Japan surrendered. They had slightly different impacts – Hiroshima was flat, Nagasaki hilly – but both took a ghastly toll of human life.

▶ The bombing campaign against Germany in 1943–45 was mounted by RAF Bomber Command and the 8th and 15th USAAF. Bomber Command replicated the German campaign against the UK of 1940–41 with its "area bombing" of German cities. The USAAF concentrated on specific industrial and military targets.

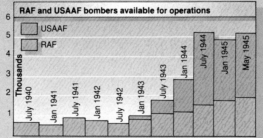

RAF and USAAF bombers available for operations
- USAAF
- RAF

(July 1940, Jan 1941, July 1941, Jan 1942, July 1942, Jan 1943, July 1943, Jan 1944, July 1944, Jan 1945, May 1945)

V1 and V2 attacks
- People injured
- People killed
- Bombs sent

(V1, V2)

▶▲ In November 1943 the RAF began a major assault on Berlin, the German capital. Increasing numbers of planes were sent, but losses mounted and soon the "Battle" had to be called off. Hitler's "secret weapons", the V1 flying bomb and the V2 rocket, also created initial shock but low casualties overall.

RAF raids on Berlin 1943-44: planes sent

(18 Nov, 22 Nov, 23 Nov, 26 Nov, 2 Dec, 16 Dec, 23 Dec, 29 Dec, 1 Jan, 2 Jan, 20 Jan, 27 Jan, 28 Jan, 30 Jan, 15 Feb, 24 Mar)

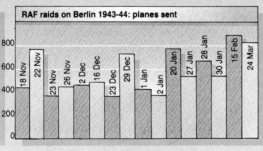

RAF raids on Berlin 1943-44: planes lost

(18 Nov, 22 Nov, 23 Nov, 26 Nov, 2 Dec, 16 Dec, 23 Dec, 29 Dec, 1 Jan, 2 Jan, 20 Jan, 27 Jan, 28 Jan, 30 Jan, 15 Feb, 24 Mar)

In January 1942, when the Japanese were advancing toward Singapore, some 600 civilians were killed and over 1,500 injured by bombs. A report in the Melbourne *Herald* of 19 January stated: "Europeans here have given up talking about 'white' and 'coloured' races... The European ARP workers, who braved death alongside Singapore's splendid body of Asiatic wardens, roof-spotters and fire-fighters, have learnt things not easily forgotten. European women shielding children in the same shelter with Chinese mothers, who have exchanged smiles of relief as a stick of bombs passed a few hundreds of yards away, have discovered many things which will not vanish when Singapore's ordeal has passed."

The rhetoric here may seem eerily familiar. Substitute "middle-class" and "working-class" for "white" and "coloured" and this would read exactly like many reports filed by anti-Nazi US pressmen in London in the fall of 1940. The Australian reporter's optimism was wholly ill-founded. Not only did Singapore fall, but the "Asiatics" whom the Europeans called "coolies" tended to desert their work when air raids were threatened in Japanese broadcasts and leaflets: little had been done to provide shelter for them.

The effect of high explosives on human flesh is horrible. Is every use of it against civilians morally evil? What if these civilians, in "total war" are proud to be "frontline" fighters like their soldiers, as was said of Londoners during the Blitz? Such questions require debate. Bombing in World War II was used in several different ways: with precision against nonhuman targets of military significance; like artillery against enemy troops; in cooperation with land forces; or in deliberately indiscriminate assault on enemy populations.

Aerial bombardment was less than 30 years old in 1939. It was first used by Italians against Turks in Tripoli in 1911-12. In the Balkan wars which followed, a Bulgarian aeroplane dropped 30 bombs on Adrianople in one day, causing only six casualties. The technique appeared somewhat futile. But in January 1915, zeppelin airships of the German navy opened the first "strategic" air offensive. By the end of the war there had been 52 raids by these slow and vulnerable dirigibles, which killed 498 civilians and 58 military and injured 1,357 people. In May 1917, 21 Gotha bomber planes appeared over Kent and killed or injured nearly 300 people in 10 minutes. Twenty-six more Gotha raids in the next 12 months brought the tally of casualties to over 4,000 civilians.

Douhet and theories of bombing

As air forces expanded after the war, extrapolation from such figures suggested that the bombing of cities could cause huge of casualties and

THE BOMBING OF CITIES

◀▼ Some scenes of war are almost interchangeable. This fire, left, happens to be in London (1940–41). Moscow citizens, below, took shelter in the underground railroad system. The photograph insists that there was good order in Stalin's Metro.

came prime minister of the UK, the long-range RAF bombers had been unleashed; the UK had committed itself to a policy of "strategic" night bombing of Germany. That the British raids on the Ruhr in May and June 1940 were wholly ineffectual should not obscure the fact that they happened.

The UK and the Blitz
Fortunately for the UK its fighter command was just able to withstand the assault of the short-range German Messerschmitts. Confusingly the British date the start of their "Blitz" from the point where German Blitzkrieg faltered. Goering should have continued to concentrate the German air force's attack on fighter aerodromes. But on 7 September, London was the target. Huge fires blazed in the city's East End. The officer in charge of an inferno in the Surrey Docks involving 100ha (250 acres) of timber sent a message to his superiors: "Send all the bloody pumps you've got; the whole bloody world's on fire." There were over 2,000 casualties on the first night of

that defense against it was difficult if not impossible. In 1930 an Italian, General Giulio Douhet, crystallized thinking with his claim that armies and navies were now best used for defense while air forces first destroyed opposing fleets in the air, then killed, maimed and demoralized the enemy populations till their clamor forced governments to sue for peace.

Events in the 1930s gave credence to Douhet's predictions. The bombing of Shanghai by the Japanese in 1932 caused Stanley Baldwin, the British Conservative leader, to conclude that "the bomber will always get through. The only defence is offence, which means that you have to kill more women and children more quickly than the enemy if you want to save yourselves." The British Royal Air Force developed long-range bombers. However, the attack which seems most to have focused fears of aerial bombardment was conducted by German pilots cooperating with an army offensive by General Franco's troops in Spain (and also carrying out an experiment in the effect of their current weapons). On 26 April, 1937, a market day, the center of Guernica, the Basque capital, was destroyed, at a human cost of 2,500 casualties.

In Germany Hermann Goering had been impressed by Douhet's ideas, but his air force, in 1940, did not comply with their requirements. It was designed for close cooperation with fast-moving German armies, in Blitzkrieg, "lightning war", and lacked long-range bombers. However, the Dutch capitulated swiftly when their capital and Rotterdam were bombed.

Meanwhile, in May 1940, after Churchill be-

▲ A street in Clydebank, near Glasgow in Scotland, after the Blitz of 13–14 March 1941. The photographer's skill has given the shot a hint of optimism. No other British town suffered such extensive damage. But this was Scotland's only really severe experience of bombing.

▲ A British rescue worker carries a raid victim. Many of those employed in rescue teams had been building workers in peacetime, intimately acquainted with the construction of dwellings – and with hard physical toil.

the Blitz, 430 of them dead, and thousands of East Enders were made homeless. For 76 consecutive nights (barring November 2) London was raided, usually heavily.

Again, had the German air force concentrated on bombing the East End, with its poor and ethnically mixed population, working-class morale might have been decisively affected. Some government ministers feared that it was anyway. But the sheer range of places in the vast city hit by accident or design encouraged the conviction that all Londoners were in it together. As it was, the war in the air turned in fighter command's favor in mid-September. Hitler decided to postpone invasion of Britain and turned his attention to the USSR. London was given ample chance to prove that sustained bombing of a nation's capital was not enough in itself to bring victory.

The Blitz on Britain falls into four main phases: (1) from 7 September to the end of the month, when invasion was still possible; (2) October and November, when Londoners' morale was under siege until ... (3) The heavy raid on Coventry, an important center of war industry, on 14 November, which marked the beginning of a phase where the capital was only one target among many; (4) January to May 1941, when London was still much visited, but when bombers tended to concentrate on the western ports which

were termini for British supplies from America.

Many quite small places, especially on the east coast, were raided heavily relative to their size. From Orkney to Cornwall, few areas of Britain were really remote from the bombing. The Blitz became a national experience. But London – most would have thought this appropriate – took the first heavy blows and set examples of civilian behavior and morale for the rest to follow.

Why did London's morale remain high, and attract admiration from the whole English-speaking world, including, importantly, the USA, where Roosevelt, standing for his third term, had to convince Americans that his anti-German posture was justified? In the first place, during the "Battle of Britain", many parts of London had been bombed as the German air force searched for fighter-command aerodromes. Awesome though the September Blitz was, people had seen bomb damage and heard of casualties before. Civil defense and post-raid preparations, though much criticized, proved just adequate. Furthermore, the earliest phase of the Blitz coincided with victory for fighter command. When Churchill broadcast to the people on 11 September, he announced that present events compared in importance with the crises in which England had seen off the Spanish Armada in 1588, and Britain had stood firm against Napoleon. One of his younger

Early last evening the noise was terrible. My husband and Mr P were trying to play chess in the kitchen. I was playing draughts with Kenneth in the cupboard... Presently I heard a stifled voice "Mummy! I don't know what's become of my glasses." "I should think they are tied up in my wool." My knitting had disappeared and wool seemed to be everywhere! We heard a whistle, a bang which shook the house, and an explosion... Well, we straightened out, decided draughts and chess were no use under the circumstances, and waited for a lull so we could have a pot of tea.

LONDON, NOV. 1940

▶ ▲ **Work continues after the air-raid warning has sounded, in this shelter located under a hairdressing establishment in London's fashionable West End. Carefully posed pictures such as this helped sustain the conviction that normal services must and would continue. However, a barber whose small shop had disappeared might well have been angered by the contrast with his own lot.**

▼ **Britain's "Queen's Messenger" convoys of mobile canteens – 18 fleets of 12 vehicles each, ready to rush to any bombed town were almost all provided by American generosity. They went into action in 1941, but this one is helping out after a V1 has struck, in July 1944.**

female subjects had already committed to paper feelings which many shared. A couple of nights before, frightened sitting indoors by the thump of bombs, she had gone out to survey London from Hampstead. "It was a beautiful summer night, so warm it was incredible, and made more beautiful than ever by the red glow from the East, where the docks were burning. We stood and stared for a minute, and I tried to fix the scene in my mind, because one day this will be history, and I shall be one of those who actually saw it. I wasn't frightened any more..." In this context, even the behavior of those people, mostly poor, who sought illicit shelter in the deep underground stations of the London Tube, mysteriously became acceptable. The 177,000 Londoners who were sleeping in the Tube in late September, simply by being in the city, were Making History, as they calmly arranged their bedding on station platforms. Special trains were soon taking better-off people to Chislehurst Caves, in Kent, which had been developed as a paying private enterprise. They had their own church, electricity, barber and entertainment.

But it is impossible to say whether London "morale" would have stood up under any circumstances. The only safe conclusion is that it was volatile. The flow of adrenalin might enable individuals and groups to endure, even perversely enjoy, flames, wrecked buildings, corpses in the open, but depression might well follow. In this connection it was crucial that the German raids were not only relatively light by standards achieved by the RAF itself over Germany later in the war, but widely dispersed over a very large city.

By contrast, Coventry was a smallish city out of which, on 14 November, the German air force seemed to have ripped the heart – to express which German propaganda coined a new verb, *coventrieren*, "to coventrate". Casualties were over 1,400; 40ha (100 acres) of the city center were destroyed. Several hundred shops were put out of action. As refugees – "trekkers" – poured from the city, those who stayed had to eat from emergency mobile canteens.

Coventry set a pattern for the Blitz outside London at its most severe, in two respects. Firstly,

morale was severely affected by the hammering of a city's center, especially if, as in the case of Plymouth in March and April 1941, the raiders came back again and again. Even in the huge Merseyside conurbation which included Liverpool, eight successive nights of bombing – the "May Week" of 1941 – produced torrents of trekkers and wild rumors of huge casualties and social collapse. But, secondly, as in Coventry, "war production" was little affected.

Events in the small shipbuilding town of Clydebank, near Glasgow, exemplify why this was so. Before two successive nights of raiding hit Clydebank in March 1941, labor relations in the important John Brown's shipyard had been conspicuously bad. Now all but seven of the town's 12,000 houses were damaged; 35,000 out of 47,000 people were homeless; the night population dropped to 2,000 as the inhabitants took to the moors. Yet "a good proportion" of John Brown's men turned up for work on the morning after the Blitz, and the vast majority came back after an average absence of a fortnight.

The Allied onslaught on Germany

If London could take it, Berlin could take it. If Coventry could survive heavy bombing, so could Hamburg. The British learnt only after the war that the policy of "area" bombing by night, which was favored by Churchill and his favorite scientist, Frederick Lindemann, who argued that flattening German working-class houses would break morale and bring victory, was ill-conceived – and immensely wasteful of the lives of brave bomber crews.

In April 1942 RAF bombers raided Rostock, a beautiful old town. They destroyed a lot of buildings, but killed just 204 people. Rostock was back to nearly a hundred percent production after only two days. On 30 May of that year, 1,043 bombers flew for Cologne. That this was a "Thousand

The Bombing of Dresden

The raid on Dresden by British planes on 13–14 February 1945 became at once a fiercely controversial episode. Harris, head of bomber command, believed that terror raids on German cities could win the war. The USSR wanted sharp raids to assist its westward advance. Churchill, at this stage, was actively in favor. In two successive attacks 805 British bombers poured 2,600 tons of bombs into Dresden's center. The second attack was carried out in excellent conditions and achieved exceptional accuracy. The Americans followed this up with daylight raiding which pinpointed the railway yards.

So far, so rational. But even before the full scale of the raid's results was appreciated, Churchill began to recoil from it, referring to it in a minute as "a serious query against the conduct of Allied bombing." Why was this?

First, though Dresden was a major center of communications through which German troops might have passed to get to the Russian front, it was not obviously an important target. Secondly, its population was swollen, not only with wounded troops and refugees who had fled before the Soviet advance or from other bombed cities, but with Allied prisoners of war. Thirdly, the former capital of Saxony was a very beautiful town, hitherto unbombed, a historic center for art and music. Fourthly, while Harris liked attacking such old German towns – "built", as he had said of Lübeck, which his men had destroyed in 1942, "more like a fire-lighter than a human habitation", Portal, chief of air staff, wanted to attack German oil supplies, and so prevent their planes and tanks from moving. Fifthly, the firestorm in Dresden was horrific. It is impossible to establish exactly how many died: 50,000 seems a reasonable estimate – a much greater toll relative to population than that of the Hamburg firestorm.

▶ The devastated center of postwar Dresden.

Bomber Raid" mattered to the British public, who were thoroughly restive over military reverses in the Far East and North Africa. Of the air crews involved, 898 actually claimed to have reached the city: they dropped nearly 1,500 tons of bombs. When Goering heard this phenomenal figure, he refused to believe it. Yet in return for the loss of 291 British airmen, only 474 Germans were killed. There was great destruction, but the official British historians conclude that "Within two weeks the life of the city was functioning almost normally."

However, Churchill believed that British raids were having "a devastating effect", and told Roosevelt so. In January 1943 a joint Anglo-American bomber offensive was agreed. While the USAAF would attack targets of key military importance with precision, by day, the RAF would keep up "area bombing" by night. So from March 1943 to March 1944 the "strategic" employment of air power independently of other arms reached its European wartime peak. Assault by bombers seemed the only way to hit Germans at home so as to give support to the USSR. Initially, British night raids concentrated on the Ruhr.

◀ May 1945, Berliners flee their burning houses as the Soviet army pours millions of shells and rockets into the small area still defended, and uses flamethrowers to incinerate soldiers and civilians alike. Land forces could still match the havoc caused by bomber planes.

My mother and I went into an open field. I remember lying between the furrows watching the Christmas trees – the target markers dropped by the pathfinders – falling slowly down... like huge, very bright, silvery fir trees hanging in the sky, one in each corner of the square, which was the target, Halberstadt.

PETER SAABOR
APRIL 1945

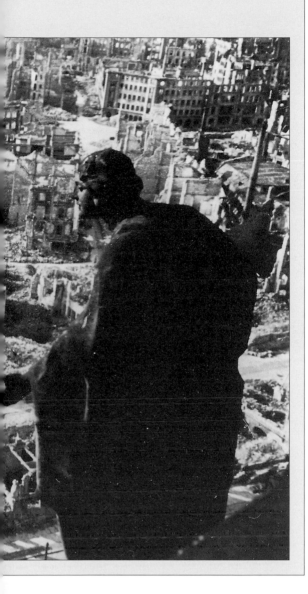

more than 400,000 people were homeless for over a month. By 17 December, a quarter of Berlin's total living accommodation was unusable. But German fighter planes were excellent, German air defense in general subtle. The RAF grew increasingly ineffectual.

What about the effects on German arms production? It tripled between 1942 and 1944. Tank production, 760 a month at the start of 1943 when the Allies agreed on their air offensive, had reached 1669 by July 1944.

One hope of patriotic Germans was that Hitler had secret weapons up his sleeve. He did: unmanned aircraft. In summer 1944 the VI "Flying Bombs" were unleashed and sent puttering and growling across the channel to southern England. The British disliked them intensely, but neither these nor the later V2 rocket bombs had significant effect except on individuals whom they killed or maimed and their families.

In Europe Douhet's theories seemed to be disproved. Neither steady bombing over a long period, nor sudden devastating attack on a key city, nor even the use of shock secret weapons had made decisive impact.

Bombing finally brings results

The Japanese experience might suggest that Douhet's theories received a new lease of life. In fact it completed their supersession. Japan, by August 1945, had suffered the most traumatic exposure to air power yet seen – its air defense was so weak that it had trained suicide pilots to ram the huge bomber planes which were destroying the country. Yet it was by no means clear that all, or even most, of its people were ready to surrender. The weapon which brought surrender was indeed a bomb, but one of a type which made obsolete in a second previous notions about international conflict.

Bar a gallant little raid by B-25s taking off from an aircraft carrier in April 1942, which had landed 16 tons of bombs on Tokyo and shocked the Japanese at the peak of their fortunes, the US air offensive began on 29 June 1944, from western China. The B-29 Superfortresses which made a few long journeys from China to Japan were the

▼ After a raid on Mannheim in 1944, when the town experienced frequent "light" raids by RAF Mosquitoes. For the victim of a "light" raid the experience might be fully as traumatic as seeing a huge city crashing around one. Young children might suffer nightmares well into adulthood.

▼ USAAF precision bombing – a German aircraft factory smashed on 22 February 1945. It was revisited several times before VE Day.

Then, in late July and early August came the Battle of Hamburg. Bombers wrought vast damage and created the first "firestorm", an effect produced on July 27-28 by an attack with incendiaries on a residential area. Twenty-two sq km (8.5sq mi) became a "lake of fire" with air temperature up to 1,000 degrees centigrade. Huge suction was created. Trees were uprooted. People were flung alive into the flames by winds of over 240km/hr (150mph). While high-explosive bombs forced people to shelter, once inside they suffocated, and were reduced to ashes as if in a crematorium. Calculation of the casualty numbers was impossible. Refugees with apocalyptic stories poured from Hamburg into nearby provinces. But most of the workers soon returned. Meanwhile, the US Eighth Air Force, which had made two daylight raids on the city, had lost 43 bombers, about a sixth of its effective force.

Sir Arthur Harris, head of British Bomber Command, believed that he could win the war by devastating Berlin. Impressive damage was caused: Wilhelmstrasse and Unter Den Linden battered, the Chancellery and many other famous buildings destroyed. After the November raids,

▲ Bombs fall toward Kobe, Japan. The USAAF bombing program attacked 65 Japanese cities. The number of planes involved rose steadily – 45 in May, 600 in June, 800 in August. Millions of leaflets warned Japanese in advance as to which cities were next in line. By the end, Allied battleships, too, were able to sail close to shore and bombard ports and industrial centers with impunity.

This outrage against humanity calls for the intervention of the civilised world. This is not war, not even murder, it is pure nihilism. But it will not in any way alter the Japanese war aims... but merely strengthen the will to fight to the last.

JAPANESE RADIO, SINGAPORE
MID AUGUST 1945

biggest bombers of the war, and altogether remarkable. They could fly for 6,500km (4,000mi) at 10,700m (35,000ft) carrying 7.5 tons of bombs at the same speed as a Battle of Britain fighter. Once they got bases which were easier to supply, on the Mariana Islands, within 2,400km (1,500mi) of Japanese cities, they were in a position to achieve spectacular results.

Japan was exceptionally vulnerable. Its air force had been destroyed. Its crowded cities were largely built of matchwood and paper. Attacks by day began on 24 November, 1944. In March 1945, night attacks using incendiaries commenced. The first destroyed about a quarter of Tokyo in a firestorm. In this case 14 US bombers were shot down – thereafter losses were negligible. Similar raids on Yokohama, Osaka, Nagoya and Kobe followed. By the summer Japan's industries had been laid to waste. A quarter of its dwellings had been destroyed. Rural people who were by 1945 eating only four-fifths as much rice as in 1941, now had to cope with 10 million refugees from the bombed cities. Famine was imminent. On 25 March 1945 the government had ordered the mobilization of all people over 13 and under 60 (except pregnant women and the sick) in a "People's Volunteer Corps." If invasion came, they were to fight with bamboo spears for want of other weapons. It was still feared that this remarkable people might fight to the last, taking perhaps half a million Allied soldiers with them on their way to self-destruction. This was the logical basis for Truman's decision to use the atomic bomb, though there were also other motives. Many have since doubted whether this experiment would have been inflicted on a "white" population.

Hiroshima

On 6 August 1945 one bomb, 3m (10ft) long and 0.7m (2ft) in diameter, exploded 500m (1,600ft) above the city of Hiroshima. The temperature at the hypocenter of the explosion was three times that needed to melt an iron bar. Uranium 235 was the agent of destruction.

People suffered skin burns 3.5 km (2mi) away. Of 76,000 buildings near the hypocenter, 70,000 were destroyed beyond use. After the initial slaughter, more people died of burns, blast injuries, and radiation effects. The city's population was swollen with Korean workers and military personnel, to perhaps 420,000. The exact death toll will never be known, but at a high estimate, 140,000 people had died from direct exposure to the blast by the end of 1945. Effects of radiation thereafter may have brought deaths to 200,000 by 1950.

On 25 March 1945 the Japanese government had ordered a general mobilization of all people over 13 and under 60. Schoolgirls in Hiroshima were detailed to do simple physical tasks connected with civil defense in the city center. Shigeko was one who survived, terribly burnt. She was still heavily scarred when she told her story 40 years later.

"I was thirteen years old; I was ordered into the center of the city to clean up the streets. We were working about 1.6 meters from the hypocenter. I heard the aeroplane; I looked up at the sky – the plane had a pretty white tail, it was a sunny day, the sky was blue. This had happened many times before, so I didn't feel scared. Then I saw something drop – white I think – and pow! – a big explosion knocked me down. Then I was unconscious – I don't know for how long. Then I was conscious but I couldn't see anything, it was all black and red. Then I called my friend, Toshiko; then the fog goes away but I can't find her. I never see her again. Then I see people moving away and I just follow them. It is not light like it was before, it is more like evening. I look around; houses are all flat! I could see straight, clear, all a long distance. I follow the people to the river. I couldn't hear anything, my ears are blocked up – or maybe my consciousness is blocked out. I am thinking – a bomb has dropped!

I heard a baby screaming – that woke me up and I could hear things, but nothing sounded loudly. Then I heard a man say, "let's go to the hills" and I thought maybe I should go back to school. People started to push; I was afraid I would fall into the water, and I wanted to leave with the others. There was an old woman on the ground and people were stepping on her. I couldn't help her up! I didn't know my hands were burned, nor my face. Very very difficult...all these years my regret...why couldn't I help her? It still hurts me.

Someone gave me oil for my hands and face. It hurt; my face had a swollen feeling, and I couldn't move my neck. My eyes were swollen and felt closed up. I got to my school yard and sat down, put my head back against a wall and – unconscious again."

Shigeko's parents had survived and found her at the school after four days searching.

For over a year after the Hiroshima bomb fell, few Westerners had more than a vague impression of the horrors it had caused. Then on 31 August 1946 the *New Yorker* abandoned

satire, cartoons and fiction and devoted an entire issue to a reconstruction by John Hersey of the experiences of six people who had survived. It did so in the conviction that few of us have yet comprehended the all but incredible destructive power of this weapon, and that everyone might well take time to consider the terrible implications of its use.

One of Hersey's interlocutors was the Reverend Tanimoto, pastor of the Hiroshima Methodist Church. He quoted a letter from Tanimoto, reporting the unshaken patriotic faith shown by citizens after the explosion. Thirteen-year-old schoolgirls sang *Kimi ga yo*, the national anthem, as they died under a heavy fence which had fallen on them. A Methodist professor was temporarily buried under this burning house with his student son. The boy said, "Father, we can do nothing except make our mind up to consecrate our lives for the country. Let us give *Banzai* to our emperor." Then the father followed after his son, *"Tenno-heika, Banzai, Banzai!"* As a result, Dr Hiraiwa said, "Strange to say, I felt calm and bright and peaceful spirit in my heart..." The pastor concluded, "Yes, people of Hiroshima died manly in the atomic bombing, believing that it was for the emperor's sake."

▲ ◀ Hiroshima, seen (above) after the bombing, had stood on a plain. Nagasaki's site was hilly, its population smaller and less concentrated, and this led to different effects when the second atomic bomb hit it three days later. Hiroshima's bomb used Uranium 235, producing explosive force equal to 13 kilotons of TNT. Plutonium 239 gave Nagasaki's bomb the equivalent of 22 kilotons, but produced fewer casualties. These victims (left) may have been among up to 70,000 who died at Nagasaki by the end of 1945. The city had just before suffered two "conventional" raids, without, in either case, the prior warning normally given by the USAAF.

Datafile

In both Asia and Europe the occupying Axis powers made intensive attempts to utilize the economic and manpower resources of defeated enemies to fuel their own war machines. Their approach was overtly exploitative, and in every instance it was pursued against a complex background of collaboration or resistance by small minorities and unwilling participation by the bulk of the subject population.

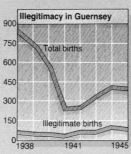

Exploitation of Korean coal

Other coal imports to Japan

Production in Korea

Imports of Korean coal

Millions (tonnes)

1940 1942 1944

Tributes levied by Reich

Reichsmarks (millions)

France
Netherlands
Belgium
Denmark
Italy
Others

1940 1941 1942 1943 1944

◀ **Germany levied direct contributions on the European countries which fell under its sway. France, the largest and most prosperous of its client states, was the most prominent contributor, but the burden fell heavily on every area in which the Germans were able to erect the machinery of exploitation.**

▶ **One product of military occupation was the disruption of normal patterns of family life and procreation. In occupied Guernsey, the birth rate fell steeply to approximately half the prewar norm, while the percentage of illegitimate births rose even more abruptly — from 5.5 percent in 1938–39 to 21.8 percent in 1944.**

▲ **Japan strove hard to extract essential raw materials from its subject peoples to fuel its resource-poor domestic industrial economy. Japanese control over the sources of supply was total and uncompromising, but supply difficulties (eg sinking of merchant ships) placed severe constraints on the economic returns.**

Illegitimacy in Guernsey

Total births

Illegitimate births

1938 1941 1945

▼▶ **At the peak of Axis fortunes in 1942, the zones of occupation covered immense areas of the globe: all but a tiny portion of mainland Europe and Scandinavia and the western part of the USSR were in German hands, while approximately half the Pacific islands, most of Southeast Asia and the East Indies, and the northeastern quarter of China had fallen to the Japanese. In many areas occupation lasted for years and was underpinned by extensive administrative and police systems.**

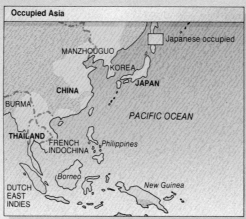

Occupied Asia

Japanese occupied

MANZHOUGUO
KOREA
CHINA
JAPAN
BURMA
PACIFIC OCEAN
THAILAND
FRENCH INDOCHINA
Philippines
Borneo
New Guinea
DUTCH EAST INDIES

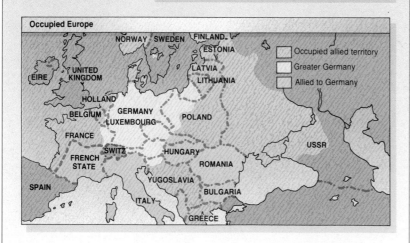

Occupied Europe

NORWAY SWEDEN FINLAND
ESTONIA
LATVIA
LITHUANIA
EIRE UNITED KINGDOM
HOLLAND
BELGIUM GERMANY POLAND
LUXEMBOURG
FRANCE
USSR
SWITZ HUNGARY
FRENCH STATE ROMANIA
SPAIN YUGOSLAVIA
BULGARIA
ITALY
GREECE

Occupied allied territory
Greater Germany
Allied to Germany

During World War II the Japanese ruled two areas of China: first, Manchuria in the north and northeast; second, a very large but continually fluctuating zone along the coasts and rivers of the south. The Chinese experience of Japanese occupation during World War II was characterized by a level of brutality, cynical exploitation and social, political and economic dislocation that was exceeded only by the horrific ordeal of European Jewry.

Japanese treatment of Chinese territories

Manchuria had been occupied in 1931. It served as the testing ground for the machinery of domination and exploitation which was later to be employed throughout Japanese-conquered territories.

The Japanese established a nominally independent state, Manzhouguo, under the Chinese-led regime of the restored emperor, Pu Yi. The occupiers sponsored a massive inflow of settlers and capital, which resulted in new cities and industries, but they treated Manchuria as a zone of economic exploitation. Resources were ruthlessly stripped away to meet the needs of the Japanese war machine.

The regime of Pu Yi attempted to ape the glories of the former Manchu dynasty, but it was an empty sham. Government officials up to the highest level were pawns in the hands of their Japanese advisors, and real power rested with the local Japanese army, the Guandong army, which contained most of Japan's radical imperialists. The trappings of Manchurian independence were only a thin veil for the intolerance of any effort to better the lot of the populace or any resistance to the demands of the occupiers.

The Japanese occupation of China itself was even more overt in its disregard of local needs or sentiments. The government of Weng Jing-wei, made up largely of nationalist rivals of Jiang Jieshi, marked only a belated realization that full conquest was best pursued through the mobilization of local political elements hostile to both Jiang and his communist enemies. No real power was transferred to collaborators and they were soon given every reason to rue the misguided nationalism which had placed them in Japanese hands.

The brutal apparatus of military occupation operated unchecked throughout the war, with the daily record of routine persecution being occasionally interrupted by outbursts of the utmost savagery. The efforts of the Japanese to realize the economic potential of the large cities and of their rural and riverine hinterlands were often hampered by their very rapacity, by the consequent flight of much of the population and by Chinese sabotage.

OCCUPATION AND RESISTANCE

Notwithstanding the territorial gains of the Japanese in 1937-41, much of China remained a fluid war zone throughout the conflict. At its best, Japanese military treatment of Chinese civilians in contested areas was characterized by indifference to safety and casual brutality. At its worst, it degenerated into murderous savagery. When Nanjing fell in December 1937, the conquerors exposed the prostrate city to a month-long reign of terror which left a third of it in ashes and hundreds of thousands of inhabitants dead. Later in the war, when attempts at creating an alternative collaborationist focus for civilian loyalties failed to stem the spread of communist guerrilla activity, the Japanese instituted the infamous "Three All" policy: take all, burn all, kill all. They laid waste entire rural areas and exterminated all who did not flee.

The immediate effect of Japanese atrocities was often a form of shocked compliance. In the long run, however, the occupiers only succeeded in catalyzing the hitherto muted nationalistic sentiments of the population. Nor did the massive structural damage inflicted on Chinese society advance the cause of Japanese hegemony. Mass destruction and death, and the even more massive internal migrations these forced, did heavy damage to the old traditions of village life. The administrative, intellectual and economic centers in the great cities were similarly battered out of shape by military onslaught and then strangled by exploitation.

The end result, again, was only to render Chinese civilization more receptive to 20th-century ideas of nationhood and populist political action. It would be simplistic to view the postwar history of Chinese communism as the direct result of Japanese occupation, but there can be little doubt that the heavy hand of the invader helped set loose the social and political forces that would bring Mao Zedong and his colleagues to power within four years of the war's end.

Japan's imperial dream

The dazzling series of victories won by Japanese armies in 1941-42 left a huge area, stretching from Burma through Malaya over the Dutch East Indies and up to the Philippines and Hong Kong, to be administered by the conquerors. Japanese objectives in establishing their rule were confused and to a certain extent contradictory, but they did revolve around three basic principles: first, the eradication of European and American influence, be it cultural, economic or political; secondly, the exploitation of mineral, agricultural and manpower resources for the benefit of the Japanese war effort; thirdly, the establishment of Japan as the leader of Asia in all walks of life with the new territories grouped around it as satellites,

subject to varying degrees of control from the center. In a sense Japan was attempting to assume the role once played by Imperial China on the wide Asian stage.

Japanese propaganda stressed the pan-Asiatic nature of the war effort from the start. The war itself was called *Dai Toa Senso* (the Greater East Asia War) and its objective the establishment *Dai Toa Kyoeiken* (the Greater East Asia Coprosperity Sphere). Peace and stability were to be restored to the area, which Japanese arms would protect from Anglo-American exploitation, and all of the constituent peoples would cooperate to fashion a self-sufficient economic zone. The major proponent of the scheme was the semidictatorial prime minister, General Hideki Tojo, who overcame entrenched foreign-office resistance to create a new Greater East Asia Ministry in November 1942. This body's policy role tended to be minimal, the naval and military commands retaining a firm grip on major political and administrative decisions, and while it did provide some manpower to replace ousted colonial officials, its prime mission was cultural. Huge efforts were made to replace the various European tongues with Japanese as the second language of the captured territories, and a series of conferences, group study tours and goodwill missions were staged in an attempt to prove that Japanese

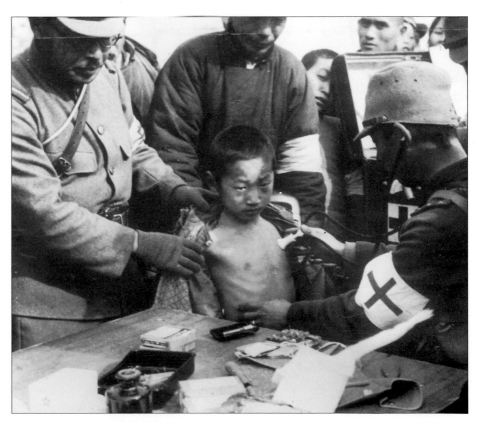

◀ False humanity. A Japanese propaganda picture of a Chinese boy receiving medical attention from the occupying forces. The reality was far different: apart from cynical attempts to promote collaboration through some measure of correct treatment, the Japanese treated Chinese civilians either with callous indifference or murderous savagery, the latter being particularly common when any form of resistance was encountered.

culture was at once more natural and more dynamic than that of the decadent West. Japan's attitude to and treatment of the heterogeneous territories under its sway varied according to past history and strategic importance. By the time of the Greater East Asia Conference in Tokyo in the autumn of 1943, five countries had been recognized as independent allies of Japan: Manzhouguo, China, Thailand, Burma and the Philippines. In the first two cases, the areas in question had been under Japanese control for years. In the third and fourth cases the Japanese were able to establish collaborationist governments in the existing political framework of countries with long histories of independent existence. In the Philippines another puppet government was eventually set up, but the occupying forces never really broke through the barriers of a heavily Europeanized culture and an active resistance movement.

Elsewhere Japanese policy followed a different line for reasons which were primarily economic. The conquest of Malaya and the Dutch East Indies gave Japan direct access to the tin, rubber and oil resources it required for self-sufficiency. The occupying forces were very slow to move away from direct naval or military rule, or to encourage any sort of nationalist movement. Initially at least, promises of greater control of their own efforts were made only to limit obstruction to and encourage participation in Japan's exploitative economic policies. As the war progressed, and as the possibility of Japanese defeat became more and more real, the occupation forces began to foster nationalism in a more wholehearted fashion, hoping thereby to create some form of united Asian front against advancing Anglo-American forces.

The realities of Japanese occupation

All over the conquered territories Japanese rule was brutally exploitative. However elaborate the pretence of independence or self-government, the military used coercion to meet its ends and responded violently to any form of resistance.

European civilians were herded up and confined in conditions little better than those prevailing in Japan's notorious prisoner-of-war camps. Eurasians were treated with harsh suspicion as polluters of indigenous ethnic purity, and Chinese communities were singled out for systematic oppression. Regular occupation troops were responsible for much of the almost routine violence of the system, but any overt or suspected sign of recalcitrance or resistance was dealt with by the *Kempeitai* (Japanese military police). Their cruelty was paralleled only by Hitler's Gestapo. The military police were particularly fond of pulling out their prisoners' fingernails, which soon gave rise to the grim joke: "Do your nails need a manicure?"

The labor demands of Japan's overextended war effort were met in part by the mass conscription of native labor. Despite the fact that they were often citizens of countries in national alliance with Japan, these laborers were forced to work in conditions of great deprivation and brutality. Thirty thousand Burmese civilians

◄ **Foreign manpower for the Japanese war effort. Japanese policy was characterized by the massive use of impressed labor from occupied zones. These Korean youths are under training in a Japanese agricultural school – other races received no such tutelage but were simply herded straight to their task.**

◄▼ **The Sino-Japanese conflict had a peculiar ideological dimension. The Japanese made periodic attempts to convert disgruntled nationalists to the spurious doctrines of coprosperity, while the Guomindang and their communist rivals devoted as much time to propaganda attacks on each other as to countering Japanese efforts.**

died while helping build the Burma–Thailand railway, the worst but by no means the only example of forced human sacrifice inflicted on the Asian population. Economic policy was equally rapacious. Trade between Japan and its new dependencies was almost entirely one way – a flood of raw materials being sent to the home islands without any adequate reverse flow of manufactured goods (commodities which most areas had formerly received from prewar European trading partners). The Japanese also debased local currencies, causing runaway inflation through their habit of printing money as required for their own needs. Whatever their reaction to the initial Japanese arrival, few Asians were able to sustain ideas of liberation or Japanese friendship for very long. Even the behavior of the departed European overlords seemed preferable to the new "coprosperity".

The motives of those East Asians who collaborated with the occupying forces were generally mixed. A minority may well have swallowed the initial Japanese message of liberation, friendship and prosperity, but few were paying it any more than lip-service after even brief exposure to the realities of occupation. Some collaborated in the hope of shielding their countrymen from the worst excesses of Japanese rule, and in one case at least there is some evidence to suggest that the puppet regime was giving covert support to the guerrilla resistance. While there was widespread approval of the defeat of the white colonial powers, the response to the forced importation of Japanese culture was rarely positive. By the last years of the war, all but the blindest were collaborating only in the hope of Japan's defeat bringing true independence rather than a return to colonial rule or European domination.

The Dutch East Indies

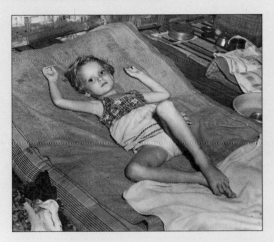

◄ **The savagery of neglect: a girl of seven in a recently liberated internment camp in Batavia. The Japanese interned the resident European populations in the colonial countries which fell under their sway.**

▼ **Indonesian sailors of the Dutch East Indies squadron before the successful Japanese invasion of 1942. The Japanese occupation heightened nationalist sentiment, and when the Allies attempted to reimpose Dutch rule in 1945, they were confronted by armed nationalist resistance.**

The Japanese occupation of the Dutch East Indies provides an interesting study in contrasts and paradox. Rich in natural assets, particularly oil, on which the whole Japanese economy depended, the area was viewed foremost by the Japanese as a strategic asset. After the Japanese conquest the islands were kept under firm military or naval control.

The Dutch East Indies had no tradition of national unity save that imposed by the colonial power. These ties were violently severed by the Japanese, by the defeat of Allied forces, by the removal of all colonial administrators from their posts and by the imprisonment and deliberate humiliation of the resident white minorities. The long-term Japanese goal was the creation of new, notionally independent states under their own hegemony. The military and naval commands, however, were loath to surrender control over such important resource areas, and in the short term the islands were subject to rigid Japanese administration. But imported bureaucrats proved unequal to the task and effective power devolved on their native subordinates. This, and the necessity of using Indonesian as the official language, fostered nationalism in spite of Japanese conservatism.

Two factors combined to accelerate the move toward Indonesian statehood. The first was the collapse of the plantation economy under the strains of the failing Japanese war effort. The native population became united in opposition to the occupiers. The second was the series of defeats suffered by Japanese forces in 1943–44 which made the occupiers more prepared to make concessions to nationalist leaders like Sukarno, in the hope of rallying the Asian population.

On 17 August 1945 Sukarno and his followers proclaimed the independence of Indonesia. While this was premature according to the Japanese schedule, the occupying forces made no move to intervene. In violation of the surrender terms, which required them to retain control until the arrival of Allied forces, the Japanese allowed the nationalists to take over administrative functions (including the guarding of interned Dutch nationals) and actually supplied the new republic with arms.

▲ German victories were accompanied by conspicuous triumphalism, like this daily military parade down the Champs Elysées in Paris. This high profile, with a German military presence in provincial as well as metropolitan areas, was calculated: it made resistance activity both more difficult and more hazardous. But, as defeat loomed and resistance forces gained in confidence, this committed German troops to policing large areas – a costly exercise for a conqueror with severe manpower problems.

► Even in countries where there was little attempt to conciliate the native population, Nazi propaganda tried to elicit compliance by stressing the possibility of a worse fate. With the Red Army's counterattack in 1943, Poles were warned that "only the German soldier can save Europe in the struggle against Bolshevism".

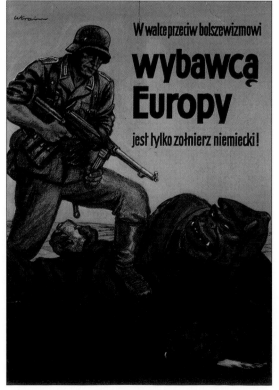

W walce przeciw bolszewizmowi
wybawcą Europy
jest tylko żołnierz niemiecki!

Occupied Europe: Hitler's New Order

Hitler went to war in September 1939 not merely to recoup the losses imposed on Germany by the Treaty of Versailles in 1919 but to create a "New Order" in which Germany would dominate continental Europe, take over Russian territory, and destroy its twin enemies: Jews throughout Europe and Russian "Bolsheviks". Nazi ideology propagated the idea of a "New Europe" in which European nation-states would accept German hegemony as being in their own best interests, with Germany leading a European crusade against communism. In most countries which came under German rule during the war, this vision had its enthusiasts.

To create his "New Order" Hitler was determined to secure "living space" (*Lebensraum*) for the German "master race", including non-German "Nordic" or "Aryan" peoples like Norwegians and Dutch. Non-"Aryans", in both western and eastern Europe, would have the task of serving the "master race" within a large-scale economic bloc (*Grossraumwirtschaft*). Germany's needs could thus be given priority; above all, its food supply would be guaranteed against any future blockade, as a vital part of Hitler's overall strategy. (See p.114.) In order to acquire "living space", German forces would have to take military and political control of virtually all of Europe, either directly or else through puppet surrogates.

Through prewar annexations and wartime conquests Germany secured mastery over most of Europe. From fall 1939 to fall 1944 German soldiers fought on fronts outside the borders of the Reich, extending and defending an empire which at its zenith in 1942–43 had some 180 million inhabitants. This "Greater German Reich" stretched from the Atlantic to the Caucasus, from Scandinavia to the Mediterranean. Only Switzerland, Sweden, Eire, Turkey, Spain and Portugal were neutral; the last two were clearly pro-German and, like Turkey and Sweden, they supplied Germany with vital raw materials for most of the war. Switzerland exported machinery and armaments to Germany; the USSR, too, provided Hitler's war machine with essential supplies, including fuel oil, until the German invasion in June 1941. Finland was nominally neutral and independent, but inclined to favor Germany once the invasion of the USSR had begun; this was a case of "my enemy's enemy is my friend", after the bitter Russo-Finnish War of 1939–40. (See p.49.) Romania, Bulgaria, Hungary and Slovakia were allied to Hitler, nominally sovereign but entirely subordinate to him.

Mussolini's Italy was initially an ally which shared (belatedly) in the French campaign and then in the invasion of the USSR. But Italy's disastrous campaigns in Greece and North Africa made it a liability, and the price of a German rescue in both these areas was Italian acceptance of German domination. Italy's defection in July 1943, after Mussolini's fall, brought German invasion and occupation. Thereafter, Italians, in the north of their country especially, were as much at the mercy of German brutality as were citizens of other countries.

The redeployment of German peoples

The *Lebensraum* Hitler sought was more than simply extra territory: it was assigned the status of a "promised land" of prime territory, stretching across Europe and inhabited by "Nordic" peoples, along with enough non-"Nordic" workers to service their requirements. The most fertile, mineral-rich, industrialized and climatically benign areas would form the "Greater German Reich", with most Slavs and other non-"Nordic" peoples banished to the wastes of Siberia or other inhospitable areas. The permanent need for vigilance along the borders between the two kinds of territory would, Himmler believed, keep Germans alert and strong.

These plans required a vast movement of peoples from one part of Europe to another. While the Soviet-German pact was in force, from August 1939 to June 1941, hundreds of thousands of "ethnic Germans" left eastern European countries like the Baltic States, Romania or the USSR itself, to settle either in Germany or in land annexed to the Reich from Poland. Citizens of the Reich, too, were encouraged either to settle in the former Polish territories or to undertake a tour of duty there to assist new settlers. At the same time, many Poles and other non-German inhabitants of this area were deported to the "General Government", the residue of Poland after German and Soviet annexations. Once German forces had conquered most of European Russia, in 1942, Himmler dreamed of settling Germans there, as frontiersmen. And from 1941 there were mass deportations of Jews from all over Europe "to the east", that is, to extermination camps (see p.164).

These migrations occurred over and above complex military operations and, like them, required manpower, transport and fuel. It is a measure of the primacy of the ideological goal of

► A Ukrainian woman reading a Nazi poster. In the USSR the native population was mostly treated as hostile. But in the Ukraine Germany's struggle against *Russian* Bolshevism was portrayed as a common cause. This was contradicted by German policy, which alienated Ukrainians who had at first welcomed German soldiers as liberators from Stalinism. But German refusal to rehabilitate Christianity and to dissolve the collective farms was crucial in forfeiting the support of the major disaffected nationality in the USSR.

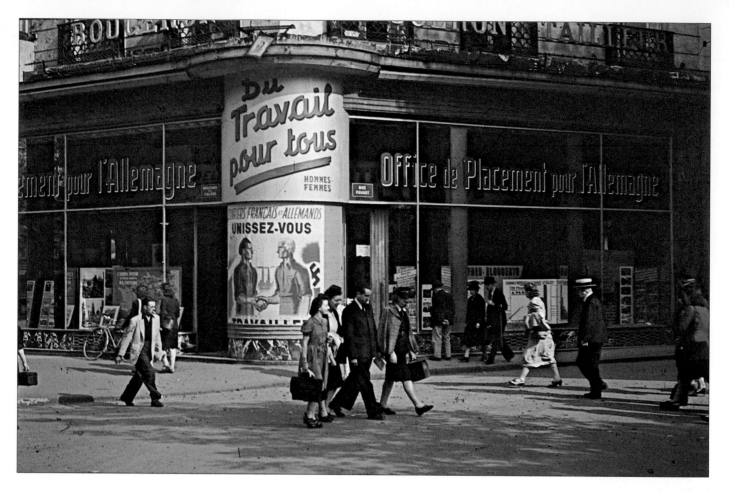

Lebensraum that Germany's already scarce resources were depleted by the demands of Nazi programs of settlement and genocide. Even in 1944, with the Allies closing in on Germany, precious fuel and transport were utilized to ensure that Hungarian Jews were conveyed to the death-camps at Auschwitz.

The pattern of occupation

All countries under German rule suffered expropriation and exploitation of resources, both human and material. Their peoples suffered the humiliation of being at best second-class citizens in their own land, and many were forced to assist the continuing German war-effort. Their material resources were worked mercilessly for the same purpose. In some cases, industrial plant was dismantled and removed to Germany, followed by the "voluntary" migration of workers from, for example, France or Belgium seeking employment. Poles had been forcibly drafted into work in Germany from late 1939, often as farm labor, and, especially from mid-1942, forced labor from the USSR was put to work in Germany. As the war turned against Germany, from 1942, compulsion was increasingly used to draft foreigners into Germany, where they worked mostly either in factories, fueling the German war-effort, or in agriculture (see p.116). France was the principal source of skilled labor, while the unskilled came chiefly from the USSR.

For no two countries was the experience of German occupation identical, and in each country German rule was in a state of flux throughout the period of occupation. Structures of government were constantly being adapted to meet changing circumstances, such as the initial conquest, levels of collaboration and resistance, and ultimate military defeat. But for any country German occupation was a deeply degrading experience. Western European countries, it is true, were mostly spared the barbaric brutality meted out in eastern Europe. There, Nazi racial prejudices branded Slavs as "inferior", fit only to serve "Aryan" Germans and to live, consequently, at a much lower standard than the "master race". This mirrored the treatment of Polish and Soviet forced labor in Germany itself. Above all, most of Europe's 9 million Jews were to be found in the east, chiefly in Poland and the USSR, with fewer

▲ Before forced labor conscription began in 1942, the Germans encouraged western European men and women to migrate to work in Germany. This recruitment office in Paris gave the impression that French and Germans were equal partners in the venture. Nothing could be further from the truth.

▼ In 1940 France was divided into two: the German-occupied area in the north and along the western seaboard, and the southern Vichy zone. French people could move between the two areas only if their identity papers satisfied German border police.

The Netherlands

In May 1940 the queen and cabinet escaped to Britain and formed a government-in-exile. A German civilian Reich commissioner was appointed – Arthur Seyss-Inquart, who was personally responsible to Hitler. Early German rule was conciliatory: the occupiers believed that the Dutch, as a "Nordic" people, would collaborate in their racial war. At first Dutch laws remained in force and Dutch civil servants continued to administer government. They issued identity cards, photographed and fingerprinted everyone, distributed ration cards, and issued a racial questionnaire. Thus German authority and Nazi ideology were gradually imposed, although Dutch officials tried to mitigate their worst effects.

The chief collaborators were in the Dutch national socialist movement (NSB). Its leader, Anton Mussert, was a useful pro-German propagandist, portraying the Dutch as the "second strongest branch of the German tree", but he lacked real power. He helped to organize the Netherlands Legion, which fought on the Eastern Front. There were also collaborators, who, often unknown to their friends and neighbors, spied and informed. But, in greater measure, there was opposition to German rule virtually from the start, from communists, the Church, the universities, among many others. Symbolic items signifying loyalty to the royal family – white carnations, the color orange – were widely displayed. London-based "Radio Orange"

encouraged subversion and a boycott of all German or pro-German events, from radio programs and concerts to football matches. Antisemitic measures, however, provoked both open and clandestine resistance. Jews were identified and segregated, and sometimes brutally attacked in the streets by the NSB. Revulsion at one such incident in Amsterdam in 1941 led to a 48-hour strike and demonstrations there and elsewhere. Many Dutch families concealed Jews to prevent their deportation. But some 104,000 out of 140,000 Dutch Jews perished, with Seyss-Inquart a zealous executor of Nazi racial policies. He also brutally tried to eradicate resistance. Nevertheless, it flourished: underground newspapers spread information and boosted morale; German offices and vehicles were blown up; several leading NSB members were assassinated. Five million Dutch workers were sent to Germany, but 300,000 fugitives were concealed and given forged ration cards by resistance groups.

Winter 1944–45 brought unspeakable suffering. To assist the Allied advance into Holland, the Dutch government-in-exile called for a railroad strike to cut German supply lines. The response was massive, as were the German reprisals. Some 16,000 died of cold and hunger as the occupier refused to allow food supplies to towns in western Holland. Liberation by the Allies was completed only in early May 1945.

▲ Nazi propaganda attempted to persuade other "Nordic" peoples actively to embrace Germany's struggle. This poster calls on "volunteers from Germany, Netherlands, Flanders, Denmark, Norway to apply for the Waffen–SS", under the slogan: "Peoples of similar blood fight together against the common enemy".

---

than a million in the west. German conquests made Jews throughout Europe an easy prey: almost 70 percent of all European Jews perished in the Holocaust, including 90 percent of Polish Jews.

Apart from their implacable attitude toward Jews, the German occupiers in western Europe were more conciliatory, especially while Germany was still victorious. They exhorted French, Dutch and other western Europeans to recognize their alleged common cause, and, especially after the German invasion of the Soviet Union in June 1941, propaganda urged western Europeans to support Germany's campaign to eradicate "Bolshevism". With Hitler's initial insistence that "none but Germans shall bear arms", it was their duty to provide munitions and other supplies for the German army by hard work in factories, whether in their own country or in Germany. But the insatiable demands of the German army led to appeals for western European volunteers for the "struggle against communism", and many joined units of the Waffen-SS.

Occupied peoples and their rulers

Nazi racial theorists regarded Norwegians, Danes and Dutch, especially, as "Aryan", and therefore worthy of a favored place in the "Greater German Reich". Propaganda was directed at "educating" them to accept their destiny. But most western Europeans continued to prize national independence above a mirage of loosely defined superiority under Nazi control. In every western occupied country and some eastern ones,

however, there were collaborators prepared to accept German hegemony and German plans for their future. There were also in every occupied country – in east and west – groups of resistance fighters, who would not accept German rule, and who engaged in activities from sabotage to helping Allied agents in a plethora of small local counter-offensives against the German occupiers.

But collaborators and resisters were at the extremes of reaction to German occupation: in both cases, they were very much in a minority. The vast majority of citizens in occupied countries simply tried to survive, accommodating themselves to German demands where refusal to do so could bring severe retribution. Especially in eastern Europe, the occupiers were quick to take reprisals, usually in response to acts of resistance. The total destruction of the Czech village of Lidice in 1942 was a particularly barbaric example. But there were also martyrs in western countries like France, where the massacre of women and children at Oradour-sur-Glane in 1944 was perhaps the most notorious example. Major atrocities were perpetrated elsewhere, notably in both Italy and Serbia (the German-occupied area of Yugoslavia).

On the whole, western civilians tried to maintain as normal a way of life as possible. This was not the same as collaboration: it was merely pragmatism, given a seemingly invincible German army. Until 1943 it looked as if German occupation might last for 50 or 100 years – for a lifetime. Accommodation to the "New Order" was the obvious option in western Europe, after German forces had quickly destroyed countries' actual and

We now experience the grotesque spectacle that after the tremendous starvation of prisoners of war, millions of foreign laborers must be recruited to fill the gaps which have appeared in Germany. With the usual unlimited abuse of Slav people, "recruiting" methods were used which can only be compared with the blackest periods of the slave trade. (They are allowed only the most limited education, and can be given no welfare services.) We are interested in feeding them only insofar as they are still capable (and they are given to understand that in every aspect we regard them as inferior).

DR OTTO BRÄUTIGAM
REICH MINISTRY OF THE
EASTERN TERRITORIES
25 OCTOBER 1942

▲ In the USSR armed partisans used local conditions to telling effect in harassing the invader and sabotaging communications.

▲ The requirement that Soviet citizens constantly and conspicuously wear an identification number emphasized their relegation by the German occupiers to the status of subhumans. Place-names and road signs appeared only in German; the victors required information, the vanquished victims merely awaited commands.

▶ In every occupied country, the Gestapo rapaciously sought out opponents. Resistance leaders soon realized that well-informed agents could, under torture, reveal enough to destroy an entire network. To avoid this, the information given to each agent was kept to an absolute minimum, so that there was very little for him or her — involuntarily — to reveal.

German oppression

The level of German oppression in western Europe clearly depended on Germany's fortunes during the war. Until 1942, with the prospect of German victory seemingly both assured and imminent, the demands of the occupiers were relatively mild. For example, the voluntary migration of labor to Germany sufficed not least because forced labor was conscripted from Poland and, from 1942, the USSR. But the failure to win quickly in Russia in 1941-42 strained existing resources. The need for increased numbers of workers for German industry led to the compulsory recruitment of hundreds of thousands of French, Dutch and Belgians for work in German industrial cities. At the same time, rations in the occupied countries declined to a level of around three-quarters of the calorie intake of Germans, whose rations were decreasing. Much of Germany's food supply came from France, whose contribution was as great as that of all the eastern occupied territories together.

In the east, as in the west, resources were plundered for the benefit of Germany. If yields were lower in the east, it was because resources were poorer and the methods of exploitation, while no less ruthless, were often mutually contradictory. The brutality and inhumanity which characterized German treatment of Poland's land and people from autumn 1939 clearly indicated what other Slav populations could expect at Germany's hands. The major difference between occupation policy in Poland and that in western Europe was the prominent role played by the SS in the east. Special SS "task forces" (*Einsatzgruppen*) were attached to German army units, charged with eliminating actual and potential Polish leaders, including the intelligentsia, army officers, the clergy and the nobility. In the areas absorbed into Germany, Poles were to form a docile class of manual laborers for unskilled work. Young Poles were to receive only the rudiments of education necessary for the menial tasks assigned to them. On the other hand, Polish children of "good blood" were to be educated in Germany, with or

without their parents' consent. In the General Government, conditions were only slightly better. Any sign of dissidence among Poles was countered with conspicuous brutality.

If German conduct in Poland was barbaric, it plumbed new depths in dealing with the peoples of the USSR, who became, in German parlance, *Untermenschen* (sub-humans). Here the SS "task forces" were used on a large scale. Unleashed to massacre Jews and Communist Party officials, they also indiscriminately murdered thousands of ordinary Russians as well. This was not some unintentional byproduct of expropriation and exploitation: it was deliberate brutality and mass murder. It often actually ran counter to German interests: at a time when labor was scarce on the German home front, huge numbers of Soviet prisoners of war were rounded up and left to starve or freeze in primitive camps. The zeal with which Red Army soldiers (all classed as "Bolsheviks") were liquidated in 1941-42 as racial and political enemies was that of the fanatic. But the failure to win a quick victory in Russia gave the initiative to pragmatists who saw in Russia's millions the kind of basic manual laborers who could work for the German war-effort.

At the start of the Russian campaign, German forces had a strong potential advantage: the many subject nationalities within the Soviet Union were implacably hostile to Russians generally and to Stalin and the Communist Party in particular. But this opportunity was thrown away in an orgy of killing and destruction. The Ukrainians who welcomed the German "liberators" in 1941 received a cool response. Here, however, there was an exception to the Germans' normally hostile attitude to eastern Europeans: an appeal was made to Ukrainians, as to western Europeans, to serve the anti-"Bolshevist" war-effort by working in German armaments factories. Even so, the saddest comment to be made about German occupation policy in the USSR is that, for ideological reasons, it was in practice no better, and often even worse, than the horrors recently experienced by Soviet citizens at Stalin's hands.

Yugoslavia

Yugoslavia came into being at the end of World War I. Land from the dismembered Austro-Hungarian Empire was added to Serbia to create a south Slav kingdom in which the Serbs dominated some eight subject nationalities, of whom the Croats were the largest and most vociferous. Inhabiting the western half of the country, the Croats were Roman Catholic, while the Serbs, in the east, tended to be Orthodox Christians. After the German invasion and victory in April 1941, small parts of the country were hived off to Germany, Italy, Hungary, Romania and Bulgaria. German domination of the residue could not disguise the internecine war waged between different "Yugoslavs". A large, nominally independent Croatia was placed under the Ustaše, a Croatian separatist group led by Ante Pavelić, which unleashed a lengthy reign of terror, chiefly against Jews and Serbs. German rule in Serbia, through the puppet general Milan Nedić, was challenged by two resistance groups, the Četniks, led by the Serbian nationalist, Draža Mihailović, and the partisans under the leader of the outlawed communist party of Yugoslavia, Tito (Josip Broz). The partisans harassed Italian and German troops, engaging in sabotage, capturing towns, and tying down substantial numbers of occupying troops; when the odds were against them, they escaped to the rugged mountain areas. They attracted support from Croats and Bosnians revolted by the Ustaše atrocities, as well as from Serbs and Slovenes, giving them bases in all parts of the country. From the very start, they constructed a system of local government in areas they liberated. This confirmed the Četniks, representing the royal government-in-exile, in their hostility to the partisans whom they saw as no better than the invader; the result was civil war of a particularly bestial and brutal kind. Believing the widespread anti-German guerrilla activity to have been instigated by the Četniks, the Allies sent them aid in the hope that Mihailović would unite the opposition to German occupation. Only in 1943 did they accept that Mihailović was serving German interests while the partisans were fighting single-mindedly against German forces. The strength of Tito's partisans was evidenced when they were able to seize Italian arms and Yugoslav territory held by Italy, when Italy changed sides in September 1943. Their 250,000 soldiers controlled most of northwestern Yugoslavia, and in 1944 they were on the offensive, besieging German garrisons in several towns. On 20 October 1944 Belgrade fell to the partisans. Alone among occupied countries, Yugoslavia was liberated by indigenous effort, and Tito's prestige and popularity enabled him to rule for over 30 years after the war.

▼ Tito (Josip Broz, foreground right) was the Yugoslav communist partisan leader who fought successfully against both invaders and native rivals. He and his men lived and planned campaigns in hideouts in the rugged mountain regions of Yugoslavia, inflicting damaging guerrilla attacks on foes who often outnumbered them. From 1943, Allied aid strengthened his forces, which in 1945 liberated Yugoslavia.

The Soviet victory at Kursk in July 1943, and the western offensive based on the D Day landings in Normandy in June 1944, were only the beginning of the end of the "New Order". Liberation in both east and west brought rejoicing, but was achieved at a terrible cost to civilians as well as combatants. Towns in northern France were bombed by France's allies. The Warsaw uprising against German rule was denied Soviet aid by Stalin. Tenacious German military resistance virtually to the end condemned most occupied countries to suffer further destruction.

The new Europe

With the Treaty of Rome in 1957, a mere 12 years after the war, a "new Europe" was created in the west. Had the wounds of war already healed, enabling five countries which had suffered German occupation – "Benelux", Italy and France – to cooperate with a part of Hitler's former Reich? More realistically, the desperate economic problems faced by all of them, reinforced by American pressure, promoted economic cooperation. Further, the Franco-German rapprochement, the basis of the European Community, was welcomed as a device for tying part of a divided Germany into an international community, to prevent any future German aggression. In eastern Europe the formidable military victory of the Red Army ensured that countries which it had liberated from German thrall would be controlled by Moscow, to prevent a future invasion of the USSR from the west. Soviet authority ensured that in the east, too, several countries which had suffered German exploitation and barbarism should cooperate with a part of Hitler's former Reich. Perhaps Soviet pressure alone ensured that Czechs and Magyars and Poles would live peaceably as neighbors, not only with each other but also with a truncated German state, the German Democratic Republic. However much the experience of occupation was officially forgotten, there clearly has been no desire on the part of the former victims to pursue a reunification of Germany.

I led the peasants to Tito, without announcing their visit. Tito interrupted his work and spoke at length and warmly with them about the suffering of the people, about the prospects of ending the war, about postwar reconstruction. And we leaders admired the unpretentiousness and eloquence of our supreme commander. But we also waited impatiently for the conversation to end, our hungry eyes fixed stealthily on the roast lambs leaning against the beech tree.

MILOVAN DJILAS
CROATIA, 1943

THE FRENCH EXODE OF JUNE 1940

In June 1940 the population of northern and eastern France was gripped by a collective panic that came to be known as the "Exode" or Exodus. Some 5 million people, possibly more, fled from their homes to avoid the invading Germans; 2 million left the Paris region alone between 10 and 14 June. Some remembered the German occupation of northern France during World War I; others had heard of Nazi atrocities in Rotterdam and Guernica; most were simply swept along by the tide of humanity. Entire towns and villages were emptied of their inhabitants: it is estimated that the population of Chartres fell from 23,000 to 800, Troyes from 58,000 to 30. One Burgundy village was totally deserted apart from one family, which committed collective suicide.

This was no orderly evacuation. The panic of the population mirrored the disarray of the authorities. In Versailles the town hall provided no more than the following help: "The mayor invites the population to flee". The government itself left Paris on 10 June. Panic increased as the refugee columns were raked by German machine-gun fire. With France's roads clogged by fleeing refugees, military operations were hampered. But the Exode was essentially a response to defeat, not a cause of it. The refugees headed for what they presumed to be the safety that lay on the other side of the Loire, although by 19 June the last bridge over the river was down. Those who did get across swelled the populations of southern cities, creating administrative problems and social tensions: Bordeaux's population grew from 258,000 to 800,000, that of Cahors from 13,000 to 60,000.

The Exode was soon over. After the signature of an armistice on 22 June, the German authorities allowed most people to return home – except those from certain designated areas of the northeast, especially the so-called "forbidden zone" – and even provided petrol to help them do so. But the psychological effects of the Exode were more enduring. Members of families became separated and for months afterward newspapers carried advertisements from parents seeking the whereabouts of lost offspring. (A postwar French film, *Forbidden Games*, described the plight of a city girl who lost her parents in the Exode and ended up being cared for by a peasant family.) The sight of this civilian suffering had played a large part in Pétain's desire to sign an armistice; he portrayed himself as the protective father of a suffering nation. The Exode was an experience of trauma and dislocation for millions of people. They had felt abandoned by their leaders: the avuncular Pétain and his Vichy regime offered reassurance and authority. Families had been split up and children gone astray: Vichy stressed the importance of the family. Treasured private possessions had been lost or bundled ignominiously onto carts for public gaze: Vichy praised rootedness and the values of home and hearth. Pétain was a revered figure in 1940: the Exode offers one explanation why this was so.

▼▶ Desperate to escape from the invaders, families piled their belongings onto every conceivable form of transport: carts, bikes, barrows, etc. (below). Those fleeing by car ran out of petrol or became caught in queues. The novelist Antoine de Saint-Exupéry, viewing events from the air, described "roads black with an interminable treacle running on forever" (right). Children often became separated from their families (far right).

▼ The map shows the movement of population from north and east to south and west, as well as the retreat of the government. One participant remembered that he had felt like a leaf swept along by a whirlwind. After such turmoil the cult of Pétain offered security. His benign countenance (below) was a ubiquitous presence. The regeneration of France – or National Revolution – that he offered took as its slogan: Work, Family, Fatherland.

REVOLUTION NATIONALE

Exode 1940

Tourcoing
Seine
Oise
Marne
Paris
Chartres
Troyes
Orléans
12 June
Seine
Loire
Doubs
Tours
13 June
Loire
Saône
Vichy
1 July
Périgueux
Clermont-Ferrand
30 June
Rhône
Dordogne
Brive-la-Gaillarde
Durance
Bordeaux
14 June
Agen
Cahors
Garonne

- - - Département boundary
→ Government migration with dates
━━ "Forbidden zone"
Evacuated area
☐ late May
☐ 10–14 June
Area settled by refugees
☐ by 19 June
☐ after 19 June

Datafile

Popular concern about war crimes is a 20th-century phenomenon, a natural product of mass politics and total warfare. Their trial and punishment was made exceptionally possible by the unconditional surrenders of 1945. The job could be done by the victors, with categories of criminality suitably enlarged to match the enormity of some of the things done. More numerous by far than unlawful methods or means of combat, the classic core of war crimes, were maltreatments of prisoners and civilians: for instance, starvation and slaughter of populations in occupied territory, forced labor there or by deportation and extraordinary neglect of the law on prisoners by Germany dealing with Russians, by Japan dealing with everyone. New as an international offence was "crimes against humanity", the best title that could be devised to describe Germany's treatment of the Jews, whether in its own territories or in conquered ones.

Mining work force

1941
12%
88%

1945
64%
32%
2%
2%

Japanese
Korean
Chinese
POW

Civilians executed

◀ **Civilians executed in occupied Holland.** The steep rise in the figures – all the steeper when it is remembered that "1945" here means less than half a year – vividly suggests how the atmosphere changed from the relatively easy-going first phase to the nervous and vindictive savagery of the last few months.

▲ **Mines and quarries were a favorite scene of forced labor.** Most of the work was unskilled, and the high rate of inevitable accidents and mortality was held to be of no account. Japan, chronically short of manpower for its armed forces, especially exploited prisoners and civilian deportees this way in the home islands.

▼▶ **Statistics for the Nazis' attempted extermination of Europe's Jews** can never be better than approximations, varying according to definitions (for example, many Jews in France were not French nationals) and border baselines (Poland, for instance, takes on quite different shapes according to date). But a cloud remains a cloud even if it has a fuzzy edge. Difficulty with precise figures cannot obscure the enormity of what was attempted and the scale of what was actually done.

Jewish victims

53%
37%
10%

Surviving
Victims
Possible victims

Jews in eastern Europe

1938 population
Victims

USSR
Poland
Czechoslovakia
Hungary
Yugoslavia
Romania
Greece

Millions

Jews in western Europe

1938 population
Victims

Germany and Austria
France
The Netherlands
Belgium
Luxembourg
Italy
Norway

Hundred thousands

People who experience invasion, occupation and domination by enemy forces usually have a bad time. What happened during World War II was so bad, and often so atrocious, that many wartime acts of the Germans and Japanese and their allies were later categorized as criminal and punished. Some were clearly war crimes by the strict definition of the term: acts positively forbidden by the international laws of war. But the letter of those laws, as stated in the Hague Conventions of 1907 and the Geneva Conventions of 1929, did not cover all the vicious deeds that had to be dealt with after the war. New categories of crime were therefore formulated – crimes against humanity, notably the crime of genocide – so that the worst could receive the punishment and universal reprobation they deserved.

Attitudes to subject peoples

Germany and Japan alone need be considered. Their war aims included the exploitation of the human and material resources of the territories they intended to conquer. Both major aggressor powers sought to enlarge their economic empires. The Japanese fancied themselves as the hub of the Greater East Asia Coprosperity Sphere, the Germans as the middle mass of a Greater Germanic Estate. People in subject territories would be made to do whatever work and live in whatever degree of servitude might suit their masters' needs and convenience. This ordering of peoples and things came readily to many Germans and Japanese because they had clear ideas about their own racial superiority and consequent right, by their way of thinking, to dominate "inferiors". In the German case this idea extended to the extermination of some groups.

Occupation by an Axis power usually followed a standard pattern: first, the immediate seizure of useful materials and equipment; second, the gradual conversion of the economy to the occupier's exclusive benefit, with the occupied country bearing the costs of the occupation. Both Germans and Japanese were indifferent to the well-being of subject peoples, but there were important exceptions at each end of the conquerors' scale. At the milder end, a certain degree of consideration was shown to peoples felt to be "kith and kin": the Germans had such regard for the Danes, Norwegians, Flemings and Dutch, Estonians and Latvians. Peoples believed to be politically sympathetic also benefited: the Japanese, anxious to be welcomed as the liberators of Asians from white imperial rule, dealt leniently with Indonesians and Malays. At the other end of the scale were peoples viewed with such indifference or contempt that the reduction of their numbers by sickness and starvation was positively welcomed. The Japanese cared little for

WAR CRIMES

what happened to Chinese whom they encountered throughout Southeast Asia as well as in China itself and were scarcely more concerned about the European whites in their prisoner-of-war and internment camps. The Germans had little concern for Slavs, whom their ideologues told them were too plentiful, and for whom the designated places in the Nazi Thousand Year Reich were those of serfs and slaves. The Jews were a special case altogether. (See p. 166.)

Slave labor and atrocities against civilians

Toiling in your own country for the benefit of the conqueror was one thing. Being taken to toil in his country was another. Germany was a populous and productive country, but the demands of an all-out, many-fronted war drove it to boost its work force with foreign labor. In the summer of 1939 foreign laborers constituted only

about one percent of Germany's work force; five years later, about 20 percent – around 7 million foreigners in all. The great majority were there because they had been forced by one means or another, most of them nasty. Many hundreds of thousands of laborers were worked to death in mines, factories, and construction sites; most of the deaths were intentional. This was particularly the case with the millions of people who were processed through Auschwitz and Majdanek, which began as concentration camps providing and organizing slave labor and only subsequently acquired extermination facilities. All concentration camps in fact became work camps as time went on, and the SS's industrial concerns (part of their ramshackle empire-within-the-empire) relied integrally on them. Another form of enslavement – less intentionally cruel, but enslavement nonetheless – was forced labor in

▼ A Chinese patriot being prepared for execution by Manchurians who, with Koreans, often assisted the Japanese in the same way.

German industrial concerns, most notably Krupps and I.G. Farben.

In Japan 1.5 million despised Koreans were forced to do hard labor but did not suffer so badly. Only about 4 percent died on the job.

Many atrocities were committed against civilians involved – or believed to be involved – with the Resistance. International law concerning civilians under occupation was ambiguous. Nevertheless it did require that effort should be made to distinguish between passive civilians and those attempting to resist the occupier. Decent armies try to observe this distinction, but often the German armed forces and security services did not. Of these various organizations the SD, the SS and the parts of the army most influenced by them were the worst, but severity of treatment also varied according to region. On the Eastern Front terror was regularly resorted to in an attempt to produce a cowed quiescent civilian population. There and in the Balkans the killing of a single German was met with the execution of hostages in their hundreds, whereas in the west a handful often sufficed. The Wehrmacht normally killed only adults, but the SS was not so discriminating. In spring 1944 the northern Greek village of Klissura was the scene of a partisan action in which two German soldiers were killed; the SS's retaliation included the murder of 30 villagers over 60 and 38 under five. Other notorious reprisals, in central and western Europe, occurred at Lidice in Czechoslovakia and Oradour-sur-Glane in France. In retaliation for the assassination in a Prague suburb of the SS official Reinhard Heydrich, in May 1942, all the males of Lidice were murdered, the children were sent to a concentration camp and the women imprisoned – despite the lack of evidence that either village or villagers had anything to do with Heydrich's death. The killing of about 550 French civilians in Oradour (400 of them women and children burnt and blown up in the church) by the Waffen SS on 10 June 1944 was apparently intended to produce a general unresisting numbness throughout the regional population. Such atrocities could work,

▲ This incinerated man was one of the 150 or so Russian, French, Polish and Jewish "political prisoners" burnt alive by the SS at Gardelegen (Germany). They were herded into a huge barn and made to sit down on petrol-soaked straw. The straw was set afire and the barn door locked.

◄ This picture is typical of those taken in the immediate wake of the Allies' arrival at sites of atrocity and horror in 1945. Highly indignant and largely incredulous at German civilians pleas of innocent ignorance, the victors often compelled local inhabitants to share in the exhumation of victims and photographed them with the evidence of what had been done in their name.

► Civilians murdered by Germans in the Crimea, discovered in early 1942. Slav peoples suffered bad times at the hands of the German invaders because of the low place accorded them in traditional German racialist theory (of which Nazi dogma was only an exaggerated version with a specially nasty antisemitic twist). Jews apart, Slavs were held to be the least valuable of noncolored races, a primitive and "animal" sort of people, fit only for serfdom within the new German empire.

Wartime Medical Experiments

Camps managed by the SS provided an opportunity for so-called medical experimentation of which SS doctors were quick to take advantage. Committed in any case by the code of their corps to subordinate all other feelings and principles to the supremacy of their race and nation, and counting among their number, as was to be expected, a high proportion of cranks and sadists, they did things which rank among the worst atrocities of the war and as shocking betrayals of medical ethics; eg maiming or, most often, killing victims by freezing and decompression.

The bulk of the evidence of these horrors emerged in 1947 during "The Doctors' Trial". Not necessarily the worst of the accused but destined to become by far the most celebrated was the one that got away, Dr Josef Mengele. He escaped to South America and died in the

1970s. Japan's counterpart atrocities had to wait many years before they were equally recognized. A handful of the army doctors who had done similar things to Chinese and other prisoners at "Unit 731" near Haerbin, Manchuria, were tried by a Soviet military tribunal at Khabarovsk in late 1949. But the bad faith engendered by the Cold War worked in two ways to dampen the effect; the Russians were concerned only to highlight the experiments in biological warfare (in which they suspected "the west" to have an unhealthy interest), and "the west" was unwilling to believe anything that came out of a Soviet court. Only in the 1980s did it become generally recognized that the findings of the Khabarovsk tribunal were essentially true, and that they were by no means the whole of the ghastly truth.

but no civilized person could count a war won by such means as any sort of victory.

Destruction of the Jews

The wartime atrocity of the greatest magnitude was the Nazis' attempt to kill all European Jews. The Jews were not the only group the Nazis sought to exterminate. They also attempted to exterminate gypsies and killed about 250,000. They sought to exterminate all "degenerates" (by which they mainly meant homosexuals) and all communists they could identify. But Jews were their principal and most prized target.

Antisemitism in various forms was common throughout Europe, but German hostility to the Jewish people went far beyond ordinary antisemitism. The Nazis' paranoid world-picture allowed some sort of place for every other "race" (as they liked to put it) but none for Jews, whom they imagined to be not only "impure" but also actively and menacingly dangerous – to such an extent that even the sight of helpless Jewish children and feeble graybeards caused well-indoctrinated Nazis to shiver with a fear of what damage might be wrought by the hidden powers of "world jewry". They believed Jews to be potentially so dangerous that they could not even safely be enslaved. It sounds crazy, and indeed it was as absurd and vicious as could be, but that is what dedicated Nazis had in their heads. They had taught themselves to believe that the Jews constituted a colossal "problem", and from the winter of 1941–42 they devoted much effort to what they liked to call its "final solution", *die Endlösung*.

This came as the culmination of a variety of antisemitic measures of mounting monstrosity. Until the war in Europe began in September 1939 nothing was possible beyond causing German Jews to wish to emigrate as the Reich expanded. Grandiose plans were aired for the mass departure of the Jews to some distant foreign land (Madagascar was the favorite); while they remained on Reich soil their lives would be made miserable and a select few killed in concentration camps. The invasions of Poland, of the Low Countries and France in the west and most of the Balkans in the southeast in 1939–41 brought much mortality and anguish to the large, scattered Jewish populations that fell within the German grasp. German Jews were expelled eastward, Jews everywhere else were corralled into ghettos and labor camps, and murderous maltreatment was accorded to Jewish prisoners of war. But still nothing as grandiose as the "final solution" was heard of until the summer of 1941. It first appeared among the plans for the invasion of the USSR (which would begin with the invasion of the lands the USSR had annexed in 1939) and for the Germanization of the vast territories thus in prospect. These, it was thought, could not be properly "German" while Jews still inhabited them. They had to be "cleansed", made *Judenrein*. What was then to be done with all those Jews? In the minds of the Nazi ideologues and specialists in violence the idea began to materialize of systematically exterminating them; not just the Jews of eastern Europe but also, as opportunity permitted, the Jews of every other part of Europe.

▲ This poster of the French "Institute for the Study of the Jewish Question" expresses the extravagance and fantasy of populist antisemitism. The age-old stereotype ghetto graybeard is used to symbolize ultra-modern international finance.

▶ A bureaucratic refinement from Dachau, close to Munich, the archetypal SS concentration camp from 1934 until its liberation by appalled American troops on 25 April 1945. Prisoners were elaborately classified and color-coded, with such results as are shown on the trouser-leg in the lower-right box.

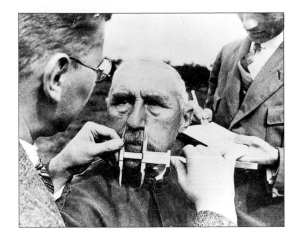

◀ German officials measure a nose with a view to judging whether its owner was properly "Aryan" or not; an instance of the bogus-scientific absurdities into which there fanatics were commonly led.

Work began on the Jews of eastern Europe in the wake of the German invasion. Spearheading it were the *Einsatzgruppen*, "special action groups" in the plain translation of their typically euphemistic title, but more accurately called murder squads: their main task was, simply, to massacre Jews and other listed undesirables. With the cooperation of the German and allied armies (some of whose more decent officers did not like what they saw or heard about and to their credit complained about it) and the often enthusiastic assistance of local police and militias, the *Einsatzgruppen* machine-gunned or otherwise did to death all the Jews they could lay their hands on, usually after first herding them into ad hoc camps and ghettos. There were innumerable scenes of horror. One of the worst was the filling of the Babi Yar ravine outside Kiev with nearly 40,000 dead or dying bodies.

Murder on an industrial scale

None of this was enough to meet the needs of the *Endlösung*. Much more planning had to be done. The work of the *Einsatzgruppen* and their local auxiliaries was patchy and piecemeal – and very messy. Killings so numerous and hasty were not easy to cover up, and the Nazis wanted to conceal their intentions from Jews still at liberty. Technology offered a less bloody and more secret means of mass murder: poison gas. Bureaucracy and efficient modern administration would surmount the other difficulties. A new master plan was developed, the details of which SD-leader Reinhard Heydrich explained to the heads of all involved agencies at a secret conference at Wannsee, a Berlin suburb, on 20 January 1942. The story would be spread that Jews were to be "resettled" eastward. The railroad systems of the whole continent would be geared to delivering trainloads of Jews (plus such others as were to be exterminated) to camps from which they would never emerge. Some would be sent initially to labor, the rest straight to newly constructed gas chambers. To handle the expected volume of business, additional camps with specialized extermination facilities would be constructed; the names of Chelmno, Treblinka, Sobibor, Belzec and Auschwitz now entered the gazetteer of Nazi infamy. The three camps at Auschwitz (Auschwitz I,

An open grave had been dug and they had to jump into this and lie face downwards. And sometimes when one or two rows had already been shot, they had to lie on top of the people who had already been shot and then they were shot from the edge of the grave. And Himmler had never seen dead people before and in his curiosity ... was looking in.

SS GENERAL KARL WOLFF
MINSK, 1941

▼ A scene from the final hours of the Warsaw ghetto, conquered by the Germans at last, after four weeks of extraordinary resistance, in mid-May 1943. What little was left of it was then razed to the ground.

Auschwitz-Birkenau and Auschwitz-Monowitz) were large industrial complexes. At its busiest period, handling Adolf Eichmann's big haul of Hungarian Jews in 1944, Auschwitz-Birkenau was managing to kill and cremate as many as 24,000 a day.

But death did not come only at that end of the railroad line. The journey itself and its staging posts were fraught with pain and terror, notwithstanding the Nazis' avowed intention to persuade victims that the very worst was not happening to them until that terrible moment of truth when gas began to come through the pipes in the "bath houses". The brutal round-ups and entrainments, the long-drawn-out journeys (food- and water-less in goods- and cattle-trucks), not to mention the steady starvation that had earlier marked life in the ghettos, brought death in many other ways, all by intention horrible. It speaks volumes about Nazi mentality that its *Endlösung*, although designed to kill its victims efficiently, had to

terrify, humiliate and torture them as well.

The "final solution" did not wholly succeed. But the Nazis and their collaborators got fearfully close to their goal. About 300,000 of those in camps were still (just) alive when the Allied armies reached them in 1944 and 1945. Over a million more had not (yet) been "resettled". This was in part because the exterminators had not had enough time, in part because some Jews had managed to stay in hiding or had been hidden by courageous Gentiles, while a few of the thousands who had joined the partisans survived to tell their tale. It was, however, also because of the resistance to their deportation offered in varying measure by peoples and administrations all over occupied Europe. The rabid antisemitism sometimes shown by inhabitants of occupied countries, which was often of essential help to the occupier, was sometimes matched by ordinary decency and moral principle. One of the many weaknesses the Nazis identified in the Italians

▲ ▶ Disposing of the bodies was a problem the exterminators never solved entirely. The *Einsatzgruppen* relied mainly on burial, but that, whether in graves the victims were made to dig for themselves or in natural landscape features, tended to be doubly inadequate: there was not enough space, and they were difficult to cover up. To fill in this mass grave at Belsen demanded hard work. Crematoria ovens therefore became the preferred method. Tending the furnaces and removing the ashes (in which much tell-tale bone nevertheless remained) was done by prisoners themselves, as seen in the picture (right) from Dachau's tiny installation.

as allies was their lack of anti-Jewish viciousness. The Jews of Denmark (admittedly, only about 7,000 strong) were spirited away to Sweden on the eve of their roundup. The 48,000 Jews of German-dominated Bulgaria owed their lives to extraordinary demonstrations of public solidarity. It diminishes not at all the luster of that noble example to reflect that other peoples, no matter how much they might have wished to do likewise, would have found it formidably difficult. A preindustrial unpopulous nation with few railroads and many mountains, at the far corner of the continent, might get away with noncooperation but this was utterly beyond, say, the people of the Netherlands. Of their 140,000 Jewish fellow-citizens, three-quarters were killed. When the fighting at last stopped in 1945 over two-thirds – some 5.75 million – of Europe's prewar Jewish population was dead.

The perpetrators of these monstrous deeds never doubted that their actions were right for their nation and race (the only segment of humankind they cared about). But as defeat drew ever nearer in 1944 and 1945 they became worried about their effects on the feelings and temper of the likely victors. They therefore attempted to obliterate all traces of them. Demolitions were carried out whenever time permitted, the camp inmates were herded by road or rail away from the shrinking borders toward the interior of the expiring Reich. Not all were Jewish but most were. The last hundreds of thousands of Holocaust victims before the liberation were those who were shot, beaten, sickened or starved to death in course of this extemporized mass migration. But more than enough of camps and survivors was left for the world abruptly to learn, with a sense of moral shock greater for most Britons and North Americans than any experienced so far, the appalling facts about the concentration and death camps, and to take at last the full measure of the foe they had been combating. The impact of these revelations was twofold. They destroyed whatever small chance there was that public opinion would wish to show that "Magnanimity in Victory" recommended by the British prime minister Winston Churchill, and they rallied public opinion in victorious countries solidly behind the war-crimes trials which were soon to begin.

From war crimes to human rights

The British and North American publics had known little about the Holocaust and its associated horrors while they were being perpetrated. Allied governments, however, had known, and made plans for dealing with the perpetrators. Culpable individuals would be punished but they intended also to shape a new world order in which such antihuman horrors could never happen again. It is probably true to say that the present worldwide regime of concern for human rights would never have been launched without World War II's extraordinary and unprecedented denials of them. The charter of the International Military Tribunal for the Trial of German Major War Criminals, known to history from the place of its assembly as the Nuremberg Tribunal, proposed to hear indictments for three categories of crimes: crimes against peace (planning and waging aggressive war); war crimes (to include "deportation to slave labor" and "killing of hostages"); and – this was the one that prefigured the Universal Declaration of Human Rights – "crimes against humanity; namely, murder, extermination, enslavement, deportation and other inhumane acts commited against any civilian population. . .".

While the United Nations was formulating basic human rights legislation, war-crimes tribunals were established in the zones of occupied Germany and in every formerly occupied country. In the American, British and French zones between 1947 and 1953, 10,400 were tried; 5,025 were sentenced; 506 executed. It is largely from the superabundant evidence offered at the trials of, for example, Heydrich's successor Ernst Kaltenbrunner (before the IMT itself, the only SS/SD defendant there), the *Einsatzgruppe* commander Otto Ohlendorff (at a military tribunal in the American occupation zone) and Rudolf Hoess the commandant of Auschwitz (in a Polish court), that the war crimes of World War II – crimes against human rights in general, the Holocaust in particular – are so copiously documented.

With the limelight so much on concentration and death camps, little indignation was aroused in "the west" by what happened in German prisoner-of-war camps – which in any case, so far as British, Commonwealth and American servicemen were concerned, were relatively not so bad. Very different was the case with those taken prisoner by Japan. Not much was known of the conditions of life, labor and death in Japanese camps until Allied forces overran them in, mostly, the last weeks of the war, or even after it had been formally ended. The fury which followed the disclosure of those atrocities, kept hot through many years to come by the stories of the survivors when they got home, made the trials of the International Military Tribunal for the Far East (brief title, the Tokyo Tribunal) and the other war-crimes trials accompanying it even more engrossing to many in the victorious nations than their European counterparts.

REVENGE AND JUSTICE

It was predictable that many among the victorious nations – especially in those which had experienced enemy occupation – would wish to punish the authors and beneficiaries of their woes. Less predictable was the resolve that such punishment should be judicially determined. But vengeance and justice are bad bedfellows. The forms which vengeance took in the wake of the Allied armies' arrivals were inevitably nasty. That justice took rough forms in the confused interim between liberation and the restoration of regular government was not surprising. What was surprising was that the settlement of accounts nevertheless had some fair-minded and discriminating aspects.

In a class of its own was the expulsion of Germans from the east European lands where their name now stank. Some of them had perhaps long lived there, others had only recently been lodged there in place of evicted Slavs. Now the tide turned, the USSR and Poland moved their frontiers westward and Czechoslovakia became again what it was before "Munich". Huge numbers of German-speakers had (or felt they had) no choice but to flee westward into the Allied-occupied zones: 1.5 million from the Sudetenland, about 7 million from beyond Poland's new western frontier, and so on.

Rough and questionable justice was meted out by lynch-mobs and people's courts directly after the departure of occupying forces. These were hazardous weeks for persons reputed to be traitors and collaborators, many of whom were summarily and often savagely dealt with before regular courts could consider their cases more dispassionately. The damning word "collaborator" was too readily attached to people who had reckoned that they could best serve their country by cautious cooperation with the occupier. Many relatively innocent men and women were unjustly done to death, and opportunity was freely taken for settling all sorts of old scores.

Justice was better served in the multitude of courts, civilian and military alike, which were soon trying alleged war crimes right across Europe from the Pyrenees to the Urals and all over East and Southeast Asia. Their quality of justice was of course conditioned by ideology and circumstances, but over-severity and bias were certainly not universal. Leniency and acquittals became more frequent as time went by. The International Military Tribunals which crowned the whole unprecedented business had mixed aims: to punish the guilty, but also to put on record the criminality of the men, organizations and regimes responsible, in the victors' view, for causing the war and for making it so horrible. In some of these aims they succeeded. "The Nuremberg Principles" asserted the superiority of international over national law and the personal responsibility of even the highest-placed breakers of it. The traditional law of war was reaffirmed and new human-rights law was helped by the creation of a new category of "crimes against humanity".

►▲ The Tokyo courtroom (right): 28 defendants face the bench of judges (one from each of 11 victors) with ample space for translators, press and camera men. At Nuremberg the USA, USSR, UK and France tried 22 defendants. Goering (above) was the most important Nazi tried, and one of the sharpest. The proceedings were free enough for him to be able to give the prosecution lawyers some sticky moments.

►▼ Vengeance and cruelty are more conspicuous than justice as the corpses of Mussolini and his mistress hang upside down at a Milan filling-station and a batch of Belgian women who have been going with German men are publicly humiliated. Below, May 1945, refugees in Berlin.

ACKNOWLEDGMENTS

Picture credits

14–15 US forces unloading supplies, Iwo Jima, February 1945: PF
82–83 Troops boarding plane, Ipswich, Australia, September 1942: RHL
106–107 Shipyard workers, Bethlehem-Fairfield shipyards, Baltimore, Md, May 1943: LC
138–139 People looking for their dead, Kerch, USSR, 1942: Alexander Meledin, Moscow

7 FSP **11** AP **16–17** USNA **17t** PF **17c** HDC **17b** Mainichi Newspapers, Tokyo**18** AP **19t** USNA **19c** CP **19b** HDC **20tl** AP **20br** PF **22–23** CP **22b** PF **23** LC **24–25** AP **25r**, **26bl**, **26tr** ADNZ **26br** BPK **29t** PF **29b** UB **30t**, **30b** IWM **31t** BPK **31c** ADNZ **31b** CP/IWM **32–33** RF **33t** Mainichi Newspapers, Tokyo **33b** PF **35t**, **35b**, **36t** USNA **36b** TPL **37t** USNA **37b** US Air Force, Washington, D.C. **38b**, **38–39** USNA **41** HDC **42** Bison Picture Library, London **44** Royal Australian Air Force Association Aviation Museum, Bullcreek, Western Australia **45t** India Office Library, London **45b** IWM **46t** PF **46b** TPL **47t** IWM **47b** TPL **49** UB **51tl** John Erickson, Edinburgh **51tr** Anatoli Garanin **51cl** ADNZ **51bl** APN, Novosti, Moscow **52** Georgi Zelma **53t** UB **53b** RHL/IWM **54–55** Alexander Meledin, Moscow **55b** IWM **56** FSP **57t** John Erickson, Edinburgh **57c** UB **57b** RHL **58–59** CP **59r** RHL **61t** CP **61c** PF **61b** TPL **62–63**, **62tl** RHL **62bl** ADNZ **63** RHL **65tl**, **65bl** IWM **65r** USNA **67tr**, **67br** IWM **67c** RHL **67bl** PF **69** BPK **71t**, **71b** USNA **72t** Bison Picture Library, London **72b** IWM **73** US Army/USNA **74t** IWM **74c** RHL **74b** US Army/USNA **75l** BPK **75r** IWM **76–77** PF **77**, **78tl** USNA **78cl** US Naval Historical Center, Washington, D.C. **78bl** PF **78br** RHL **80t** USNA **80b** IWM **81** US Army/USNA **85**, **86**, **86–87** RHL **87t** Bison Picture Library, London **87b** BPK **88** RHL **88–89** David King Collection, London **90** RHL **90–91** CP **91bl** RHL **91tr** TPL **91br** BPK **92t** TPL **92b** HDC **93l** RHL **93r** PF **95** USNA **96** RHL **96–97** IWM **97** PF **98**, **99b** USNA **99t** PF **101** PF **102–103** MARS/IWM **103t**, **103b** PF **104l** USNA **104r** RHL **104–105** IWM **105** PF **109t** RHL **109b** PF **110** Mainichi Newspapers, Tokyo **111t** PF **112t**, **112b**, **113b** Mainichi Newspapers, Tokyo **113t** Pictorial Press Ltd. **115** BPK **116t** AA **116b** UB **117** BPK **118–119**, **119** UB **121** University of Reading, UK **122t** PF **122b** HDC **123t** Futile Press/IWM **123b** IWM **124t**, **124b** PF **124–125** HDC **125** The Labour Party, London **127**, **128t**, **128–129** Alexander Meledin, Moscow **129t** John Erickson, Edinburgh **130** Alexander Meledin, Moscow **131**, **131 inset** John Erickson, Edinburgh **133** LC **134t** IWM **134b**, **135t**, **135b**, **136**, **137t**, **137b** LC **141 l** RHL **141r** Alexander Meledin, Moscow **142t** Glasgow Herald **142b** AP **143t** PF **143b** IWM **144–145** BPK **144b**, **145t** UB **145b** LC **146l** IWM **146r** AA **147** RHL **149** PF **150t**, **150b**, **151t**, **151b** Pictorial Press, London **152–153** Magnum/Zucca Tallandier, London **152b**, **153** BPK **154t** Magnum/Zucca Tallandier, London **154b** Roger-Viollet, Paris **155** RHL **156t** Nationalmuseet, Denmark **156b** ADNZ **157t** IWM **156–157** Roger-Viollet, Paris **158tl**, **158cl** John Erickson, Edinburgh **158br** RHL **159** IWM **160** J-L Charmet, Paris **160–161t** Roger-Viollet, Paris **161t** RHL **161r** IWM **160–161** Bundesarchiv, Koblenz **163** HDC **164t**, **164b** IWM **165** David King Collection, London **166t** Roger-Viollet, Paris **166b** Bundesarchiv, Koblenz **167t** HDC **167b** AP **168–169** IWM **169b** HDC/Bettmann Archive **170t** TPL **170b** BPK **170–171** USNA **171t** FSP **171b** HDC

Abbreviations
AA   Andromeda Archive
ADNZ   Allgemeiner Deutscher Nachrichtendienst, Zentralbild, Berlin (East)
AP   Associated Press, London
BPK   Bildarchiv Preussischer Kulturbesitz, Berlin (West)
CP   Camera Press, London
FSP   Frank Spooner Pictures, London
HDC   Hulton-Deutsch Collection, London
IWM   Imperial War Museum, London
LC   Library of Congress, Washington DC
PF   Popperfoto, London
RF   Rex Features, London
RHL   Robert Hunt Library, London
TPL   Topham Picture Library, Kent, UK
UB   Ullstein Bilderdienst, Berlin (West)
USNA   United States National Archive, Washington, D.C.

t = top, tl = top left, tr = top right, c = center, b = bottom etc.

Cartographic advisers
Duncan Anderson, Royal Military Academy, Sandhurst; David Parry, Imperial War Museum, London

Editorial and research assistance
Matthew Jones, William Philpott, Mike Pincombe, Elaine Welsh

Artists
Chris Forsey, Alan Hollingbery, Colin Salmon, Mick Saunders, Dave Smith

Photographs
Shirley Jamieson, Alison Renney

Cartography
Maps drafted by Alan Mais, Hornchurch; Euromap, Pangbourne; Lovell Johns, Oxford

Typesetting
Brian Blackmore, Anita Wright; OPUS Ltd, Oxford

Color origination
Scantrans, Singapore

Production
Clive Sparling

INDEX